TRAVEL CULTURE

ESSAYS ON WHAT MAKES US GO

~

Edited by
CAROL TRAYNOR WILLIAMS

Westport, Connecticut
London

Library of Congress Cataloging-in-Publication Data

Travel culture : essays on what makes us go / edited by Carol Traynor Williams.
p. cm.
Includes bibliographical references and index.
ISBN 0-275-95727-6 (alk. paper)
1. Travel—Philosophy. I. Williams, Carol T., 1935- .
G151.T65 1998
910'.01—dc21 97-32996

British Library Cataloguing in Publication Data is available.

Library of Congress Catalog Card Number: 97-32996
ISBN: 0-275-95727-6

First published in 1998

Praeger Publishers, 88 Post Road West, Westport, CT 06881
An imprint of Greenwood Publishing Group, Inc.

Printed in the United States of America

The paper used in this book complies with the Permanent Paper Standard issued by the National Information Standards Organization (Z39.48-1984).

10 9 8 7 6 5 4 3 2 1

Copyright Acknowledgments

The authors and publisher gratefully acknowledge permission for use of the following material:

Judith Adler's chapter, "Origins of Sightseeing," is adapted and reprinted with permission from *Annals of Tourism Research*, vol. 16, no. 1, pp. 7–29, 1989, Elsevier Science Ltd, Oxford, England.

Excerpts in Michael Bryson's chapter from *The Song of the Dodo: Island Biogeography in an Age of Extinctions* by David Quammen. Published by Scribner, 1996. Reprinted with the permission of Renee Wayne Golden, Esq. for David Quammen.

Excerpts from David Tomlinson's chapter from the unpublished typescript "The Log of the Stargazer," by Olive King. Reprinted with permission of Margaret Argent, daughter of Olive King.

Poetry from Beatriz Badikan's chapter excerpted from "Poem for the Young White Man Who Asked Me How I, an Intelligent, Well-Read Person Could Believe in the War Between Races" from *Emplumada*, by Lorna Dee Cervantes, © 1981. Reprinted by permission of the University of Pittsburgh Press. "Moon in Hydra" and "Letter to Iona from the South of France," from *My Wicked, Wicked Ways*. Copyright © 1987 by Sandra Cisneros. Published by Third Woman Press and in hardcover by Alfred A. Knopf. Reprinted by permission of Third Woman Press. All rights reserved. Reprinted by permission of Susan Bergholz Literary Services, New York. All rights reserved. "In My Country" from *My Father Was a Toltec*. Copyright © 1995 by Ana Castillo. Published by W. W. Norton & Co. Reprinted by permission of W. W. Norton & Co. All rights reserved. Reprinted by permission of Susan Bergholz Literary Services, New York. All rights reserved.

To
Ray and Pat Browne—
"Mom and Pop" of Popular Culture—
And All Their Children,
And to Susan Weiss,
Extraordinary Traveler Through Life,
In Memorium

Contents

Acknowledgments

LIKE ALL EDITIONS, this one owes the most to its contributors and to other "friends of the subject." Travel culture's best friend is surely Ray B. Browne, who asked me in 1994 if I would write about teaching travel culture for his edition about popular culture in the twenty-first century. Could I really *write* about my favorite bedtime reading, travel adventures? Ray and Pat Browne have gone on supporting the new subculture of popular culture with sections on travel culture I have chaired at the national Popular Culture Association conferences; a number of the pieces in this book, and their authors, were met at these, the *fun* conferences.

I am grateful to my dean, Al Bennett, and to the Roosevelt University faculty committee, which awarded me a faculty research leave that allowed me to put this book together at my home in Southwest Harbor, Maine. In Maine and the East, I thank Anne Street of New York City and Janet Reed of Tremont, Maine, for oral histories (which have turned out to be mostly for the next book), and Heidi Bliss, of the Harvard Department of Visual and Environmental Studies, who gave me books and papers on travel and film, including the essay by Tom Gunning that is reprinted in this collection; for that, for finding (with the help of the Tozzer Library staff) the unfindable source during production—and, most of all, for her friendship—I am very grateful.

Thanks to Nichols Fox, of Bass Harbor, Maine, for research leads; to Sheila Wilensky, for Oz Books and help (good teacher that she is) in clarifying what cultural anthropology does; to Lorraine Saunders and the staff and volunteers of the Southwest Harbor Library, for finding "everything" almost always at the last minute; and to Doug Hodgdon, for listening, talking, and reading (for editing the editor)—and for naming the book.

Praeger convention manager Marietta Yannetti, and editors Nina Pearlstein, Elisabetta Linton, and vice-president Jim Sabin were helpful, as were my copyeditor, Suzanne Solensky, and my production editor, Deborah Whitford.

A number of colleagues at Roosevelt University stepped into the breaches—to type, fax, mail, or do a computer thing (always at the last minute). Thanks particularly to my secretary, Sophia Thomas. The contributors to this book contributed beyond their essays; they chased permissions and changed copy, format, and whatever else I asked them to do. The Chicago contributors held my hand when I held my head, and to them I am especially grateful—as I am to the caring of Joe, Megan, and Christopher Williams, and to many friends, who put me up in *my* travel culture and fed me in many ways, in many places, on this, that turned out to be an odyssey, a voyage like all of them, full of change.

~

Introduction

CAROL TRAYNOR WILLIAMS

HUMAN HISTORY IS the story of a traveler, an Odysseus. In *The Songlines*, his narrative of traveling Australia to know its Aborigines, Bruce Chatwin says that travel is innate because humankind first evolved as hunters walking through the grasslands. And, like our history as a whole, the history of travel is a tale of ever growing democratization. The first humans who sallied forth from the mouth of the cave started a stream of us who have caught the caravan. We have looked for new herds, fresh soil, free land (or a free land), a mate not incestuous; we have searched fearfully for warmth, water, safety from the *wargus*—in Middle Latin, *wargus* is both the wolf and the stranger—but we have also moved out curiously, for new tribes to trade with, for novel congress. We have quested for the Grail and for gold, but also just for the sight around the bend. And that surprise has been searched for often enough, and by all kinds of men and women, from the most ancient times, so that we can be sure that to move and to change are human habits, as inborn as the other habit: to settle, to nest.[1]

In the last half of the twentieth century, after the end of World War II, democracy and travel have run rampant. Ironically, war has been the great travel opportunity for the average Joe. Technology, especially of transportation and communication, also spurs travel, but these technologies grow from war (or "peace-keeping" missions). The Civil War uprooted and urbanized rural and small-town America. How would we keep them down on the farm after they had seen "Paree"? the World War I song asked, and World War II "expatriated" fourteen million American men and women. The Vietnam War lies behind the current boom in Asian travel. In the wake of post–World War II wealth, first in the United States and then worldwide, churned travel or, more democratically, tourism. As the world traveled, willy nilly and unwitting of itself as sea changer, it slowly grew more "international": from hamburgers to Wimpy's hamburgers in old Paris; from hamburgers to the French dip, tacos, sushi, tapas, and so on. In the early 1960s, when I crossed the Appalachians, moving away from the Atlantic Ocean for the first time in my life, the only fish I could buy in Oxford, Ohio, was the frozen rectangle of Booth's "ocean perch."

I am typical in that unwittingly my life in roughly the last half of the century has partaken of tourism's taking over the economy and culture. It looks now as if I lived my life to write about the coming of the travel culture, but many who lived in this time could say the same if they thought about it. All my life, at least in the summers, I have lived in resort towns on the Atlantic Coast: Manchester-By-The-Sea, Massachusetts, at the base of Cape Ann, north of Boston, where the rocky coast of New England starts; the Jersey shore (which means north Jersey) and Cape May, at the southern tip of New Jersey; and, since 1971, Southwest Harbor, on Mt. Desert Island in Maine, just south of where Down East starts.

"Off season," I lived a lot of my childhood in Rutherford, New Jersey, under enormous, ancient trees—elms, oaks, walnuts, maples—whose roots raised the old slate slabs of sidewalk and whose leaves met over Lincoln Avenue, Van Ness, Sylvan Street. I scorned landlocked Rutherford, but from the hilltop of my street (Pierrepont), straight across six miles of the Secaucus "meadowland (swamp) stood the Empire State Building, tallest in the world. My mother and my fairy godmother maiden aunt took me to the Bronx Zoo, where I rode on the top of an elephant, and to Grant's Tomb, the Cathedral of St. John the Divine, F. A. O. Schwartz (whose doll house "tilt top" tables and radio consoles in those days were solid walnut), and, best of all, plays with Katherine Cornell, *South Pacific*, Radio City Music Hall, and Longchamps restaurant, with chocolate "maple leaves" and unbelievably green peas even in winter, because they were the new Birdseye's. My father took me to Brooklyn, on the Hoboken ferry, and one time he bought me a baseball and Jackie Robinson signed it. Once he took me to Yankee Stadium, because even though we were Dodger fans, he thought that I should see Joe DiMaggio—once.

All this I took for granted. One of my first memories is of an airplane sticking out of the Empire State Building. On a foggy Saturday morning (thank God it was a Saturday, not a work day), a plane flew into the seventy-ninth floor, and Aunt Ebba, as was her derring-do wont, trundled me off to see the wonder. I am in awe to remember that in 1945, our bus from New Jersey went to the city (Newark was "Newark," but "New York" was only "the city") on a two-lane road across the wetland and through the Lincoln Tunnel and left us in an alleyway next to the (puny) Woodstock Hotel on West 43rd Street. When, after the war, they built Route S-3 (now Route 3), from the west into the city, all those wide lanes made craters in our neighborhood, and then "lakes," for which we built, and then embarked on, rafts and got in great trouble with our mothers. Did I have any idea that this was the democratization of travel? Or the ending of a world? Of course not.

Now I see with a little surprise that even when I was not in a "beautiful" place—for me, a seashore place—I was still part of travel and tourism. By moving to Chicago in 1965, I have also lived through that city's slow, unstoppable change from hub and crucible of farm animals and steel to a worldwide tourist venue. (What other city do you know, north of Rio, where you can swim—cleanly—from beaches in the middle of downtown?) I even went to college in another kind of tourist spot, the historical, in Gettysburg, Pennsylvania. And, like most everyone else in the "developed" world at the millennium, whenever I can, I travel. I, who typically of my generation was closer to forty than twenty when I first went to Europe, travel regularly for work (for academics, that means conferences or research) and for fun—to San Antonio, Sanibel, the San Juan Islands, Big Sur, Vegas, Venice, and Santa Marguerita. In 1997, I used my airline award miles for Australia. Also typically, my three children outdo me. Among them, they have hitch-hiked across western Europe; semestered in Ireland; taught English in Taiwan for a year in order to travel India; driven an old orange Saab from Mexico to the Panama Canal; jetted round and round the world in three weeks—Torino to Toronto, Tokyo, Mendoza, Harare, Paris—producing a series of rock concerts for human rights; and, in a three-month odyssey, driven and camped the American Great Plains, Northwest mountains, Pacific Coast, and Southwest canyons and desert (this was my daughter)—and more. In my generation's children, our travel gene runs amuck.

When I cannot travel, like so many others, I read travel literature. It is my bedtime reading, my vicarious travel, and how this collection came into being. Hospitality is the world's number one and fastest-growing business, and so Ray Browne, creator of popular culture, was eager to bring it into a text, *Preview 2001+: Popular Culture Studies in the Future* (1995). Ray asked me to write about my humanities seminar for Roosevelt University's hospitality management students, and as I got into what Ray aptly called the "travel culture," I became amazed how widely it ranged and reached both in our world and our worldview, in the lives we live and the philosophy by which we understand and order our lives.

Travel culture covers travel and the faraway places and also everything that goes with travel: all the media and artifacts connected with the Orient Express or the "small, small world" of Disney; the hype, trappings, and general milieu of a Princess cruise or a Smithsonian expedition. It is a field primarily of anthropology and sociology, but it is also a perspective on history, a metaphor for the human psychological "passage," and when human beings are looked at in the aggregate, rather than as individuals, it is a philosophy or metaphysic. In 1996, it was even an analogy for cosmetic surgery: "real life morphing, traveling in place, a palliative—more lasting than a mere change of clothes or a new hairdo—for our growing inability to sit still in our own skins."[2]

Eric J. Leed, in a provocative, encompassing criticism, *The Mind of the Traveler: From Gilgamesh to Global Tourism* (1991), classifies the whole structure of life (the journey) into departures, passages, and arrivals, which he charts psychologically, using mythical and literary travels such as Odysseus's journey. In Leed, the psychological becomes the metaphysical (and gender study as well: the traveler wears the "masculine persona" [219], freeing himself through moving on). Seminal in contemporary travel culture criticism, as he is generally in understanding the second half of the twentieth century, is Daniel Boorstin, in his essay "From Traveler to Tourist: The Lost Art of Travel" (in *The Image*, 1961). Also key is Paul Fussell's *Abroad: British Literary Travel Between the Wars* (1980). Note that the field is literary art; traditionally, travel criticism has been literary criticism. More and more, however, critics—like those in this collection—look at travel in relation to the culture in all its parts: economic, political, international, and particularly the popular culture, which, unlike the literary, looks at mass action such as tourism appreciatively. Judith Adler, for example, draws from seventeenth- and eighteenth-century history the notion of travel as experimental, or sensory-based history: source of the first factual history based on first hand observation, for example, in shops and factories, to note the labor of ordinary men or customs and the popular culture in general.[3] Sociology joins aesthetics in the contemporary spate of travel scholarship connected to the postmodern focus on participant-observer relationships. Travel culture, for example, looks at the complex interactions of the "native" and the "tourist": Who is the insider? Who is the outsider in today's voyeuristic world? In *The Tourist Gaze*, John Urry weaves a complex theoretical travel culture history of the "developed" world from the nineteenth- and twentieth-century romantic-capitalist-consumer society, through modernism's celebration of the masses, to postmodernism and "post-tourism," in which a "new petty bourgeoisie" (quoting Bourdieu, *Distinction*, 1984) lives antiboundaries (of class or social group) and antimemory (history) and is afraid of bonds; their attitudes—including their ideas of travel—put novelty above all and, as Urry suggests, grow from a new snobbery or elitism, this one not of class or intellect but of particular lifestyle, such as conservationism. (See in particular Urry's Chapter 5.)

But in spite of its growth, this rich field of travel culture analysis is still relatively new and small, still in the academic fringe of the interdisciplinary. Until just a few years ago, the term "travel culture" would have meant "travel literature," and almost all of that was bypassed as "light," even though much of it was written by "serious" writers such as Mark Twain, Henry James, D. H. Lawrence, and Evelyn Waugh. Of course: it was the *elite* who traveled, and what do the "cultured" do in the face of beauty and novelty? They write about it (or paint it). In the last twenty years, however, travel writing has burgeoned; Paul Theroux's sunflower-sized seed, *The Great Railway Bazaar*, was published in 1975. Michael Kowalewski, in his introduction to *Temperamental Journeys: Essays on the Modern Literature of Travel* (1992), notes rightly that "the resurgence of interest in travel writing [is] unequaled since the twenties and thirties" (1). Yet, as Kowalewski also says (and this text's annotated bibliography shows), twentieth-century travel criticism "has been scanty," particularly of "American travel narratives" (1). Reviewing travel writing in the fiction form—specifically, *A Fine Balance* (1996), Rohinton Mistry's tale of modern Indian history—A. G. Mojtabai writes:

> Those who continue to harp on the inevitable decline of the novel ought to hold off for a while. The unique task of the genre, after all, is truthfulness to human experience in all its variety, and thanks to the great migrations of population in our time, human variety is to be found in replenished abundance all around us. The displacements, comminglings and clashings of peoples and cultures have released new energies, strange pollens; indeed, the harvest has barely begun.[4]

Of course it is democratization that has "released new energies"—the democratization of "displacements [and] comminglings," of movement, of travel. This has enlarged the field for study, the body of travel writing. Some of the enlarging is in the content of the traditional travel writing genres, the memoir and the novel; for example, politics is more than ever the content of travel books. Travel writing is generically political; the fresh eye, looking anthropologically, that is, wholistically, is innately radical, inevitably subversive. But in this era when the observer-eye is less on the Grand Tour and more often on a Third World region (and not uncommonly, if American, is the eye of someone who started his or her traveling in the Peace Corps), the politics are generally stronger. Christopher R. Cox's journey *Chasing the Dragon: Into the Heart of the Golden Triangle* (1996) is typical: it is plotted with poor opium farmers; rich, "indifferent" heroin dealers; rebels who scheme to free Myanmar (Burma) or rule it; and a "supporting cast" of, for example, AIDS sufferers and Thai child prostitutes. In another characteristic 1996 memoir, "*Exterminate All the Brutes*," Sven Lindqvist hitchhikes and buses across the Sahara not as a lark, a religion, or a romance (as earlier travel memoirists have trekked this region), but as part of a political history showing the roots of genocide, particularly the German genocide of the Jews, in European imperialism, especially in Africa. Lindqvist's title quotes Kurtz, Joseph Conrad's King Oedipus in the Congo, colonizer in the *Heart of Darkness*, fatally flawed by elitism, the snake in every traveler's paradise.

Travel writing, then, is much more than the light trippings up the Orinoco of yore. But the genres of travel writing have also broadened beyond the personal narrative, fictional or factual. Most noticeably, travel guides—and there are more and more of them—are becoming more people's favorite "read." A 1996 *New York Times Magazine* piece on them estimates the U.S. market for guidebooks at $200 million a year; many of them, such as the Lonely Planet series (216 in 1996), which the *Times* focuses on, are empathetic with the cultures they write about, aimed at audiences of "independent travellers, . . . from all backgrounds," and stylishly written.[5] In the summer of 1996, ABC's Catharine Crier reported on a new series of travel guides written by "outed" KGB spies about the regions they had spied in. As the Soviet agent in London said to Crier, the KGB agents really had to get to know their cities! (*ABC Evening News*, July 26, 1996).

Travel guides from the KGB may be bizarre, but beside the Lonely Planet or Harvard's *Let's Go* series, most of you probably have more than one guidebook like those in my current file: on Nevada, Alaska, Australia, *The Pine Island [Florida] Visitor's Guide*, and so on. Or you may have your city's equivalent of the quarterly *Newsletter* from The Savvy Traveller in Chicago. Such stores offer bags of all sizes and gimmicks of all sorts, usually miniaturized, neon-ed, or otherwise made travel-savvy. The Savvy Traveler gives travel talks and sells videos and, most of all, literature, from guides and traditional narratives (e.g., *Twilight Over Burma: My Life as a Shan Prince*, by Inge Sargent), to the practical: a section on "handicapped travel"; the "Culture Shock" series on "the social, cultural, governmental and business climate" and the "language and lifestyle" of (in 1996) almost forty countries; *Teaching English Abroad: Talk Your Way Around the World!*, or *American Ways: A Guide for Foreigners in the United States*, and even Sarah Anderson's *Travel Companion: A Guide to the Best Non-Fiction and Fiction for Traveling* ($65), for what

The Savvy Traveller says are "what *we* think are the best guides, histories, travel literature, fiction available" (Fall 1996 *Newsletter*).

What we think. It *is* one small, small world. As this smattering from The Savvy Traveller *Newsletter* makes clear, the key fact of travel at the end of the twentieth century is that it is a worldwide web. Travel talk is all over the Internet (I booked a room for July 1997 at a cheap but funky motel a friend told me of, on the outskirts of Port Douglas, Australia. Travelocity, on the World Wide Web (http://www.travelocity.com) is 200,000 pages big, can book reservations for airplanes, hotels, car rentals, and so on, and if you need really basic help, Chats and Forums is there, as is Merchandise (luggage, videos, and so on).[6] But travel today is also a web in ways that are both more traditional and more fanciful. In May 1996, Ruth Carrington, the veteran journeyer whose early traveling steps are recounted in this text, sent me a postcard mailed to her by two friends: "Greetings from Honduras! We've done some hiking in the interior and saw howler monkeys and lots of birds." On the card to me, Ruth wrote: "I wonder if they had read David Yeadon," because she had read my essay in *Preview 2001+: Popular Culture Studies in the Future* (1995), the title of which, " 'And then I saw the monkey . . . ,' " is taken from Yeadon's account of canoeing through the Costa Rican jungle humbled by his intrusiveness but blessed joyously by his sighting, at last, of "just one" rare howler monkey (*The Back of Beyond*, 98–99). Ruth had shared with her friends Chris and Ken the meaning I took from David Yeadon and they had sent back to her their story, and she sent it to me, and so a new loop in the web was knit—as it was when Steven M. Newman "rerouted" his walk across America to include Robin Morris's third grade in Bozeman, Montana, because they had sent him (in Melbourne, Australia), a "huge" letter, three feet by three and one-half feet, "[c]overed on both front and back with dozens of very intelligent questions about my worldwalk" (*Worldwalk*, 503). One world of walkers.

~

For the 1995 Popular Culture Association Conference, Ray Browne and I sent out a call for papers on "travel culture" and got enough good ones for a full day's worth of panels, saving the last time slot for the best: a forum among paper-givers and listeners, making connections and brainstorming for the next year's conference—and for this collection. All of the essays here are original, except for Judith Adler's and Tom Gunning's; and most come from the 1995, 1996, and 1997 Popular Culture Association conferences. In this text, as in the conference sessions, we have strived for variety and an introductory flavor, rather than a "true believer" and "last word" tone: we want to open up this new field, travel culture in popular culture.

In this collection, we have history, and typical of travel writing, we have historical essays taking off from someone's personal story: "Touring America in a Model T," in which David Tomlinson reports from an unpublished diary by Olive King of her honeymoon trip from Missouri through the West in the early 1920s ("One has to cultivate a tra-la-la feeling and take what comes"). Terri Ryburn-LaMonte writes of America's popular culture icon, Route 66, but she also stimulates the teacher in us by recounting how she taught Route 66 to college students and how she herself became a scholar of the international visitors on "the Road." The knowledge of

America's history held by these "foreigners," and their respect for history, should humble and teach us—and give new meaning to that commonplace put-down, "tourist."

Marielle Risse, in "White Knee Socks Versus Photojournalist Vests: Distinguishing Between Travelers and Tourists," also takes issue with the habitual scorn of the "masses." Risse looks historically at the differentiating criteria, for example, "physical toughness," money and class, and knowing the language. She uses a rich library of travelers, from Montaigne through Paul Fussell, to help in her subtle (and humorous) defining: for example, shouldn't we applaud the "simple" traveler who spurns the tour bus to wander at length and casually, really living in the host land? Not if we remember that these "simple" travelers can do that only because they have the money that buys such freedom.

Exemplifying the importance of personal history, especially in a new field such as travel culture, is Montanan Ruth Carrington's story of the start of her life as a twentieth-century traveler, teaching in postwar Asia. This is perhaps a small piece of history, but it has been a lost one: the occupying servicemen, their dependents, the teachers and other civilian workers on the U.S. bases—growing in number from one hundred thousand in 1950 to five hundred thousand in 1960—and above all, the Taiwanese, Philippine, and other "native" people Carrington met and writes about. As she says, "From these contacts began my introduction to the realities of international politics, a view of the world that had never before concerned me." This view was to change the life of this seventy-plus-year-young woman just back from her latest Fulbright teaching, this time in Sri Lanka. Hers is one of what should be a whole book's worth of histories of the true makers of the travel culture.

Robert D. Kaplan, one of the best political travel writers (*Balkan Ghosts, The Arabists*), judges that "[t]he ultimate test of a travel writer may be political savvy." V. S. Naipaul's books, for example, as Kaplan says, foreshadow "[African] disasters like Rwanda, Zaire and Liberia more effectively than did some misguidedly benign depictions of that continent."[7] This collection has political travel culture studies that focus on the roots in American history and popular culture of today's dilemmas of multiculturalism and changing gender roles. Lynn Y. Weiner's " 'There's a Great Big Beautiful Tomorrow': Historic Memory and Gender in Walt Disney's Carousel of Progress" looks at perhaps the "major purveyor of popular history throughout the twentieth century," the Walt Disney Corporation, and specifically at the changing picture of women and the family in the Carousel of Progress in, first, Disneyland in California and, after 1975, Disney World in Florida. Weiner's "Carousel" shows the impact of feminism and then of the current backlash against it. Her essay raises again the central question of popular culture: how much do the Disneys of our world create our "collective memory" (Weiner's words) and how much do they just reflect it? The answer, of course, is both: because of the gigantic scope of its reach, the popular has to "show" and cannot help but "tell" or teach. (Travel agents tell us that the television series *The Love Boat* created the mass cruise business.)

In "Lawrence and Beauvoir at Tua-Tah: European Views of the Heart of the World," Tamara Teale looks into an earlier part of the twentieth century, when the elite culture had more stature than it does in our global culture. Specifically, Teale goes to the 1930s and 1940s, when, first, D. H. Lawrence and then, briefly in 1946, Simone de Beauvoir visited Taos, New Mexico, and the Tua-Tah pueblo of the Tiwa Native people. The by now familiar clash of cultures focuses here on Lawrence's observation of "the old, amusing contradiction between the white and the dark races"—he saw himself as neither and hence an "outsider . . . of the game"—and Beauvoir's disrespect for a *khiva*, a place sacred to the Indians and barred to tourists. Teale is keen to the subtleties of the cultural insider-outsider "game" ("[Beauvoir's] need to 'slip away from the group' seems to be an elite tourist move"), without losing sight of the general ironies of the natives' dilemma (" 'We live by these damn tourists' ").

In "D. H. Lawrence in Taos: High Pilgrimage, Low Pilgrimage"—a companion to Teale's essay—John W. Presley tells the tale of his meeting with Lawrence's paintings in Taos and with their keeper, Saki Karavas. Like Teale, Presley sees the wry contradictions in the mystery of D. H. Lawrence: a "great" artist, but perhaps also an "obscene" one? In "Identity in John Lloyd Stephens's *Incidents of Travel in Central America, Chiapas, and Yucatan*" (1841), William Lenz also delves sensitively into an exceptionally popular travel writer from another "sumptuous" era of "narratives of travel and exploration." In his literary critic's reading of Stephens, Lenz brings to the surface Stephens's "unembarrassed" picture of U.S. dominance in Mesoamerica ("unembarrassed" is the reviewer Edgar Allan Poe's word) and Stephens's own erotic patronage of the proverbial dark-skinned primitives, especially the women. Like Lawrence, and like Melville in Polynesia, it is a fearful as well as a compelled gaze that Stephens flicks recklessly, feverishly, in the new world.

Tom Gunning, in an important aesthetic history, " 'The Whole World Within Reach': Travel Images Without Borders," starts from the early days of photography and one of the photographer's favorite subjects: "snapshots" of travels. Gunning charts the parallel growth in this century of travel and the filmic perspective and illuminates a world become picture, as the philosopher Martin Heidegger put it—a world of images, distancing and disjointing viewers and viewed. A world like this, Gunning makes clear, in time becomes a world in love with "transit." How can this be "one world"?

Another piece in the puzzle is Michael Bryson's "Popular Science on the Road: Adventures in Island Biogeography" which focuses on the ideas of David Quammen, particularly in his popular 1996 book, *The Song of the Dodo: Island Biogeography in an Age of Extinctions.*[8] Like Lenz and our other essayists, such as Beatriz Badikian and David Espey, Bryson explores travel literature as narrative; his point is that travel storytelling has served science and, as in Quammen's work, still richly serves it, by clarifying scientific information for a popular audience: "the excitement, the surprise, and the wonder generated by the travel aspects of a text contribute to its didactic function, its ability to provide a scientific education." And like Lenz, Bryson in his analysis emphasizes the narrative persona. Both see this persona as a simple, natural man. Lenz's is John Lloyd Stephens, a man thoroughly at home in his "manifestly" arrogant nineteenth century; Bryson's persona is the opposite: in nature he is empathetic, respectful, thoughtful, unheroic in the extreme.

In characterizing his narrator, Bryson draws on Mary Louise Pratt's *Imperial Eyes: Travel Writing and Transculturation* (1992). Quoting liberally from historical travel texts, some little known, Pratt shows us the range and depth of Eurocentrism—even in the Linnean biological ordering system—but also surprises us, for example, with the European's (properly) "humbling" discovery that the interior of west Africa, away from the worldly coast, was highly "civilized" (and as aware of Europe as the Europeans were not aware of their culture). Pratt also illuminates Lenz, for example, in showing how Alexander von Humboldt and his followers writing in the early nineteenth century "reinvented" the Spanish and English "colonies" in the Americas as a "creole" paradise, "wild and gigantic" (120), as the Romantic era fantasized the natural world. Even more provocatively, Pratt links the eroticization of the creole with the empowerment of "antislavery sentiment"; as Pratt says, the abolitionist movement is in the genre of sentimental travel writing and the survival literature popular since Europe's first foray into empire building in the fifteenth century: first-person stories of shipwrecks, castaways, mutinies, abandonments, and (the special island setting) captivities. From the old popular stories, Pratt shows us that even before the late eighteenth-century abolition movement started, survival literature had taken on as its great themes "sex and slavery"—really, as Pratt says, a single theme, often in an Arab setting and with a religious cast of many heathens and infidels. "Throughout the history of early European colonialism and the slave trade, survival literature furnished a 'safe' context for staging alternate, relativizing, and taboo configurations of intercultural [and "transracial"] contact," she says: the context was safe because "the tale was always told from the viewpoint of the European who returned." (86–87).

Pratt retells what she calls a "typical" transcultural story, similar to John Lloyd Stephens's. In the *Narrative of a Five Year Expedition against the Revolted Negroes of Surinam* (1796), John Stedman tells of his love and marriage to Joanna, a fifteen-year-old "house slave," who said no to going back to Europe with him (where he married a European woman). As Stedman's diary tells us, Joanna actually was one of several "mates" Stedman left in Surinam, but Pratt will not be simplistic in her reading. In Joanna's proud rejecting of Europe (and keeping of the special, high place she feels she holds in her culture), Pratt sees her sensitivity to the "dehumanization" Europe would subject her to (96) and her tragic placing of herself outside any world. As Pratt says, "It is easy to see [these] transracial love plots as imaginings in which . . . sex replaces slavery as the way others are seen to belong to the white man" (97). But in their details the stories show us clearly that the uncommon lovers tried, and tragically failed, to create "reciprocal . . . exchanges" that made them "individuals worthy of each other" (97). As we say, they could not talk each other's language; it is, in American culture, the age-old *Summer of '42* romance of the "native" boy or maid and the rich person from "away."

In "Childhood and Travel Literature," David Espey connects traveling to childhood. Children don't (often) travel on their own, but the seeds of travel are planted then, perhaps because it is a time of "constriction" (Espey's word). And the typical adult traveler is childlike: vulnerable, but wondrous. Espey writes, "Like a child, one discovers challenge and delight in accomplishing simple tasks like making oneself understood, ordering a meal, finding the way back to the hotel"; and he links travel writing (and reading travel writing) to "childhood autobiography": "The return to the home of one's childhood . . . is a kind of ultimate journey, a mythic return which completes the cycle begun by the departure from home. Like the literature of travel, childhood autobiography is grounded in a strong sense of place." The poet Beatriz Badikian, in "Mapmaking: The Poet as Travel Writer," charts a similar connection between travel and story-making in women writers. Badikian looks at *Maiden Voyages*, Mary Morris's anthology of writings by women travelers, and at her own poetry and that of contemporaries such as Sandra Cisneros, Lorna Dee Cervantes, and Ana Castillo. In all, she sees joined the interior and exterior journey. A journey is purposeful or destined travel, and in the journey, as in the poetry, such as her central poem, "Mapmaking," Badikian shows the blood, myth, and the history and politics of racism and injustice, melded with a journey and the artful writing, or memorializing, of it: "I measure / earth with words."

The inward look and the outward; the "thing itself," the "native"—ideally uninterpreted and thus the ultimate "insider"—versus the "objective" outsider, the student, the explorer: these mirror the dialectic of travel. History, political analysis, sociology and anthropology, psychology, literary criticism, memoir: these are the perspectives, or disciplines, of the travel culture essays in this volume. A week before the popular culture conference in Philadelphia that gave birth to a number of these pieces, at a conference on women and television in Seattle, anthropologist Ellen Strain spoke of the "crisis" in ethnography. Especially in a field and a time of nonjudgment, said Strain, perhaps the only value the scholar has is to tell the rest of us facts we do not know. And so, today, when tourism and television are close to universal, in the anthropologist's field do we not all know everything? Is the "gaze" of the ethnographer not merely the "tourist gaze" in scholarly guise?[9] Leading ethnographers such as Clifford Geertz, of the Institute for Advanced Study in Princeton, New Jersey, emphasize cultural blends, practicing "transnational" analysis. "The world . . . does not divide itself clearly at the joints into societies or traditions," says Geertz. But he also adds that the current "effort to downplay differences may not necessarily improve understanding among different cultures."[10]

Indeed it will not. In October 1996, Beatriz Badikian sent a postcard from Hanover, Germany: "Took a train from Brussels yesterday, tonight a sleeper to Paris. . . . [H]ow small the world is becoming: Television all over, shops, music, food. . . . I don't know where I am anymore when I wake up in the morning." John LeCarre writes, "Panama is a beautiful country, with splendid people, coastlines, mountains, pastures, forest and out islands. Will sloth, corruption and stupidity ruin this little paradise, as they have ruined so many others?[11] The names of many places could be substituted for Panama, could they not? But note that LeCarre's subjects are generalizations; where are the human actors? Whose "sloth, corruption and stupidity" tend to ruin paradise? It is not just outsiders, battering the gates to womblike home. Some "locals"—"natives"—also, always, want a piece of the pie. Some "transplants," some "away people," care as much for the land/town/"fortress" as the locals driven "to Florida" by last year's "awful" winter. Andrew G. Fox taught

English in a Prague high school for two years at "Czech wages," which she says, averaged $200 per month in nonconvertible currency. Fox traveled on a Czech tour bus to Italy for six days (for $150) and was humbled as a traveler:

> Despite the fuss, noise, heat, and sheer fatigue, Rome and Italy overwhelm us with beauty. Tomorrow at dawn, we will have the city of Sirmione on the shore of Lake Garda, the Roman amphitheater in Verona, and the next day the shimmering light on the buildings of Venice will enchant us. The look in the eyes of our group members when they see those things makes me feel privileged to be with them. They have spent a significant part of their incomes, and have undergone outrageous trials, for these few moments, and one cannot help feeling that as a result the intensity of these moments is greater for them. They seem to embody the whole reason for travel. No traveler in a luxury suite could gain more from Rome than these ragged, sunburned people.[12]

Is Andrew G. Fox's stand against elitism sentimental? Naive? Fox looked outward, away from himself, and so saw with a clearer, and a kinder eye. Even so, he did not break free of classism. Those "ragged, sunburned people" who "embody the whole reason for travel" reek of bathetic "enthusiasm" for the "peasant." The "one" who cannot help feeling "the intensity of [their] moments" is still formally, impersonally set off from "them."

It is a love-hate relationship between insiders and outsiders. It is, and it has been so everywhere and always—since the start of sea coast traders/raiders and fortresses erect on hills or warm hearths hidden in woods. The outsider always brings danger: captivity, plunder, disorder. But he—or she, the "mystery woman"—also brings novelty, new worlds to titillate the curiosity and creativity of men and women who in their slower, more naturally paced and isolated land-worlds have been able, perhaps, to think more fully, more deeply, than the scintillating, fast-moving trader-pirate. It could be, should be, a balance and a complement between mover and stay-at-home, but it rarely is.

The insider always spells "arrival," not "departure": Penelope waiting and spinning for Odysseus stands for "journey's end"; "home free"; "made it." Ah, but the outsider signals freedom. Loosing, losing, bonds, bounds. Travelers use words like "fresh . . . sweet, like a return to very early youth," "a sense of morning, . . . even of innocence" (the novelist John Knowles, 1964), but they also use "madness" (Goethe, 1788)—disorder.[13] We can only see things when they are outside; inside, our world of objects becomes a medium, not a place of substance.[14] Home and the insider are comforting, cozy—and, well, boring, right? The "community" means "civility" and the "social contract"—anxiety-stirring, face-yourself-in-the-mirror *compromise.* And do not forget sex. Within the fortress are no secrets—as in any small town, anytime. "Home" is monogamy, propriety, respectability, "the law," organized religion, cleanliness. "On the open road," the "open sea," "down river" (or "up"), "the other side of the mountain": all bespeak something "strange, perhaps "wonder-ful," not "settled,": liberty, movement, sometimes even lawlessness, in the wilderness wild.

"Home" is Francesca, the farmwife in *The Bridges of Madison County*; "away" is Robert, the globetrotting picture-taker—outsider and voyeur personified. He fills her with wonder when he tells her he knows her hometown, Bari, in southern Italy, because on a train en route to Brindisi, to catch the boat to Greece, he saw Bari, liked it, and got off.

Francesca: You got off the train because it looked pretty?
Robert: Sure.

And later, when he asks how long she's lived in Iowa, she answers, "You just jumped off the train without knowing anyone there?"

Robert: Yeah.[15]

Travel is the other side—the good news—of the story of Adam and Eve.

And travel is a story needing a lot more telling. For example, does tourism totally destroy the chance of cultures coming together—connecting even in clash? This is a question only broached in this text, and needing its own (several) points of view. Already travelers are squeezed by the vicious circle: tourists—travelers massed and scheduled—tramp over and crush out the solitude, beauty, and adventure the traveler seeks; and tourism, or "development," generates crime and other fears. The lonely spots on the planet either get overbooked or rate a "travelers' warning." Travelers are the visitors who really get to know a culture; they are the guests who stay for "the season." As tourists take the place of travelers, what will become of the relationship of the locals and the people from "away"? Already we have a taste of the answer: indifference at best. The tourists and natives who are ships passing in the night are sadder, if safer, than guests and hosts who bump and jar and cut with their edges as they, at least, intersect.

For there are larger questions, and we are all implicated, all part of the problem. In reviewing *The Dictionary of Global Culture*, edited by Kwame Anthony Appiah and Henry Louis Gates, Jr., an encyclopedia which bespeaks the growing importance of the field of travel culture, James Shapiro sounds a death knell many of us welcome: the *Dictionary* "demonstrate[s] . . . there is no going back, no retreat to a time when Western cultural achievement could be artificially severed from non-Western." And then Shapiro states, "The real—and unspoken—battle now is no longer between West and non-West, but between global culture and a multinational consumer culture that threatens to obliterate regional diversity, if not identity" (7).

If this stark iteration is the right way to put the "battle" ahead—and I think it is except for "unspoken," as our Annotated Bibliography shows—then we can see clearly that travel culture is at the center of understanding; for it studies, and would limn, both the global culture (jazz, kabuki, the Yoruba) and the consumer culture—Shapiro names the "icons" of McDonald's, cyberspace, MTV, Nike, the Miss Universe contest, and the like. "Should this mass culture be considered part of global culture?" Shapiro asks. How can it not be? But how to untangle the joy of a trip to Disneyland, the *lift* of a pair of Nikes, from what they "threaten? Nike, "ironically, has depended upon exploited Indonesian laborers," Shapiro notes. What if the regional diversity embraces female circumcision? What if the particular culture's identity needs to sell rare, radiated tortoises? ("We do this to eat. We are human. We need to eat," says the tortoise catcher in Madagascar, where both the land and the sea have been made barren by human farming.)[16] Let our answering these questions not be thought of as a battle, but, rather, a dilemma—a global one all us travelers are knotted up in. Tourists and natives all, we must do more than just pass in the night.

We will at least get a snapshot of the edges where we touch in the selection of essays on the global, millennial travel culture that follow. Reading these studies over, following the trains of their allusions and images, I envision them spurring more connections, new papers and collections. In the global culture, this era of "demystifying imperialism" (Pratt), may they feed the institutional curriculum struggles now under way in most American universities, "the legacy of Euroimperialism, androcentrism and white supremacy in education and official culture" (Pratt xi). But besides the serious, may the ends of these new analyses and interpretations of the travel culture be to feed our sense of wonder; open us to new peoples, ways of living, ideas; and stir us to move—to *travel.*

NOTES

1. In *The Neanderthal Enigma: Solving the Mystery of Human Origins* (New York: Morrow, 1995), James Shreeve, a contributing editor of *Discover* magazine, proposed that the answer to the "mystery of human origins" is the Cro-Magnon people, specifically their mobility, which the Neanderthal did not share, and which drove the Cro-Magnons to go afield to mate; and then to learn and create many new tools and, for the first time, symbolic expression such as cave paintings, starting around 40,000 years ago, which most paleoanthropologists say marks the start of the human race of today. Shreeve's hypothesis is new and has not won the field over the Neanderthal-ites, but what should interest us is that mobility—travel—is primary in his argument. See also the review by Brenda Fowler, "Where Did He Go?" *New York Times Book Review,* December 17, 1995, 21.

2. Charles Siebert, "The Cuts That Go Deeper," *New York Times Magazine,* July 7, 1996, 25.

3. "Origins of Sightseeing," *Annals of Tourism Research* 16 (1989): 7–29. Dean MacCannell makes a similar point on the "institutionalism" of tourists looking at ordinary, everyday work and workers, in *The Tourist: A New Theory of the Leisure Class* (New York: Macmillan, 1976), 49 (2nd ed., 1989). MacCannell's point is cited by John Urry in *The Tourist Gaze: Leisure and Travel in Contemporary Societies* (Thousand Oaks, CA: Sage, 1990), 8.

4. "An Accidental Family" (review of *A Fine Balance* by Rohinton Mistry), *New York Times Book Review,* June 23, 1996, 29.

5. Philip Shenon, "The End of the World on 10 Tugriks a Day," *New York Times Magazine,* June 30, 1996, 37. Frommer's series (1957–), is unusual today in being "for all travelers except the backpacking, sandal-wearing crowd" (37).

6. "One Stop Shopping," *New York Times*, May 19, 1996, sec. 5, p. 3.

7. "Neither Here Nor There," *New York Times Book Review*, December 18, 1994, 12.

8. See also Quammen's application of his theory of islands to national parks: "Like islands, they are places where species go [or are sent] to die." "National Parks: Nature's Dead End," *New York Times*, Op Ed section, July 28, 1996, sec. 4, p. 13.

9. "Millennium: Touristic TV and the Ethnographer's Dilemma," paper presented at *Consoling Passions: Women and Television* conference, Seattle, April 6–9, 1995.

10. Qtd. in Karen J. Winkler, "Anthropologists Urged to Rethink Their Definitions of Culture," *Chronicle of Higher Education*, December 14, 1994, A18.

11. "Quel Panama!" *New York Times Magazine*, October 13, 1996, 54.

12. "A Group Tour of Italy, Czech Style," *New York Times*, October 23, 1994, sec. 5, p. 39.

13. Qtd. by Eric J. Leed, at the opening of Chapter 1, "Reaching for Abroad: Departures," in *The Mind of the Traveler: From Gilgamesh to Global Tourism* (New York: Harper Basic, 1991).

14. Leed, 45, citing the perceptual psychologist James Gibson, *The Ecological Approach to Visual Perception* (Boston: Houghton Mifflin, 1979), 20 ff.

15. In the 1995 movie version of Robert James Waller's 1992 novel, Meryl Streep plays Francesca and Robert is played by "Mr. Laconic," Clint Eastwood.

16. James Shapiro, "From Achebe to Zydeco," *New York Times Book Review*, February 2, 1997, 7. On the global consumer culture of traffic in endangered species, see Donovan Webster, "The Looting and Smuggling and Fencing and Hoarding of Impossibly Precious, Feathered, Scaly Wild Things," *New York Times Magazine*, February 16, 1997, 26–33, 48–49, 53, 61.

PART I

SIGHTSEEING: THE TWENTIETH-CENTURY

Origins of Sightseeing

JUDITH ADLER

INTRODUCTION

EVEN A BRIEF perusal of travel literature, or a short look at contemporary tourists, is sufficient to suggest that travel practices might be conveniently grouped according to style. The conventions which, at various times, have governed the artful performance of journeys include norms pertinent to ritual preparation; modes of transportation; duration; design and pattern of itinerary; foci of attention; dress, demeanor, and social relationships to be maintained en route; and forms of discourse marking termination. The list, meant only to be suggestive, far from exhausts all possible categories of convention. The relative emphasis given any one category can be expected to vary; indeed, this variation often helps to define the distinctiveness of a travel style. But all travel conventions bear upon human movement through culturally conceived space, movement which is deliberately undertaken in order to yield meaning pertinent to the travelers and their publics. Space and time—and the traveler's own body as it moves through both—are the baseline elements of all travel performance.

This chapter explores one dimension of the human "embodiment" of the travel art. It has never been irrelevant whether a traveler set out in a male or female body, and for centuries moral treatises warned of the dangers which travel posed to women (Giles 1976). Age and health have also drawn attention, early treatises often setting an ideal age for touring, while interdicting it to those whose bodies were too young, too old, or too infirm to bear out the desired experience (Baretti 1768; Bourne 1578; Leigh 1671; Turler 1575). But one may further argue that even beyond such classifications, the traveler's body, as the literal vehicle of the travel art, has been subject to historical construction and stylistic constraint. The very senses through which the traveler receives culturally valued experience have been molded by differing degrees of cultivation and, indeed, discipline. In examining the link between a particular style of travel that flourished in the seventeenth and eighteenth centuries and a historically new, overweaning emphasis upon the isolated exercise and systematic cultivation of the sense of sight, the concern of this chapter is twofold. It attempts to suggest that the way in which the human body is exercised as an instrument of travel is deeply revealing of the historically shifting manner in which people conceive themselves and the world to which they seek an appropriate relation through travel ritual. More specifically, it urges that the strong present link between tourism and sightseeing should not be taken for granted or regarded as static in nature. For not only is sight just one of several sense modalities around which styles of travel have been elaborated, but sight itself has been differently conceived in the course of tourism history.

In a convention of Western tourism which has become so taken for granted that it risks passing without remark, it is often said that people travel to "see" the world, and it is assumed that travel knowledge is substantially gained through observation. This longstanding association between travel and vision, tourism and sightseeing, demands closer scrutiny. It has not always existed, it has undergone important modifications even for its duration, and its history offers intriguing glimpses into earlier phases of Western epistemology and subjectivity. The practices of the contemporary sightseer, so often caricatured with his camera in tow, must ultimately be understood in relation to the historical development (and eventual popularization) of post-Baconian and Lockean orientations toward the problem of attaining, and authoritatively representing, knowledge. They must be seen in relation to forms of subjectivity anchored in willfully independent vision and in the cognitive subjugation of a world of "things." Above all, they need to be understood in relation to that European cultural transformation which Lucien Febvre first termed "the visualization of perception" (Febvre 1947:473; Mandrou 1961:68–77).

TRAVEL AS DISCOURSE

Travel was first widely proclaimed as an art, and openly secular forms of tourism were first systematically practiced by European elites, in the early sixteenth century. One need only turn to the treatises on travel method produced during a period which was preoccupied with the problem of "method" in all branches of learning to find evidence that sightseeing did not always enjoy its later pride of place. The travelers that treatises addressed, scholar-courtiers and young aristocrats preparing for diplomatic and legal careers, went abroad seeking educational experience at universities in Paris, Bologna, or Padua, as well as opportunities to engage the services of Europe's foremost dancing, music, fencing, or riding masters with whom they would be forced to speak in a foreign tongue. Books played a prominent part in the preparation for a journey and their purchase was one of its objects. The aristocratic traveler who was addressed, often by his tutor, in early manuals on advice went abroad for *discourse* rather than for picturesque views or scenes. The art of travel he was urged to cultivate was in large measure one of discoursing with the living and the dead—learning foreign tongues, obtaining access to foreign courts, conversing gracefully with eminent men, assimilating classical texts appropriate to particular sites, and, not least, speaking eloquently upon his return. At a time when the social role of the nobility was being transformed and burgeoning institutions of diplomacy opened new opportunities in a courtier's career (Mattingly 1955:211), European aristocracies sustained an art of travel, explicitly legitimized by service to the state, which sought to develop international contacts, judicious political judgment, adeptness at foreign languages, and skill in oratory deemed desirable in a prince's counselor. The experience of the world at which this was aimed was understood to involve primarily a reflective and disciplined exercise of the ear and the tongue.

Advice to "confer with expert men and with many," to go a hundred miles out of one's way to speak with a wise man, rather than five to see a fair town, and to be neither credulous nor overly eager to contradict when in conference was reiterated in one early travel sermon after another (Essex 1596:13). Many travelers carried with them a book of blank pages, an *Album Amicorum,* with which they would call on men of reputation, begging them to inscribe some words (Hazard 1953:6). The young Earle of Bedford is lectured by his tutor, J. Spradling:

> Everie one can gaze, can wander, and can wonder, but to few it is given to seek, to search, to learne, and to attaine to true policie and wisdome (which is traveling indeed). . . . Now this search and inquisition I speake of is to be practiced either by reading the severall histories of those nations where you are to travell . . . or else by hearing. . . . Therefore to attaine to a more exact and perfect knowledge it shall not be amiss for your Lordship to talk with the learned of the lande where you go. For albeit wisdome and safetie do wish to counsel you to silence in travelling: yet I thinke it not amiss, though you give the rains now and then to that unbridled member, the toong which you may use as occasion shall serve. (Lipsius 1592:A4)
>
> . . . And might I have leave to direct you also in the subject of your talk, in mine opinion nothing were more meet for one of your honorable estate then to question and discourse of the fashions, lawes, nobilitie, and kind warfare of the people where you travell. (Lipsius 1592:B2)

Elaborating further upon the advantages to be gained through "conferring with the wise," the tutor affirms that mere contact with eloquence "will make a man much more rhetoricall and civil in speech" and concludes by anchoring his travel program in human anatomy: "Learning . . . is obtained either by the eare, or by the eie: by hearing (I meane) or by reading" (Lipsius 1592:B3). Both senses are given equal weight, but, far more tellingly, sight is exclusively equated with reading, or at best with the confirmation of classical texts. For in traveling, a man "shall have occasion to call into remembrance that which is set down in Livy, Polibius, Tacitus, etc. [and] see before his eies the trueth of their discourses and the demonstration of their descriptions" (Lipsius 1592:XC).

The word, not the image, the ear and the tongue, not the eye, stand at the center of such treatment. Any sightseeing which takes place remains at the service of textual authority. Preparation for travel involved gathering information at home for exchange abroad, learning foreign languages, compiling systematic lists of questions, obtaining the letters of introduction necessary for access to high-status settings of conversation, and above all, reading.

Still in this tradition, Richard Lassells's *An Italian Voyage* (1697) features travel as a means of undoing the curse of Babel and restoring universal discourse.

> [It] takes off in some sort that aboriginal curse which was laid upon mankind . . . the confusion of tongues . . . [or] diversity of language [which] makes the wisest man pass for a fool in a strange country, and the best man for an excommunicated person, whose conversation all men avoid. Now traveling takes off this curse and this moral excommunication by making us learn many languages and converse freely with people in other countries. (Lassells 1697)

Similarly:

> It contents the mind with the rare discourses we hear from learned men. It makes him [the traveler] sought after by his betters, and listened unto with admiration by his inferiors. It makes him sit still in his old age with satisfaction; and travel over the world again in his chair and bed by discourse and thoughts. . . . In fine it's an excellent Commentary upon histories; and no man understands Livy and Cesar, Guicciardin and Monluc, like him who hath made exactly the Grand Tour of France and the giro of Italy. (Lassells 1697)

For Lassells, a Catholic tutor, the world figures metaphorically as a book after the manner of Plotinus and Augustine, and travel through it is treated as a commentary upon other texts. In a formulation to be repeated by other writers until the end of the nineteenth century, he writes, "They that never stir from home read only one page of this book; and, like the dull fellow who could never learn to count farther than five . . . dwell always upon one lesson." Conversation with eminent men, assiduously sought out abroad, becomes a prime technique for "reading" the world, and in old age the traveler can hope to "travel over again"—not, it is worth noting, through a store of pretty scenes which have been squirreled away in memory, but through thoughts and discourse.

THE ASCENDANCY OF THE EYE OVER THE EAR

The notion of travel as an exercise in universalizing discourse, particularly fitting to scholastic notions of how knowledge was to be sought, endured for a long time. But it was increasingly overlapped and eventually eclipsed by another tradition, which gave preeminence to the "eye" and to silent "observation." To a modern reader, one of the most anomalous features of sixteenth- and seventeenth-century travel sermons is the consistency with which they digress into human anatomy, rhetorically arguing the superiority of the eye over the ear. With inevitable juridical reference, travel is praised through favorable contrast between "eyewitness" and "hearsay" as legally admissible evidence and ground for valid judgment. Auricular knowledge and discourse identified with traditional authority, Aristotelianism, and the Schoolmen are devalued in favor of an "eye" believed to yield direct, unmediated, and personally verified experience. The shift accompanies a new naturalistic orientation and attains its purest expression in the seventeenth century, when it is nurtured by a fashion in courtly circles for Natural Philosophy and an epistemological individualism which enjoins every man to "see," verify, and, in a sense, "create" the world anew for himself.

R. Dallington opens *A Method for Travell* with a recommendation of both discourse and observation: "Plato . . . thought nothing better for the bettering of our understanding than travels as well by having a conference with the wiser sort in all sorts of learning as by the eye-sight of those things which otherwise a man cannot have but by tradition: a sandy foundation either in matter of science or conscience" (Dallington 1605:1). Dallington goes on to recommend that the traveler carry no books with him, but only "the papers of his own observation, especially a Giornale wherein from day to day he shall set down . . . [whatever] his eye meeteth by the way remarquable." Even more significant, like other seventeenth-century English Protestants who urged travelers to take protective measures against Continental Catholicism and its "infection of errors," Dallington warns against auricular openness: "The next caveat is, to beware how he heare anything repugnant to his religion; for as I have tyed his tongue, so must I stop his eares, lest they be open to the smooth incantations of an insinuating seducer, or the suttle arguments of a sophistical adversarie" (Dallington 1605:1–2).

In a contemporaneous sermon, *Quo Vadis? A Just Censure of Travell as It Is Commonly Undertaken by the Gentlemen of Our Nation*, Joseph Hall warns against the spiritual dangers of discourse abroad. "While our ears are open and our tongues free, they [Catholic adversaries] will hope well of our very denials" (Hall 1617:3). In the face of doctrinal difference, when English travelers to the Continent might be suspected of treasonist sympathies with Rome (Einstein 1902:155–75), travel treatises warned, "Though you hear the discourses of all . . . discover your mind to none" (Peacham 1622:162). The eye found favor as affording a more detached, less compromising form of contact than the ear, one more conducive to judicious, but socially distant appropriations. The wise traveler kept his eyes open and his mouth closed.

Comparing the well-traveled man to an "opticke Glasse, wherein not only the space of three or tenne miles, but also . . . of the whole world itself may be represented," or to a "true watch-tower" from which all may be viewed, Kirchnerus opens his "Oration in Praise of Travell in Generall" (1611:C2) with an affirmation of the importance of seeing things with one's own eyes. In this conceit, he is echoed by the Scottish traveler William Lithgow, who writes in the prologue to his *A Most Delectable and True Discourse of a Peregrination in Europe, Asia, etc.*: "This laborious work . . . is only composed of mine own Eie-sight and occular experience: (pluris est occulatos testis unus, quam auriti decem) being the perfect mirror, and lively portraiture of true understanding" (Lithgow [1614] 1632:B). Lithgow repeats this association between eyesight, as direct "test" and "mirror" of reality, and epistemological grounds for certainty in *The Pilgrim's Farewell: The Joyes and Miseries of Peregrination* (1618).

> I see those things, which others have by eare:
> They reade, they heare, they dreame, reporters affect,
> But by experience, I trie the effect.

The discourse "of the advantage and preheminence of the Eye" which opens James Howell's *Instructions for Forreine Travell* (1642) argues the new sensory bias in detail.

> To run over and traverse the world by Hearesay, and traditional relation, with other men's eyes, and to take all things upon courtesie, is but a confused and imperfect kind of speculation, which leaveth but weake and distrustful notions behind it; in regard the *Eare* is not so authentique a witness as the *Eye*; because the *Eye*, by which as through a clear christall casement, wee discerne the various works of Art and Nature, and in one instant comprehend half the whole universe. . . . I say the eye . . . taketh in farre deeper Ideas, and so makes firmer and more lasting impressions.
>
> And although one should reade all the Topographers that ever writ of, or anatomized a . . . Country, and mingle Discourse with the most exact observers . . . Yet one's own *ocular* view, and personall conversation will still find out something new and unpointed at by any other . . . and so enable him to discourse more knowingly and confidently and with a kind of *authority* thereof; It being an Act of Parliament among all Nations *that one eye-witness is of more validity than ten Auricular.* Moreover, as everyone is said to *abound with his own sense*, . . . so in each individual man there is a differing faculty of *observation* . . . which makes that every one is best satisfied and most faithfully instructed by himselfe, I do not mean solely by himself . . . but *Books* also . . . yet . . . a collation of his own optique observations . . . work much more strongly. . . . And indeed, this is the prime use of Peregrination. (Howell 1642:2–3, 5–8, emphasis in original)

The "prime use of peregrination" is to make a "collation" of one's own "optique observations." Howell's redundancy makes the preoccupation with sense modality unambiguous. The gentleman traveler to whom these and similar remarks were addressed is increasingly encouraged to treat himself as a detached and "curious" eye and his journey as an exercise in accurate observation. When John Evelyn made his exemplary Grand Tour of the Continent, he employed a "sightsman" in Rome (Hodgen 1964:118). Other seventeenth-century travel relations described places in terms of those things in them which were "most observable" (Bromley 1693), often ignoring people altogether (Mazouer 1980) or simply classifying them as "amongst the living objects to be seen" (Lister 1699:20). By the eighteenth century some travelers were calling for guides which, by cataloging "the best articles to be seen in every town in order of merit," would bring the rationalization of sightseeing effort to its final, modern conclusion (cited in Curley 1976:242).

ORIGINS OF EARLY SIGHTSEEING METHOD

For a long time, aesthetic interests played little or no role in European sightseeing practice. Architectural monuments and sumptuous pageantry received some attention, but references to painting and sculpture, as well as to landscape beauty, are almost nonexistent in travel literature of the sixteenth and seventeenth centuries—even in travel accounts of Italy where these arts were flourishing. Rather, the norms which defined early sightseeing can first be discerned in the writings of sixteenth-century humanists who compiled regional topographies and ambitiously encyclopedic "cosmographies" of the known world (Strauss 1965). The new geographic description was self-consciously empirical: "For I myself have walked from one end to the other of this splendid land, and have, to the limits of my ability, measured it and recorded the sights," one German scholar assured his readers (Strauss 1958). "Wandering, or traveling, as long as not business or gain but learning is the motive" was praised as a mark of supreme scholarly effort (Strauss 1958:94). In Italy, Germany, the Low Countries, France, and England the project was devised of combining minutely comprehensive descriptions of both domestic and foreign regions, based upon eyewitness accounts, to create a "polyhistory" which would include all branches of knowledge within its scope. Such projects, invariably relying upon the collaboration of amateurs, with whom their authors sought correspondence, were explicitly formulated in visual terms. Regions were to be described in the manner of painting—"picturae similitudine observata prosequitur" (Strauss 1958:99)—resulting in a speculum or looking glass mirroring a country in all its aspects. By making it possible to "envision" whole countries through a detailed inventory of their flora, fauna, antiquities, and monuments, such projects undoubtedly participated in the "national awakenings" of the period, and the travel researches upon which they were based have some of the color of a patriotic rite (Moir 1964).

It took some time for the authors of these new empirically based "polyhistories" to break decisively with the past, insisting that seeing was better than reading and that travel should precede rather than follow the interpretation of established texts. A "method" of travel comprised of excerpts from Belgian and Danish geographers, translated into English and presented by one John Woolfe in 1589, still betrays a note of the earlier deference to traditional authority. Comparing his pamphlet on travel method to a "grammar," without which a traveler would be like a foolish youth, aspiring to be a Latinist without study, Woolfe promises: "I doubt not but that if our men will vouchsafe the reading, portage and practice of this pamphlet of notes . . . the thicke mistes of ignorance, and harde conception will soon be scattered, and the same converted into a quick sight and illumination of the senses" (Meirus 1589). But after translating Albertus Meirus's long lists of what a traveler should observe, Woolfe ends the tract on a humbler note, with a translation of a passage from Ortelius's *Itinerarium Belgiae:*

> If in our peregrinations and travels we shall observe and note in our tables or papers those things which . . . seem worthie of regard, we shall make our journies and voyages in great measure pleasant and delectable unto us: *not thinking that our diligence can search and mark anything in any place, which other men before us have not seene,* but to discourse and record anything, rather than to passe the way and spend the time in idleness. (Meirus 1589, emphasis added)

Gradually, travel methodologists became less deferential in proclaiming the advantages of direct observation. Their long checklists of things worthy of notice came to be adopted by courtesy writers offering advice on education to an aristocracy which was finding it increasingly necessary to secure their status on the basis of claims to "noble" accomplishments. In the seventeenth century, a courtly ideal of the gentleman scholar, or virtuoso (an Italian term then enjoying widespread European currency), made publicly applauded proficiency in an investigative art of travel a desirable status embellishment (Caudill 1976; Houghton 1942; Leigh 1671; Sorbière 1660). The culture of the virtuosi was sustained by princes, courtiers, physicians enjoying royal patronage, lawyers (particularly in France), and—in an intellectually central but socially marginal position—the tutors of the aristocracy (Frank 1979; Hunter 1981; Mandrou 1978). It centered upon the value of "curiosity," a word which had gradually moved away from its medieval denotation of vice to signify instead a virtuous passion for secular knowledge, as well as scrupulous observation and concern for accuracy of detail (Elliott 1970:30; Howard 1980:23; Zacher 1976). The virtuosi came in time to be known as "curious travelers," travel handbooks marking objects for their attention as "curiosities," and designing itineraries which might "gratify the curiosity by degrees."

The royal academies and scientific societies, which sprang up in many European countries during the seventeenth century, not only fostered an international travel culture, but helped to provide an institutional infrastructure for elite travel throughout the following century—leading one French historian of the Enlightenment to refer to them, along with Masonic lodges, as "institutions de tourisme intellectual" (Pommeau 1966:179). If the academies provided travelers with an international network of collegial support and hospitality, they were also dependent upon them for the direct contact and personal "correspondences" so important to scholarly communication at the time (Brown 1934). After having been received, a traveler might be asked to recommend his hosts, as correspondents, to eminent men of his own country or to disseminate their publications in other centers of learning (Middleton 1971:282–85). Thus, in 1661, the young Robert Southwell, later to become president of the Royal Society, writes home while on Grand Tour at age twenty-six that, wanting admission to the court of the grand duke of Tuscany, he first sought "entrance into a meeting of the virtuosi": "I put in an oar . . . and then got not only the occasion of choosing good acquaintance, but heard that at the court some favourable words passed of me" (cited in Middleton 1971:285). The acquaintance was not without price, for returning home Southwell is asked to set up a correspondence between the prince and the internationally famous Robert Boyle (commending the former on the basis of his correspondence with Parisian scholars) and he receives a letter from another of his hosts instructing him to promote the sale of that person's book in Venice, Vienna, Amsterdam, Aix, and Leyden. As a historian of the Florentine academy concludes, "there was a natural desire of [Italian] authors to obtain an even wider distribution for their works, and to do this they were quite prepared to give a good deal of trouble to foreign visitors, who might also find themselves expected to perform many other chores on the way back home" (Middleton 1971:282).

The culture sustained by the academies accorded high status to travel executed in a "serious" manner. Men were praised for being "well traveled," significant travel achievement was rewarded with honorary memberships and prizes, and erudites who shirked travel effort were denigrated as "sages of straw" (Dairval 1686:9). Travel often proved instrumental in launching international scholarly reputations (Hahn 1971:90). Not only did it afford the opportunity to establish personal contact and initiate prestigious correspondence with eminent men, but travel observations and voyage accounts were routinely publicized in the Royal Society's *Philosophical Transactions* as well as in such periodicals as the *Journal des Savants, Journal des Trevaux*, and *Mercure* (Broc 1974:188). Travelers might hope to become "traveling contributors" or "foreign correspondents" of important scientific societies and certainly received recognition for any specimens contributed to collections of curiosities upon their return home.

But most important, the academies explicitly codified and energetically propagated norms of travel discipline, providing a forum within which travel reports were publicized and criticized as well as translating and publishing "instructions" of travel method. Over the course of three centuries works with titles such as *A Booke Called the Treasure for Travellers* (Bourne 1578), *A Direction for Travaillers* (Lipsius 1592), "Directions for Seamen Bound for Far Voyages" (Rooke 1665), *De l'Utilité des Voyages et l'avantage que la recherche des Antiquités procure auz savans* (Dairval 1686), *General Heads for the Natural History of a Country Great or Small, Drawn Out for the Use of Travellers and Navigators* (Boyle 1692), *Brief Instructions for Making Observations in All Parts of the World* (Woodward 1696), "The Method of Enquiry into the State of Any Country" (Petty 1927), *Essai d'instructions pour voyager utilement* (Bernard 1715), and *Instructions for Travellers* (Tucker 1757) joined the chorus of courtesy writers (e.g., Gailhard 1678; Leigh 1671; Peacham 1622) and travel narratives to shape an internationally shared canon of observational method.

TRAVEL AS "EXPERIMENTAL" HISTORY

Throughout the seventeenth and eighteenth centuries, scholars refer to travel as a branch of history (Curley 1976:66; Volney 1788), history being understood, in opposition to fable, as a true account of the facts, based upon firsthand observation. The "facts" requiring observation constituted a heterogeneous assemblage of physical, biological, ethnological, and political information, and historians of science have noted the absence of any impulse at the time to group cultural and "natural" facts in separate domains of inquiry (Broc 1974; Hodgen 1964; Rowe 1964; Shapiro 1979). Sir Francis Bacon's *Catalogue of Particular Histories*, published with the *Novum Organum* in 1620, grouped the history of arts and trades with natural history as the study of man's work upon nature, and it was mirrored in subsequent treatises on travel method directing travelers to make careful observations of manufacturing processes. Soon, writers were exhorting aristocrats not to be ashamed to enter shops and factories in order to closely observe the labors of ordinary craftsmen (Houghton 1941). By the eighteenth century, travelers were increasingly directed to note customs and political institutions, but insofar as these were still understood to be effects of the properties of air, soil, climate, and food, social description remained circumscribed by observations of natural facts. The result, a hodgepodge of descriptive observation which violates later classifications of knowledge, is one of the distinctive characteristics of erudite travel reports during this period.

The travelers whose collaborative efforts, sustained over the course of several generations, were to be used in constructing a "new philosophy" and universal history, were not expected to be specialists. Amateur status was even believed to be an advantage. Thus Andrew Sparrman, physician, naturalist, and fellow of the Swedish Royal Academy, praised "every authentic book of voyages and travels" as "in fact a treatise of experimental philosophy," continuing, "it is . . . in the original writers of itineraries and journals that the philosopher looks for genuine truth and real observation; as the authors of them for the most part have had neither philosophical abilities, nor any other motive sufficient to induce them to report these facts, otherwise than they have presented themselves to their notice" (Sparrman [1785] 1971:v). Disciplined travel observations were regarded as "experiments," a word at the time connoting all investigations relying upon direct sensory experience, on the basis of which sound theories could eventually be inductively constructed and tested.

The helpmeets of the new philosophy sometimes received royal patronage or found support through private subscription, but most often they paid for their travels from their own purse even when undertaking public commissions. Any distinction one might make between a private tour and publicly sponsored investigation blurs when applied to societies whose elites remained defined by feudal rather than professional statuses, and in which training for public posts took place within aristocratic families rather than schools of public administration. Similarly, there is no evidence that the categorical distinction one now tends to make between narratives of New World exploration and those of European or domestic tours was made by the reading public of the time (Bideux 1981:31) or that formal publication of travel narrative can be taken as a sign of its public standing. Recent French scholarship has definitively established that a travel literature which never assumed book form (unedited diaries, letters, handwritten manuscripts) was widely circulated among intellectual elites and held a prominent place in private libraries (Broc 1974; Dainville 1940; Duchet 1971:66; Harder 1981:88–98; Michea 1945). In short, formal publication was not a precondition of significant public reputation and influence. Once the public sphere is conceived in a manner appropriate to this premodern organization of cultural life, one can better understand the seriousness with which amateur travel, along with its outgrowth in private letters and diaries, was discussed.

With the aim of disciplining an informal corps of reliable informants, travel critics castigated "untutored minds," incapable of giving any reliable account of where they had been, who moved "as if in a dream," seeing all through the mist of their own vanities and prejudices (Baretti 1768; Bourne 1578; Dairval 1686; La Lande 1769). Through both advice and praise, intellectual authorities held travelers accountable to explicitly formulated rules of observational method. John Evelyn, writing in 1669 to Samuel Pepys, who was about to embark for Paris, instructed him in one of these conventions. Upon arrival Pepys must mount the steeple of St. Jacques in order to "take a synoptical prospect of that monstrous city, to consider ye Situation, Extent, and Approaches so as to be ye better able to make comparisons with our London" (Marburg 1935:47; compare with Howell 1642:31). Having once taken the synoptical view, a systematic sightseer was expected to visit palaces, gardens, charitable institutions, libraries, and curiosity cabinets—catalogs of whose contents were beginning to be published as a subgenre of the travel guidebook (Koehler 1762; Reiske 1645). Conventional itineraries taking in important European curiosity cabinets became established, and a virtuoso making the "stations" of these early museums might win public praise for having "seen and described the contents of more cabinets than any man did before him" (Lister 1699:99). In fact, the early cataloging of Europe's museums was largely carried out by authors describing themselves as "travelers" (Murray 1904).

In evaluating both the contents of a collection of curiosities and the worth of a traveler's observations, a premium was placed upon rarity. The strange and the bizarre, natural marvels and monstrosities, precious stones, rare coins, medals, and other antiquities—like oddities of social custom—defined the focus of travel interest (Hodgen 1964:113). Landscape, appreciated for its "beauty" without reference to military or productive uses, lay entirely outside it, as did all of the arts (with the exception of architecture). In contrast to both earlier forms of pilgrimage and later styles of secular travel, the emotions aroused by travel sights received no public elaboration. The "eye" cultivated in this initial period of sightseeing was deliberately disciplined to emotionally detached, objectively accurate vision; its commanding authority could only be jeopardized by evidence of strongly colored emotional response.

GROUNDS OF OBJECTIVITY

The ideal of objective vision toward which "serious" travelers aspired was signaled by an absence of personal or autobiographical reference in travel narrative and by a sightseeing focus determined by public rather than private relevancies. Those things were worth viewing and recording, whether in letters to friends or in a journal intended for intimate circulation, which "anyone" might have viewed in the traveler's place. Moral tracts aiming to establish the utility of travel distinguished serious practitioners from idlers on the grounds of whether more than personal pleasure was their aim: "A purpose to travell, if it be not *ad veluptatem solum sed ad utilitatem* argueth an industrious and generous minde" (Dallington 1605:1). Withdrawal from the obligations of family, community, and polity, even if temporary, could be regarded as legitimate only if one traveled on behalf of others, sharing "all the rare and singular things one has seen with those obliged to remain at home" (Rogissart and Havard 1707:2).

A discourse featuring travelers as carriers of enlightenment, or—in Bacon's phrase—"merchants of Light," eventually made it plausible to order objects in terms of their moral claim to attention. One widely read eighteenth-century treatise enumerated "the objects most worthy of a traveler's discovery and investigation" in a hierarchy of descending order based upon the size of community to which they were pertinent: "In the first class belong such objects as affect immediately the welfare of Mankind, and consequently promote the universal good, and may be investigated by everyone endowed with a common share of understanding" (Berchtold 1789:19). After them in second place were objects relevant to "increasing the prosperity of a traveller's native country," followed by those which "have respective attraction from personal advantages and . . . apply to that sphere of life in which the traveler himself is destined to act" and a final class of objects relevant only to "such branches of ornamental knowledge as might be cultivated without neglecting or slighting either one of the preceding classes" (Berchtold 1789:19).

Most often, the attempt to ground objectivity of observation in public interest was simply left implicit. Between the sixteenth and eighteenth centuries, travel treatises and travel narratives focused upon similar lists of objects whose logic of construction, though unstated, mirrored fields of investigation marked out by Natural Philosophy. Sir Francis Bacon's influential essay "Of Travel" (1625) presented a prototypical list of objects worthy of observation, drawn from the works of earlier topographical writers and paralleling in significant respects the *Catalogue of Particular Histories,* with its "interrogatories" or topics of inquiry, which formed part of Bacon's plan for the advancement of science (Bacon 1620). Guided by such a list (see Newton 1669:9–11), the assiduous traveler could hope for recognition as both a patriot and a member of an international community of scholars, since the new science to be based upon impartial and objective investigation was widely proclaimed to be linked to the improvement of national wealth and welfare.

In the main, however, objectivity was understood to be a matter of observational method, rather than the focus of attention. A new epistemology, seeking grounds for certainty in the quantity and quality of impartial witnesses whose testimony was based upon direct sensory evidence, found expression in a travel discourse which stressed the importance of "on the spot" record keeping and of dated, diurnal journals. *Nulla dies sine linea,* counseled the French traveler Misson (1691), thus helping to establish a new convention for the scrupulously maintained diary. Observations recorded "on the spot" were less susceptible to distortions of memory, and a meticulous notation of the times and places in which they were made allowed for easier checks on authenticity. Advising the traveler never to be without paper, pen, and ink, methodologists of travel reportage went on to explain,

> in order to acquire an adequate idea of a variety of objects . . . it conduces not a little to know on what days they were seen. In fact, the time, manner, and the order in which things occur are accidental circumstances from which much light may be derived. But the greatest advantage accruing from this method is, that hereby it becomes easier both for the writer and the reader to distinguish what is the actual result of the author's own experience, from what he has, in defect of this, been obliged to advance on the strength of the information given him by others. (Sparrman [1785] 1971:xvii; compare with Young [1792] 1905:1–2)

So strong was the convention requiring that the acts of witness and of notation be as coincident as possible that even when travels were written up after a journey's completion, their authors often sought to create an impression of authenticity by adopting the literary form of fictive dated letters (Harder 1981:70).

Above all, the traveler was enjoined to adopt a plain, unornamented, minimalist style of report, "not to be forward to tell stories," and to answer questions with accuracy and modest brevity (Bacon [1625] 1972:56). "Truth must be religiously adhered to and elegance of expression banished" (Berchtold 1789:44). "My main aim having been to render all things perspicuous and intelligible," writes John Ray (1673:A3), "I was less attentive to Grammatical and Euphonical niceties." Declaration of the intention to speak plainly and avoid rhetoric (in fact a statement of affiliation with the new scientific culture and its stark, technical language) becomes so repetitive a feature of seventeenth-century erudite travel as to constitute, in the words of one historian, one of the "topoi" of the genre (Bideux 1981:30). Shorn of rhetorical flourish and personal romance, travel narrative could be more easily mined for "facts" which were then compiled for comparative purposes in numerous collections of travel "extracts" published during this period. Indeed, in the concern to rationalize travel reportage, narrative itself appears to have become suspect, and perhaps in part for this reason travelers strove to give their observations enumerative form.

"The use of traveling," Samuel Johnson would insist, "is to regulate imagination by reality" (Schwartz 1971:49). Touring in 1774, he carefully notes the lengths and breadths of castle rooms and counts the number of steps leading to their towers. "To count," he avers on one occasion, "is a modern practice"; and on another, "modern travelers measure" (Schwartz 1971:79). At a time when the mapping of Europe was far from complete, accurately gauging the height of a mountain or landmark steeple, correcting earlier estimations of climatic variation or of the distance between posting stations, counting the number of portals in a city's walls, or trees in a famous garden, had standing as a gentlemanly "accomplishment." Travelers were advised to prepare for their tours by learning something of mathematics, perspectives, drawing, and map-making, and to carry instruments for measuring temperature, height, and distance. Those who could afford it sometimes hired professional artists to sketch the plans of fortifications, palaces, and gardens, as well as other natural or manmade "curiosities" encountered en route. Such sketches attested to diligent observational activity and helped to defend the traveler against any suspicion of haste. The latter was important, since one strategy of travel criticism was to cast doubt upon the accuracy of observations by suggesting that insufficient time had been devoted to carrying them out. Travelers were eager to assure their publics that tours met at least minimal requirements of duration (Baretti 1768; Sharp 1767).

The final development in the effort to create a travel method capable of yielding a corpus of "objective" knowledge, based upon the observations of gentlemen scholars, was an outgrowth of techniques developed to rationalize the information-gathering practices of absolutist states. During the sixteenth and seventeenth centuries designers of an embryonic statistics developed research instruments (the preprinted questionnaire, the statistical table laid out in columns) which permitted impersonally conducted and comparable inquiries to be carried out by local authorities (Broc 1974:221; Elliott 1970:36; Petty 1927:175–78). A research technology by which state administrators attempted to inventory people and wealth had obvious bearing for a travel culture in which travel method was regarded as a branch of history. Preformed questionnaires and tables for compactly recording the kind of information deemed relevant to the "political arithmetic" of the period became appended to many travel guides. The blank tables now commanding the traveler's attention bade him observe not only climate, minerals, and soil, but also population, housing, livestock, clothing, agricultural product—in short, all the "things" which would permit him to judge the relative poverty or prosperity of a region. If it was unlikely that any single traveler could complete all the observations indicated, this did not matter so much as the fact that with the help of such tables he would be reminded of the common task (West 1978).

By the second half of the eighteenth century, guides for "patriotic" travelers and essays commissioned at official request, though still blending cultural and natural observations, thrust into focus the social and economic state of the polity and the "causes" of its health or unhappiness (Stagl 1970, 1980; Tucker 1757; Volney 1795).

> Let the traveler observe the condition of the public Inns on the great roads. . . . Let the traveler make the like observations and inquires concerning the number of wagons which pass and repass the road, the quantity and quality of the wares to be found in shops, the state of the dwelling houses, etc. (Tucker 1757:60)
>
> And during his travels he should constantly bear in mind the Grand Maxim that the Face of every country through which he passes, the looks, Numbers, and Behaviour of the People, their general Clothing, Food, and Dwelling, their Attainments in Agriculture, Manufactures, Arts and Sciences, are the Effects and Consequences of some certain causes; which causes he was particularly sent to investigate and discover. (Tucker 1757:10)

In this new concern with what later came to be called "social indicators," as well as in the further rationalization of impersonally conducted and more easily compiled observation, the history of amateur travel merges with the history of early social science (Defert 1982).

CHANGING CANONS

As the world open to gentlemen scholars gradually became exhaustively known and described, at least in its immediately apprehensible appearances, amateurs were displaced by specialized professional agents of information gathering. Already by the eighteenth century no European traveler could any longer hope to gain the kind of recognition accorded only two centuries earlier for such testimony as the observation that Genoa was *not* constructed completely in marble. By the following century, even accurate measurement of a steeple or estimate of a city's population risked parody—for example, in Anthony Trollope's caricature of the "tourist in search of knowledge" (Trollope 1866:79–80) and in Ralph Waldo Emerson's lines on the futility of "counting the cats of Zanzibar." A travel performance which had once been taken as a sign of seriousness and discipline was soon disdained as empty ritual, its epigone practitioners dismissed as hacks who simply ticked off a checklist of sights already exhaustively described by others. Once severed from the drama of publicly lauded discovery, the work of taking objective visual inventory declined in prestige. Though a precipitate of some of its conventions can still be discerned in later styles of tourism, a style of travel which had flourished for three centuries ceased to exist as elite amateur practice.

By the end of the eighteenth century, innovators had changed the dominant canon of sightseeing to serve other intentions. The traveler's "eye," hitherto bound by a normative discourse rooted in fealty to science, became increasingly subject to a new discipline of connoisseurship. The well-trained "eye" judiciously attributed works of art, categorized them by style, and made authoritative judgments of aesthetic merit, as travel itself became an occasion for the cultivation and display of "taste." Objectivity was still called for insofar as the aesthetics of the period held beauty to be an effect governed by discoverable rules of harmony and proportion rather than a matter of mere personal predilection. (In fact, the rule of taste often required a sacrifice of personal whimsy.) But travelers were less and less expected to record and communicate their observations in an emotionally detached, impersonal manner. Experiences of beauty and sublimity, sought through the sense of sight, were valued for their spiritual significance to the individuals who cultivated them. Only through communicative enthusiasm could they be transferred to the stay-at-home audience of a travel performance, and even then only in weakened and diluted form. In its aesthetic transformation, sightseeing became simultaneously a more effusively passionate activity and a more private one.

In the last two decades of the eighteenth century, the Reverend William Gilpin published a series of "picturesque tours" through England and Scotland which inventoried, along with painting, sculpture, and architecture, natural scenes satisfying pictorial canons of beauty (Gilpin 1776, 1782, 1789, 1791, 1792, 1798). Applying Sir Joshua Reynolds's academic discourses on the newly prestigious art of painting to landscape itself, Gilpin urged travelers to seek "amusement" through the "art" to be found in nature, sketching and contemplating "picturesque" scenes in addition to works of human artifice. Wide prospects and synoptical views took on different significance as a new canon of "picturesque travel" added natural landscape to the other "things" which an aesthetically trained eye might hope to grasp (Gilpin 1792). Soon tourists were carrying Claude glasses (named for the painter Claude Lorraine) through which to frame and color a view. By the following century, numerous "picturesque tours" had been published and picturesque itineraries conventionalized for entire geographical regions (Burton and Burton 1978; Nicholson 1956). Belief in the restorative effects of happily constituted scenes, and an increasingly romantic orientation to aesthetic sightseeing, eventually added their own legacy to the mass-marketed conventions of a later tourism.

Not all late eighteenth-century styles of travel centering on sightseeing involved literal vision of the scenes or objects which lay before the traveler. Early romantics often "closed their eyes" to immediate appearances in order to better see some other reality. William Beckford of Fonthill opens a travel manuscript entitled "Dreams, Waking Thoughts and Incidents" with a description of what he calls his "visionary way of gazing."

> Shall I tell you my dreams?—To give an account of my time is doing, I assure you, but little better. Never did there exist a more ideal being. A frequent mist hovers before my eyes, and, through its medium, I see objects so faint and hazy, that both their coulours and forms are apt to delude me. This is a rare confession, say the wise, for a traveller to make: pretty accounts will such a one give of outlandish countries: his correspondents much reap great benefit, no doubt, from such purblind observations. . . .
>
> All through Kent did I doze as usual; now and then I opened my eyes to take in an idea or two of the green, woody country through which I was passing; then closed them again, . . . and was happy in the arms of illusion. The sun sat before I recovered my senses. . . .
>
> I neither heard the vile Flemish dialect which was talking around me nor noticed the formal avenues and marshy country which we passed. When we stopped to change horses, I closed my eyes upon the whole scene, and was transported immediately to some Grecian solitude. (Beckford [1783] 1928:1)

Madame de Stael-Holstein's novel *Corinne* (1807), cuing a comparable closing of eyes, guided an entire European generation in tourist sensibility as well as in Italy. Its protagonists banish the present appearance of Roman sites from mind in order to invoke their past glories to an inner eye and, like Beckford, model a new fashion for nocturnal, moonlit sightseeing which leaves visual impressions muted and ambiguous. A romantic movement which, in other cultural domains, elaborated the ideal of the *Gesamtkunstwerk* sought experiences of sensory fusion and "confusion" in its travel practices as well. The more overwhelming and emotionally colored the experience, the more surely might travel fulfill its new function of affording escape from sensory immersion in degraded realities. The young Keats, planning a walking tour in 1818, enthuses, "I will clamber through the clouds and exist. I will get such an accumulation of stupendous recollections that as I walk through the suburbs of London I may not see them" (Keats 1959:269–70). Byron, marking the distance between his own travels and earlier modes of investigative sightseeing, writes of his stay in Greece: "I gazed at the stars and ruminated: I took no notes, asked no questions" (cited in Feifer 1985:153). From an exercise in acute eyewitness investigation and detached, enumerative observation to an occasion for wordless gazing, nocturnal dreaming, and provisioning against sordid realities—sightseeing had changed in significant respects during three centuries of practice.

While in its various styles of deployment sight was pivotal to the styles of travel dominating this period, it was by no means the only sense modality in which travel patterns were anchored. Among eighteenth-century tourists, for example, must be numbered the many thermalists seeking tactile contact with waters of varying mineral composition (Lowenthal 1962), as well as travelers for whom music or even olfaction played a primary role in motivating their journeys. Pre-Pasteurian theories of morbidity and health assigned the qualities of "air" pride of place (Dagognet 1959), and a longstanding vogue for aerotherapy, accompanied by complex articulations of olfactory experience, continued to affect fashions in travel destination throughout the nineteenth century. But to trace the manner in which senses other than sight were contemporaneously cultivated in minor travel traditions would take one too far afield. They bear mention here only in order to caution against drawing any exclusive link between a single sense modality and an age, the same historical period easily accommodating several distinctive travel styles, each of which may deploy the senses in different ways.

CONCLUSION

The kind of seeing first consciously cultivated by the methodologists of a post-Renaissance secular art of travel was intimately bound to an overarching scientific ideology which cast even the most humble of tourists as part of a corporate, multigenerational, heroic undertaking: the impartial survey of all creation. Such seeing, strikingly reminiscent of the taking of inventory, was accompanied by significant collecting activity, as travelers transferred antiquities and other natural and manmade "curiosities" from many parts of the world to the private estates and scientific academies of their home countries. In fact, one is struck by the fit between a form of travel which featured the world as a series of "things" to be objectively enumerated, and acts of appropriation which lifted such things from the contexts in which they were found in order to complete collections of things elsewhere.

It would appear evident that the form of seeing cultivated by erudite travelers between the sixteenth and eighteenth centuries made its own contribution to the perceptual creation of the earth as a continuous, lawfully regulated, and empirically knowable secular terrain. But one is tempted to suspect as well that during the period in which, for the first time, a single system of interrelated markers began to span the globe, a style of travel performance which privileged the eye for comprehensive inventory served as one of the rituals through which European cultural and intellectual elites sought to take title to "the whole world" then coming into view. The form of human subjectivity such travel ritual required, honed, and exalted was one which could "grasp" this vast new world of "things" without being overwhelmed by it.

ACKNOWLEDGMENTS

I am grateful for the sustained, multifaceted help of Cecilia Benoit, Volker Meja, and the late Nathan Adler. Dean MacCannell spurred the effort and Stuart Pierson offered helpful comments.

REFERENCES

Bacon, Sir Francis. 1620. *Instauratio Magna*. London: J. Billium.

——. [1625] 1972. "Of Travel." In *Essays*. London: J. M. Dent.

Baretti, Joseph. 1768. *An Account of the Manners and Customs of Italy*. London: T. Davies.

Beckford, William. [1783] 1928. "Dreams, Waking Thoughts and Incidents." In *The Travel Diaries*. Boston: Houghton Mifflin.

Berchtold, Count Leopold. 1789. *An Essay to Direct and Extend the Inquiries of Patriotic Travellers*. London: Robinson, Debrett, Payne, Jeffery and Faulder.

Bernard, J. F. 1715. *Essai d'instructions pour voyager utilement*. Amsterdam.

Bideux, Michel. [1606] 1981. *Voyage d'Italie*. Geneva: Slatkine.

Bourne, William. 1578. *A Booke Called the Treasure for Traveilers*. London: C. Burbie.

Boyle, Robert. 1692. *General Heads for the Natural History of a Country Great or Small, Drawn Out for the Use of Travellers and Navigators*. London: J. Taylor.

Broc, N. 1974. *La Geographie des Philosophes: Geographes et Voyageurs Francais au XVth Siècle*. Paris: Ophrys.

Bromley, W. 1693. *Remarks Made in Travels through France and Italy*. London: Thomas Basset.

Brown, Harcourt. 1934. *Scientific Organizations in 17th Century France, 1620–1680*. New York: Russell and Russell.

Burton, Anthony, and P. Burton. 1978. *The Green Bag Travellers: Britain's First Tourists*. London: Andre Deutsch.

Caudill, R. L. W. 1976. "Some Literary Evidence of the Development of English Virtuoso Interests in the Seventeenth Century, with Particular Reference to the Literature of Travel." Ph.D. diss., University of Oxford.

Curley, Thomas M. 1976. *Samuel Johnson and the Age of Travel*. Athens: University of Georgia Press.

Dagognet, Francois. 1959. "La Cure d'air: Essai sur l'histoire d'une idee en therapeutique medicale." *Thales* 10.

Dainville, Francois de. [1940] 1969. La *Geographie des Humanistes*. Geneva: Slatkine.

Dairval, Baudelot de. 1686. *De l'Utilité des Voyages et l'avantage que la recherche des Antiquités procure auz savans*. Paris: Aubouin.

Dallington, R. 1605. *A Method for Travell*. London: Thomas Creede.

Defert, Daniel. 1982. "The Collection of the World: Accounts of Voyages from the Sixteenth to the Eighteenth Centuries." *Dialectical Anthropology* 7:11–20.

Duchet, M. 1971. *Anthropologie et Histoire au Siècle des Lumieres*. Paris: F. Maspero.

Einstein, Lewis. 1902. *The Italian Renaissance in England*. New York: Burt Franklin.

Elliott, J. H. 1970. *The Old World and the New, 1492–1650*. Cambridge: Cambridge University Press.

Essex, Earl of. [1596] 1892. Advice to the Earl of Rutland on his Travels. In *The Letters and the Life of Francis Bacon*, edited by James Spedding, 6–20. London: Longman, Green and Roberts.

Febvre, Lucien. 1947. *Le Problème de l'incroyance au XVI-siècle*. Paris: Editions Albin Michel.

Feifer, Maxine. 1985. *Going Places: The Ways of the Tourist from Imperial Rome to the Present Day.* London: Macmillan.

Frank, Robert G. 1979. "The Physician as Virtuoso in Seventeenth Century England." In *English Scientific Virtuosi in the 16th and 17th Centuries*, edited by B. Shapiro and R. G. Frank. Los Angeles: William Andrews Clark Memorial Library, University of California.

Gailhard, J. 1678. *The Compleat Gentleman: Or Directions for the Education of Youth as to Their Breeding at Home and Travelling Abroad.* London: Tho. Newcomb.

Giles, C. 1976. "Opposition to Pilgrimage in the Middle Ages." *Studia Gratiana: post octava decteti saeculari* 19:123–46.

Gilpin, Rev. William. 1776. *Observations, Relative Chiefly to Picturesque Beauty. . . .* London: R. Blamire.

——. 1782. *Observation on the River Wye. . . .* London: R. Blamire.

——. [1789] 1973. *Observations on the Highland of Scotland. . . .* Richmond, England: Richmond Pub. Co.

——. 1791. *Remarks on Forest Scenery. . . .* London: R. Blamire.

——. [1792] 1972. "On Picturesque Travel." In *Three Essays.* Westmead, England: Gregg International.

——. [1798] 1973. *Observations on the Western Parts of England.* Richmond, England: Richmond Pub. Co.

Hahn, Roger. 1971. *The Anatomy of a Scientific Institution: The Paris Academy of Sciences, 1666–1803.* Berkeley: University of California Press.

Hall, Joseph. 1617. *Quo Vadis? A Just Censure of Travell as It Is Commonly Undertaken by the Gentlemen of Our Nation.* London: E. Griffin.

Harder, Hermann. 1981. *Le Président De Brosses et le voyage en Italie au dix-huitieme Siècle.* Geneva: Slatkine.

Hazard, Paul. 1953. *The European Mind (1680–1715).* London: Hollis and Carter.

Hodgen, Margaret T. 1964. "Collections of Customs: Modes of Classification and Description." In *Early Anthropology in the Sixteenth and Seventeenth Centuries.* Philadelphia: University of Pennsylvania Press.

Houghton, W. F. 1941. "The History of Trades: Its Relation to Seventeenth-Century Thought." *Journal of the History of Ideas* 2:33–60.

——. 1942. "The English Virtuoso in the Seventeenth Century." *Journal of the History of Ideas* 3:51–73, 190–219.

Howard, D. B. 1980. *Writers and Pilgrims: Medieval Pilgrimage Narratives and Their Posterity.* Berkeley: University of California Press.

Howell, J. 1642. *Instructions for Forreine Travell.* London: Humphrey Mosele.

Hunter, Michael. 1981. *Science and Society in Restoration England.* New York: Cambridge University Press.

Keats, J. [1818] 1959. Letter to Benjamin Robert Hayden (8 April 1818). In *J. Keats: Selected Poems and Letters*, edited by Douglas Bush. Boston: Houghton Mifflin.

Kirchnerus, Hermann. 1611. "Oration in Praise of Travell in Generall." In *Coryats Crudities, 1611*, edited by Thomas Coryats, 159–93. London: W. Stansby.

Koehler, Johann D. 1762. *Anweisung fur reisende Gelehrte. . . .* Frankfurt.

La Lande, J. J. 1769. *Voyage en Italie.* Venice: Desaint.

Lassells, Richard. 1697. *An Italian Voyage.* London: R. Wellington.

Leigh, E. 1671. *Of Travel, or a Guide for Travellers into Foreign Parts: Three Diatribes.* London.

Lipsius, Justus. 1592. *A Direction for Travaillers* [by Sir J. Spradling] *Out of J. Lipsius.* London: C. Burbie.

Lister, Martin. 1699. *A Journey to Paris in the Year 1698.* London: Jacob Tonson.

Lithgow, William. [1614] 1632. *A Most Delectable and True Discourse of a Peregrination in Europe, Asia, etc.* London: N. Okes.

——. 1618. *The Pilgrim's Farewell: The Joyes and Miseries of Peregrination.* Edinburgh: Andro Hart.

Lowenthal, David. 1962. "Tourists and Thermalists." *The Geographical Review* 52:124–27.

Mandrou, Robert. 1961. *Introduction à la France Moderne* (1500–1640): *Essaie de Psychologie Historique.* Paris: Albin Michel.

——. 1978. *From Humanism to Science 1480–1700.* New York: Penguin.

Marburg, C. 1935. *Mr. Pepys and Mr. Evelyn.* Philadelphia: University of Pannsylvania Press.

Mattingly, Garett. 1955. *Renaissance Diplomacy.* London: Jonathan Cape.

Mazouer, C. 1980. "Les Guides pour le voyage de France au XVII siècle." In *La Découverte de la France au XVII Siècle.* Paris: Editions du Centre National de la Recherche Scientifique.

Meirus, Albertus. 1589. *Certaine Briefe and Special Instructions for Gentlemen, Merchants, Students, Souldiers, Mariners, etc. Employed in Services Abrode, or in Anie Way Occasioned to Converse in the Kingdomes and Governments of Foreign Princes.* London: John Wolfe.

Michea, Rene. 1945. *Le "Voyage en Italie" de Goethe.* Aubier, France: Editions Montaigne.

Middleton, W. E. K. 1971. *The Experimenters: A Study of the Accademia del Camento.* Baltimore, MD: Johns Hopkins University Press.

Misson, F. M. 1691. *A New Voyage to Italy.* London: R. Bentley.

Moir, Esther. 1964. *The Discovery of Britain: The English Tourists, 1540–1840.* London: Routledge and Kegan Paul.

Murray, David. 1904. *Museums: Their History and Use.* Glasgow: Maclehose.

Newton, Isaac. [1669] 1959. Letter to Aston. In *The Correspondence of Isaac Newton,* edited by H. W. Turnbull. Cambridge: Cambridge University Press.

Nicholson, Norman. 1956. *The Lakers: The First Tourists.* London: Hale.

Peacham, Henry. 1622. *The Compleat Gentleman.* London: Francis Constable.

Petty, William. 1927. "The Method of Enquiry into the State of Any Country." In *The Petty Papers: Some Unpublished Writings of Sir William Petty,* 2 vols., edited by Marquis of Lansdowne. London: Constable & Co.

Pommeau, Rene. 1966. *L'Europe des Lumières: Cosmopolitisme et unité Europeene au 18 siècle.* Paris: Editions Stock.

Ray, John. 1673. *Observations Topographical, Moral and Physiological Made in a Journey. . . .* London: John Martyn.

Reiske, Johann. 1645. *Dissertatio qua pinacothecas, cimeliothecas, et societates doctorum in Europa. . . .* Guelferb.

Rogissart and Havard. 1707. *Les Delices de L'Italie.* Paris.

Rooke, Laurence. 1665/6. "Directions for Seamen Bound for Far Voyages." *Philosophical Transactions* 8:140–41.

Rowe, John H. 1964. "Ethnography and Ethnology in the Sixteenth Century." The Kroeber Anthropological Society Papers 30:1–19.

Schwartz, Richard. 1971. *Samuel Johnson and the New Science.* Milwaukee: University of Wisconsin Press.

Shapiro, Barbara. 1979. "History and Natural History in Sixteenth and Seventeenth Century England: An Essay on the Relationship Between Humanism and Science." In *English Scientific Virtuosi in the 16th and 17th Centuries,* edited by B. Shapiro and R. G. Frank. Los Angeles: William Andrews Clark Memorial Library, University of California.

Sharp, Samuel. 1767. *Letters from Italy.* London: R. Cave.

Sorbière, M. de. 1660. *De l'Utilité des grands voyages . . . Lettres et Discours.* Paris: Francois Clousier.

Sparrman, A. [1785] 1971. *A Voyage to the Cape of Good Hope from the Year 1772–1776,* trans. from the Swedish. London: Robinson.

Stael-Holstein, A. L. G. Baronne de. 1807. *Corinne; ou L'Italie.* Paris: Imprimerie des Annales des arts et manufactures.

Stagl, J. 1970. "Die Apodemik oder Reisekunst als Methodik der Sozialforschung vom Humanismus bis zur Aufklaerung. In *Fruehgeschichte der Staatsberschreibung und Statistik,* edited by Mohammed Rassem and Justin Stagl. Paderborn, Germany.

——. 1980. "Der Wohl Unterwiesene Passagier: Reisekunst und Gesellschaftsbeschreibung (vom 16. zum 18. Jahrhundert)." In *Reisen und Reisebeschreibungen im 18. und 19. Jahrhundert als Quellen der Kulturbeziehungsforschung,* edited by Wolfgang Kessler. Berlin: Verlag Ulrich Camen.

Strauss, Gerald. 1958. "Topographical-Historical Method in Sixteenth Century German Scholarship." *Studies in the Renaissance* 5:87–101.

——. 1965. "A Sixteenth-Century Encyclopedia: Sebastian Munster's Cosmography and Its Editions." In *From the Renaissance to the Counter-Reformation: Essays in Honour of Garett Mattingly,* edited by Charles H. Carter. New York: Random House.

Trollope, Anthony. [1866] 1981. "The Tourist in Search of Knowledge." In *Travelling Sketches.* New York: Arno Press.

Tucker, Josiah. [1757] 1970. *Instructions for Travellers.* New York: S. R. Publishers Ltd., Johnson Reprint Corp.

Turler, Jerome. 1575. *The Traveiler.* London: William How.

Volney, Constantin Francois Chasseboeuf, comte de. 1788. *Travels through Syria and Egypt.* London: G. and J. Robinson.

——. [1795] 1822. "Questions de statistique a L'usage des Voyageurs." In *Oeuvres Completes.* Paris: Bosange Freres.

West, Hugh. 1978. "Göttingen and Weimar: The Organization of Knowledge and Social Theory in Eighteenth-Century Germany." *Central European History* X1:150–62.

Woodward, John. 1696. *Brief Instructions for Making Observations in All Parts of the World.* London: printed for Richard Wilkin.

Young, Arthur. [1792] 1905. *Travels in France during the Years 1787, 1788, 1789.* London: George Bell & Sons.

Zacher, C. K. 1976. *Curiosity and Pilgrimage: The Literature of Discovery in Fourteenth Century England.* Baltimore, MD: Johns Hopkins University Press.

~

"The Whole World Within Reach": Travel Images Without Borders

TOM GUNNING

AS CHARLES MUSSER has demonstrated in a pioneering and penetrating essay, the travel genre was "one of the most popular and developed" genres in early film.[1] In terms of pure numbers of productions it could rank with any other form of filmmaking until about 1906. And as Musser and others have shown, it is perhaps the genre of early film that is most clearly prepared for by precinematic practice.[2] Musser's careful research into the precinematic lantern slide illustrated travel lectures of John L. Stoddard and Burton Holmes establishes that the travel film grew directly out of this form. In fact, one would be hard pressed to make a definitive separation between the two, since travel lecturers like Burton Holmes adopted motion pictures as a natural extension of the lantern slides he was already using, and soon after the invention of cinema he simply introduced films into his lectures, interspersing moving and still images. Travel films became absorbed so smoothly into the travel lecture that the older practices of lecture and explanation adapted to the new technology without a major adjustment. However, we must approach such films with caution. "Foreign views" portray not only a distant site but also a particular point of view, one from outside the land viewed. This chapter explores this tourist viewpoint as embodied in early travel films, examining both the forms this viewpoint takes, the discourses that surrounded it, and its place within a peculiarly modern experience in which the role of images has taken on a new dimension. I believe that early travel films display a mode of perception.

Travel films share with other forms of early cinema an enormous range of exhibition contexts. While travel films as illustration for a lecture may have been their privileged mode (and one with enough status and popularity to permanently influence the way travel films were made and understood), such films were also shown as brief segments in a variety format of mixed genres (in the earliest years of exhibition), projected in special theaters designed as railway cars or other means of transportation (e.g., the Hale's Tours in 1905–1906), or shown as multi-shot films known as "scenics" that formed a part of many nickelodeon programs (from 1907 or so on). Further, as Musser has pointed out, elements of the travel genre were adopted early on by fiction films,[3] with travel providing the background for fictional action, resulting in a narrativization of the genre that persists to this day (Wim Wenders's *Until the End of the World* providing a recent and interesting example).

But a thorough understanding of the travel film genre must go beyond the travel lecture as its source and place it within an extensive industry of travel images which arose in the nineteenth century. In an age of mechanical reproduction photographs of distant places and countries probably were surpassed only by portraits as the most commonly reproduced images.[4] The travel lecture illustrated by lantern slides provided perhaps the most public way of consuming these transnational images, but travel images were also displayed in the stereoscope with its illusion of three dimensions. The contrasting modes of these two forms make the importance of travel imagery in each of them more striking: from an audience in darkness in a public space watching a large, bright image under the control of the lecturer, to a single individual seated in her own home holding the apparatus in her hand, determining the order and length of each view and absorbed in an illusion of depth and recession. Yet both lantern and stereoscope were means of appropriating some distant place through an image, of seeming to be somewhere else by becoming absorbed in a "view." They attest to what Lynne Kirby has called a "touristic consciousness," a fascination exerted by foreign images that was fed by a number of different technologies.[5]

Along with the stereoscope and the magic lantern image, the postcard became by the turn of the century a major form of travel imagery (travel photographers such as William Henry Jackson or Eadweard Muybridge usually worked in all three forms). This mode of reception contrasts with both stereoscope and lantern lecture, since the postcard also functioned as *evidence* of travel, sent by a tourist en route back to friends and relatives who had not made the journey. Observers at the turn of the century described hordes of tourists ascending the Rigi in Switzerland and then rushing to buy postcards and immediately sitting down and writing home.[6] The postcard seemed to function not only as a souvenir of the journey, but as its goal and purpose. This obsession with documenting one's trip by an image brings me to the core of the issue that I believe the travel genre poses for modern perception and use of images. In the modern era the very concept of travel becomes intricately bound up with the production of images. The image becomes our way of structuring a journey and even provides a substitute for it. Travel becomes a means of appropriating the world through images.

The postcard shows that modern travel images cannot be understood without placing them in a larger context of the development of mass tourism. A Biograph catalogue from 1902 understood this and informed potential film buyers: "It will be noted also that the foreign subjects include most of the places visited and admired by tourists."[7] Images of foreign lands took on a more tangible quality when audiences knew it was possible to travel to them, even if they did not undertake the journey themselves. And this sense of the accessibility of foreign lands forms a cornerstone of the modern world view in which technology can render every distant thing somehow available to us. The creation of Cooks Tours in the middle of the nineteenth century was more than a systematic approach to making the process of traveling more rational and convenient. It had a symbiotic relation to the development of modern means of transportation (the railway and steamship, especially).[8] The new systems of transportation made tourism possible and the extension of tourism then allowed further development of transportation systems.

As the development of industrial capitalism made areas of the world more accessible, travel became more economical in term of finances, as well as energy, to a larger number of people. The production of travel images was essential to this new travel industry. A travel lecture illustrated by lantern slides or motion pictures served not only as an ersatz for actual travel for those lacking finances or energy, but as stimulant and preparation for those who had the means. One wanted to travel partly because one had already seen images of distant places. And one went to travel lectures to make sure what one should see on a journey. But travel images did more than incite journeys. As the postcard shows, they were also the end products of the journey, the proof one had been there, and the means by which one reflected on one's experience. This became even more true with the introduction of the Kodak "Brownie" camera, which made every tourist a travel photographer and, eventually, with the perfection of celluloid slides, converted family gatherings into travel lectures. In other words, we should not simply think of travel images as substitutes designed for those who cannot travel (although they can play that role). Rather, during the modern era images penetrate deeply into the process of travel itself, structuring our experience of the journey.

Returning to the turn of the century, one is struck again by the range of ways travel images were consumed by spectators, from devices that could be held in the hand and enjoyed at home, to formal and public exhibitions. The largest and most grandiose representations of travel extend beyond travel lectures to more cumbersome forms of spectacle. The idea of making the world available in the form of a spectacle stretches back to the panorama of the turn of the eighteenth century and to the world expositions of the latter part of the nineteenth. Besides bringing together the consumer products and technological marvels of the developed nations, the world expositions always provided attractions which plunged spectators into exotic environments. The Eskimo villages of the Pan American Exposition, the Cambodian temple of the Paris 1900 Exposition, Little Egypt's hoochie coochie dance at the Chicago 1893 Columbian Exposition, all presented traditional cultures within a simulacrum of their real environment, designed to give gawkers the illusion of having traveled there. These expositions were explicit hymns to the colonial expansions of the industrialized nations. They provide searing illustrations of spectacle as appropriation, as the traditions and inhabitants of the unindustrialized world were posed for the contemplation of citizens of the modern world.

It is no coincidence that such expositions also staged elaborate presentations of travel films in exhibition environments that simulated the travel experience. These presentations ranged from the Cinèorama of the Paris exhibition of 1900 (which simulated balloon flight by projecting motion pictures panoramically to an audience seated in a mock-up of a balloon's gondola) to the Hale's Tours that were inspired by the many travel attractions featured at the 1904 St. Louis Exhibition, which projected moving landscape films to spectators seated in train-car screening rooms. But these forms of cinematic simulation were often side by side with precinematic forms of travel simulation. As Emmanuelle Toulet has shown in her exemplary research on the Paris 1900 Exposition, the Cinèorama competed (and unsuccessfully, for it proved inoperable) with such precinematic means of conveying a journey as the Marèorama, in which a tilting deck, sea brine–infused ventilation, and moving canvas panoramas gave spectators the illusion of a sea voyage, or the Trans-Siberian Panorama, in which viewers sat in train cars as a moving painted panorama of landscapes along the Trans-Siberian route unfurled beyond their windows, or the Strorama, which presented an unfolding panorama of a sea voyage along the coast of Algeria.[9] Such elaborate apparatuses demonstrate the link between cinematic travel imagery and the introduction of the panorama and diorama earlier in the nineteenth century. Travel images, views of natural wonders or famous cities, also supplied the most frequent subjects of panoramas and dioramas from the end of the eighteenth century into the modern era.

All of this indicates that the production of foreign views, of images crossing borders, in early cinema must be placed in a larger context, one which extends from the travel lecture, to the postcard industry, to world fair exhibits. But as soon as this horizon is constructed, the larger social and technological forces behind these phenomena loom before us: the tourist industry, the development of modern transportation, the expansion of colonialism. But this connection involves more than traditional historical arguments of causes and influence. I would claim that rather than simply acting as underlying causes of this industry of travel images, a base to this superstructure, these forces are clearly visible within these images. In other words, travel images are more than an effect; they supply essential tools in the creation of a modern world view underlying all these transformations. One cannot understand modernity without penetrating its passion for images. Images fascinate modern consciousness obsessively, and this modern sense of images comes from a belief that images can somehow deliver what they portray. Image as appropriation dominates the modern image-making industry, and travel images provide a unique perspective onto this modern phenomenon. Lynne Kirby has pointed out that the epigraph to Burton Holmes's memoirs reads "to travel is to possess the world."[10]

If the study of early cinema can play a crucial role in the ideological analysis of the cinematic apparatus it is less because the earliest period of filmmaking represents an age of innocence than a sort of naiveté in which elements which later on became camouflaged are frankly displayed. For instance, the link between foreign views and colonialism needs no deconstructive analysis to be demonstrated. A straight reading of American film catalogues from the turn of the century suffices. The travel views that Edison and Biograph marketed directly paralleled the colonial wars of the period. Views of Cuba and the Philippines appeared along with films of the Spanish American War and were categorized as war films. For instance, in 1902 the Biograph Company released a brief film called *Aguinaldo's Navy*. The film consists of a view of Philippine native canoes on a river, but the title evokes the name of the leader of Philippine resistance to U.S. occupation. Clearly the Biograph Company wanted to attract audience curiosity to a rather bland actuality film. But the title also makes a mocking colonialist joke which equates the ability to photograph this image with U.S. dominance over the native people. Our technology (our navy, certainly, but in some sense our cinema as well) can overwhelm these simple people with their primitive boats, the film proclaims.

Travel curiosity intersected with the interest in colonial wars in a number of locales, and the genre of travel and war pictures often intersect in the catalogues of early American manufacturers. The Biograph catalogue proclaims that the camera followed the flag in these instances: "In every case our operators worked under the direct patronage and with the most perfect co-operation of the respective Governments involved."[11] The Biograph Company marketed a view of the Taku road in China by stressing that this street scene was taken "under the occupation of the city by allied forces" after the Boxer Rebellion. Likewise, Edison in 1901 announced their films of China by informing potential exhibitors that "people will eagerly appreciate any pictures that relate to the localities in which the war in China was prosecuted."[12]

The connection between early American travel films and the transportation industry is also proudly displayed in early film catalogues. There is no real dividing line between travel films and railway films in this period, and both were prominent genre headings in catalogues. In the Edison catalogue railway views are offered under the name of the railways utilized: Denver and Rio Grande, Mexican International Railway, Mexican Central Railway, Acheson, Topeka and Santa Fe, and so on. (Similarly, Edison offers a series of films under the sponsorship of the Occidental and Oriental Steamship Company, showing views of Shanghai, Hong Kong, Yokohama, Tokyo, Macao, and Hawaii.) In all cases the transportation companies mentioned sponsored these films with the specific intention of encouraging tourism along their routes. The Edison catalogue, for instance, introduces its series of Denver and Rio Grande films by saying: "Tourists who choose this route are assured of magnificent scenery and also of the very best of treatment."[13] Railways frequently not only encouraged the production of such films but organized their own tours of travel lectures using motion pictures and lantern slides to increase their tourist patronage.[14]

In the United States the Santa Fe Railway exemplifies the circuit between industrial expansion and tourism and the role travel images play in moving consumers over this route. As T. C. McLuhan has shown in her book *Dream Tracks*, in the 1890s the advertising department of the railway sought to overcome bankruptcy by aggressively promoting the line as a tourist route. To accomplish this, the corporation contracted landscape artists to paint scenic images from the great American Southwest, along with picturesque images of Native American life. These images were circulated nationwide on posters, brochures, and calendars.[15] For the 1915 Pan Pacific Exposition the Santa Fe Railway even constructed its own panorama of the Grand Canyon.[16] In addition, photographers, such as William Henry Jackson, were contracted (and provided with specially equipped photographic railway cars), and they produced still photos, lantern slides, and postcards. Eventually motion picture cameramen were also hired who shot not only the southwestern landscape but the line's greatest tourist draw, the Hopi Snake Dance at Walpi Pueblo.[17] Travel images were part and parcel of a modern advertising campaign, as were most of the early railway series filmed by American film companies (the Union Pacific provided motion picture cameraman Billy Bitzer with his own car, as well).[18]

We can see clearly, then, that the travel genre in early film occurred within a context of feverish production of views of the world, an obsessive labor to process the world as a series of images and to make those views available as never before through a range of methods: actual tourism, fairground simulations of journeys, projected images, stereographs, or postcards sent through the mail. This consumption of the world through images occurs in the context of industrial and colonial expansion, with war and the railway leading the curiosity of both photographer and spectator into new geographical realms. In short, the travel genre exemplifies what philosopher Martin Heidegger has called the "age of the world picture":

> Where the world becomes picture, what is, in its entirety, is juxtaposed as that for which man is prepared and which, correspondingly, he therefore intends to bring before himself and have before himself, and consequently, intends in a decisive sense to set in place before himself. Hence, world picture, when understood essentially, does not mean a picture of the world but the world conceived and grasped as picture.[19]

In other words, for Heidegger the metaphysical (and destructive) nature of modern Western man views the world as something which can be appropriated through becoming a picture. No better illustration of this could be conceived than the travel images of the nineteenth and twentieth century. The phrase used by a number of early film companies as their motto, "the whole world within reach,"[20] exemplifies this thinking: the world brought close as a picture and appropriated by the viewer. No longer are even the most remote reaches of the planet inaccessible. They can be brought forward and consumed as images. And this form of image consumption is not merely done *faute de mieux*. Rather than an ersatz, images become our way of possessing the world, or the universe. Does anyone doubt that on the first tourist voyage to the moon, the initial stop for tourists will be at the postcard rack to buy images produced by NASA?

But if early travel films arise from a deep context of image making that characterizes the modern world, does the fact that they are *films* add anything unique to the picture? I believe so. The unique aspect of motion pictures, the representation of movement, supplied a new way the world could be transformed into pictures. But this modern transformation of the picture itself also has its roots in the passion for images of distant places that marks the nineteenth century. This explosion of travel images which we have been tracing also transformed the nature of the picture. Although undoubtedly inspired by traditions of landscape painting and the picturesque, all the visual devices we have been discussing project the idea that there is something insufficient about the simple framed perspectival illusion. Each device tries to supplement this insufficiency in a different manner.

For instance, the panorama constructed its canvases in such a way that the limits of the picture frame seemed to be abolished. In stationary panoramas the circular form of the painting and the arrangement of lighting and architecture (which deemphasized the upper and lower edges) created a sense of an image without borders.[21] In moving panoramas the unfolding canvas (which could never be visible in its entirety at any particular moment) seemed equally to produce an image without a frame. Daguerre's diorama through sheer size also undermined the sense of its border, while illumination from behind the translucent canvas created an uncannily lifelike image which could also transform itself with a change of light, thereby exceeding the illusion allowed by a traditional landscape painting.[22] Illumination and transformation (through dissolving views) also intensified the visual power of magic lantern imagery. And the stereoscope endowed images with an illusionary depth achieved by the superimposition of two parallax images.

While traditionally these supplements are thought of as attempts at greater realism, it might be more useful to think of them as attempts to overcome the limits of the traditional picture and its frame. As such, they heighten the experience of an image by giving it either a greater visual saliency (illumination, stereoscopy) or a temporal dimension (both forms of panorama, transforming views) since the view cannot be exhausted from one viewpoint at a single moment. Clearly the cinema combines these traditions, wedding illumination with movement. But, as Jonathan Crary has demonstrated about the stereoscope, I believe all these new forms of travel images also construct a new form of observer.[23] Interestingly in all these devices the appropriation through imagery becomes somewhat agonistic, as the scale, depth, movement or brilliant illumination and transformation of the image seem to elude the viewer's grasp as much as the image offers itself up to him. All these devices in some sense create an image which overwhelms the viewer through change, scale, or intensity, or all three in concert.

Early travel films frequently make use of what they term "panoramic views." This is an extremely polyvalent term in early cinema. Occasionally it means simply a broad view of a landscape from some "panoramic" point, like a high mountain. But more frequently such films try to recreate either the circular effect of the stationary panorama or the unfolding of a mobile panorama through camera movement. "Circular panoramas" generally made use of the possibilities for *panning* (the term comes from *panorama* and denotes the swivel of a camera while in a single position) from the camera tripod; the Edison catalogue offered a number of films under this specific category.[24] Advertising one circular panorama of a Parisian street, the catalogue indicated that a view such as this provided more information about Paris than a dozen street scenes taken under the older method (i.e., with a stationary camera). Besides such arcing panning shots, "panorama" was also used to describe films in which the camera was in motion on some vehicle: railway train, trolley car, motorboat, or automobile. Lumière cameraman Promio, claimed he first hit upon the idea of this sort of motion when touring Venice in a gondola. As he recalled some twenty-five years later to the film historian G. Michele Coissac, he reasoned, "If the immobile camera allowed the reproduction of moving objects, then perhaps one could reverse the proposition and film immobile objects with a moving camera."[25]

The popularity of such moving camera shots in early travel cinema can be easily explained. First, they allowed a broader view of the landscape. Second, the actual movement seems to carry the viewer into the image, realizing what Charles Musser has called the "spectator as passenger convention."[26] It is no accident that one of the later terms for such camera movements would be the "traveling shot." Rather than simply reproducing the view, such films seem to recreate the actual penetration of space that traveling involves. Finally, a moving camera creates a sort of stereoscopic illusion as the varied rates of apparent movement of objects at different distances within the visual field provide another depth cue. Early film catalogues frequently stressed the stereoscopic nature of their moving panorama films. Like the earlier precinematic devices which the name "panorama" links them to, these moving camera films provide a supplement of effects not available in traditional landscape painting. The moving camera's ability to seem to surpass its own frame creates another image which seems to pass beyond its own borders.

These means of representing travel (both proto-cinematic and filmic) share what might be called a "sensational" approach; they attempt to increase the power of representation by addressing either more of the senses (particularly the psycho-physical sensation of movement known as kinesthesia) than traditional painting can or by making vision more intense (through illumination or stereoscopy). The manufacture of sea air in the Marèorama, Daguerre's ringing church bells in the diorama, and the sound of train whistles in the Hale's Tours, along with the kinesthetic experience of pitching boat decks or lurching train cars, are only the most extreme experiments in surpassing the landscape painting. These devices aim at direct physiological stimulation and recall Crary's definition of the modern observer as one whose body plays an acknowledged role in the creation of the illusions he or she observes.[27]

The terms which early film catalogues use to make these panoramic travel films attractive to exhibitors contrast sharply with the experience of absorption in the contemplation of nature associated with a traditional landscape painting (although they might be related to the romantic sublime landscape which pictures nature as an overwhelming force). Again and again descriptions of panoramic travel films emphasize that the camera is not only moving, but moving at a high rate of speed. The Biograph catalogue description of the film *A Panoramic View in the Grand Canal* does not invoke the somnolent sway of a gondola, but stresses that it "was taken from the front of a rapidly moving launch."[28] Likewise, the same catalogue describes *Panoramic View of Siegsalle, Berlin* as "taken from an automobile in rapid motion" and a view of the Battery of New York City was "taken from a rapidly moving tug." As much as stereoscopy or a sense of traveling, these descriptions advertise the sensation of speed. They promote a truly modern perception of landscape, one mediated by technology and speed.

Wolfgang Schivelbusch has supplied an already classic account of the way the view of the landscape from a rapidly moving train became emblematic of modern perception. Revealingly, Schivelbusch calls this new mode of perception "panoramic." Panoramic perception involves a separation between the viewer and the spectacle observed: "Panoramic perception, in contrast to traditional perception, no longer belongs to the same space as the perceived objects: the traveler sees the landscape, objects, etc. *through* the apparatus which moves him through the world."[29] As a number of film scholars have pointed out,[30] this description anticipates the mode of film viewing. In the case of early panoramic films the "panoramic" effect is doubled as the apparatuses involved include both the means of transportation and the cinema itself. Cinema in early travel films becomes itself a mode of transportation, as recent works by Guiliana Bruno and Anne Friedberg have indicated.[31]

Schivelbusch's study of the railway journey also reveals that the new form of travel initially carried with it a deep-rooted anxiety over the possibility of an accident.[32] While railway companies tried to minimize this anxiety, it is extremely curious that the descriptions provided for some early train films seem rather to maximize it (and it seems likely that such descriptions found their way into the patter of travel lecturers using these films). Take, for instance, the Edison 1902 description of the film *Panoramic View of Lower Kicking Horse Canyon* from their Rocky Mountain Panoramic Railroad Series: "Of all panoramic mountain pictures this is the most thrilling, as the audience imagines while they are being carried along with the picture the train will be toppled over thousands of feet into the valley below." Another panoramic view of the same canyon is advertised in this way: "The train seems to be running into the mountains of rock as each curve is reached and rounded, making the scene exciting from start to finish." Likewise, Edison's description of *Panoramic View of Mt. Tamalpais, Cal* vaunts this view from a mountainside train by saying: "this makes the picture most thrilling as one experiences the sensation of momentarily expecting to be hurled into space."[33]

What is one to make of these curiously masochistic fantasies so at odds with the usual genteel conception of travel as a form of contemplation?[34] Obviously the sensation of imminent danger can be offered as pleasurable entertainment because the peril is illusionary, and the spectator can have her thrill while safely seated in a theater. The viewer of travel films is not simply a surrogate of the tourist, seeking the ersatz of the traveler's original experience. The security of the cinema seat can have advantages the tourist never enjoys.

For instance, the mediation of the cinematic apparatus allows viewpoints not available to the tourist. A 1903 Edison description for *Phantom Ride on the Canadian Pacific* points out that "the view taken from the front of the train running at high speed is one that even tourists riding over the line are not privileged to enjoy."[35] Further, the cinema protected viewers against the dangers which flesh-and-blood tourists might have to face, and even presented these dangers as an additional thrill for the secure spectator. Descriptions of travel films frequently point out the danger or discomfort in which the actual tourists find themselves. A 1903 Edison description of *Tourist Climbing Mt. Blanc* gives this as one of the fascinations of the film: "as the audience views the picture it will be spellbound, momentarily expecting to see the mountain climbers fall into a chasm and be dashed to pieces."[36] Such descriptions show that early travel films often participate in the aesthetics of sensation and astonishment so basic to the early cinema of attractions.[37] The viewer is not a detached, contemplative spectator but a physiologically stimulated observer.

These images in which the audience is "carried along" by both film images and modes of transport seem to act out the aggressive appropriation of space that Heidegger finds implicit in the world picture. But the ambivalence of early cinema asserts itself; this fantasy of appropriation through images is laid bare by such nakedly aggressive visual strategies. And when the image of aggressive appropriation becomes stripped of all camouflage, could a process of demythologization be beginning? When the world comes within one's imagistic grasp so tightly, is squeezing the only option?

This unanswered question penetrates to the core of cinema's complicity with the most destructive aspects of modern perception, its links to war and colonial expansion and exploitation. But it also raises the issue of the utopian aspects of cinema, an aspect that early cinema also reveals. In Walter Benjamin's utopian conception, cinema, as a form of mechanical reproduction, overcomes all forms of distance to bring everything closer to its mass audience. For Benjamin this modern passion for nearness wields a destructive power that is also liberating, a power that smashes older forms of control and ownership of the image.[38] To express this utopian power of cinema, its ability to evade the entrapments of the older static culture, Guiliana Bruno introduces to film study a term coined by Italian philosopher Mario Perniola, *transito*, which she says cannot be translated into English by a single word. Bruno defines the term "as a wide ranging and multifaceted notion of circulation. *Transito* connotes many levels of desire as inscribed in both physical and mental movement: it includes *passages*, traversing, transitions, transitory states, and erotic circulation, and it incorporates a linguistic reference to transit."[39] For Bruno *transito* is a neglected source of cinematic pleasure, one which escapes from the strategies of containment and ideology. History teaches us that utopias provide inspiration only as long as they are situated nowhere, as they remain u-topic. Certainly to find in early cinema and especially early travel films a form that escapes the claims of ideology and entrapments of power and aggression would be the worst sort of deception. However, within these early films one also sees utopian possibilities in which cinema, like these early panoramic films, seems not only to trace the routes of power and appropriation but also to describe a line of escape and flight.

An Edison film shot in the West Indies in 1903 typifies the double nature of these foreign views, these images shot beyond our borders. A single-shot film entitled *Native Woman Washing a Negro Baby in Nassau, B.I.*, it lasts less than a minute. It is typical of a large number of travel films in which the inhabitants of other lands, particularly of less industrialized nations, are treated as curious sights not unlike the landscape.[40] The first part of the film consists of the title action, which the Edison catalogue summarizes in this way: "The baby seems to enjoy the washing until he gets soap in his eyes and begins to cry." The Edison description ends with this expression of slightly mocking and condescending amusement. But the film continues beyond this. Suddenly the camera pivots, making a swift panoramic turn. In a sort of reverse angle we discover that the process of turning the daily life of native people into a spectacle has itself become a spectacle, as the camera reveals a group of native children and adults watching the filming. Then suddenly this group of witnesses flees, dashing out of the frame, away from the camera's view.

The film says it all, balancing the horror with the escape. On the one hand, a slice of native life is seized and presented as an amusing and possibly even laughable spectacle for the delectation of viewers from another culture and race. But then the frame becomes unstable with movement and the camera discovers another context. The spectacle makers themselves have become a spectacle, the tables turned with the camera's pivot. And, finally, there comes a sublime moment as this witnessing audience refuses to become a spectacle in turn and takes off, escaping the frame and the camera, running off into unimaged space. The film captures and contains, mocks and reduces, but then it responds to its own capacity for motion and also reveals. It shows what possibly no other form of travel representation could represent, the escape of its subject, its pure *transito* and flight.

ACKNOWLEDGMENTS

This chapter was first delivered as a paper for the Second International Domitor Conference, "Images Across Borders/Images sans frontières" in Lausanne, Switzerland at the Universite de Lausanne in June 1992. I would particularly like to thank Roland Cosandey for his comments and aid.

NOTES

1. Charles Musser, "The Travel Genre in 1903–1904: Moving Towards Fictional Narrative," *Iris* 2, no. 1 (1984): 47–60, especially p. 47.

2. Musser, ibid.; and Musser, *The Emergence of Cinema*, vol. 1 of *History of the American Cinema*, ed. Charles Harpole (New York: Scribners, 1990), passim; and Musser with Carol Nelson, *High Class Moving Pictures: Lyman Howe and the Forgotten Era of Traveling Exhibition* (Princeton, N.J.: Princeton University Press, 1991). See also Lynne Kirby, "The Railroad and the Cinema, 1895–1929: Institutions, Aesthetics and Gender" (Ph.D. diss., UCLA, 1989; also Kirby's book based on her dissertation, *Parallel Tracks: The Railroad and Silent Cinema* (Durham, N.C.: Duke University Press, 1997).

3. Musser, "The Travel Genre," p. 57.

4. See Rainer Fabian and Hans-Christian Adam, *Masters of Early Travel Photography* (New York: Vendome Press, 1983).

5. Kirby, "The Railroad," p. 59.

6. Fabian, p. 339. See also T. C. McLuhan, *Dream Tracks: The Railroad and the American Indian, 1890–1930* (New York: Harry N. Abrams, 1985), p. 37, which describes a 1906 tourist train disembarking in the American Southwest: "About half the tourists jump from the train almost as soon as they stop and run from one place to another in search of souvenir postal cards, flop themselves down in the waiting room or on the brick curb and write feverishly, hunt around for some place to buy stamps and then mail their cards, and then by that time have only a few minutes left to patronize the lunch counter. Meanwhile the greater portion of the other half are taking snapshots of the hotel or station, or are posing against one of the other buildings for someone else's picture. It is as good as a circus to watch it."

7. Biograph 1902 film catalogue, in Musser et al., *Motion Picture Catalogs by American Producers and Distributors, 1894–1908: A Microfilm Edition* (Frederick, Md.: University Publication of America, 1985), p. 130.

8. Maxine Feifer, *Going Places: The Ways of the Tourist from Imperial Rome to the Present Day* (London: Macmillan, 1985), pp. 166–68. See also David Levy, "Sentimental Journeys of the Big-Eyed Sightseer: Tourism and the Early Cinema," in *Cinèma sans frontières 1896–1918: Images Across Borders*, ed. Roland Cosandey (Lausanne: Editions Payot Lausanne, 1995).

9. Emmanuelle Toulet, "Cinema at the Universal Exposition, Paris 1900," *Persistence of Vision*, no. 9 (1991): 10–37 (originally published in *Revue d'Histoire Moderne et Contemporain* 33 [April–June 1986]: 179–209). See also Tom Gunning, "The World as Object Lesson: Cinema Audiences, Visual Culture and the St. Louis World's Fair," *Film History* 6, no. 4 (1994): 422–44.

10. Kirby, "The Railroad," p. 112.

11. Biograph 1902 film catalogue, in Musser et al., *Motion Picture Catalogs*, p. 138.

12. Edison 1901 catalogue, in Musser et al., *Motion Picture Catalogs*.

13. Edison 1900 film catalogue, in Musser et al., *Motion Picture Catalogs*.

14. McLuhan, *Dream Tracks*, p. 39.

15. Ibid., pp. 18–33.

16. Kirby, *Parallel Tracks*, p. 44.

17. McLuhan, *Dream Tracks*, pp. 33–40.

18. G. W. Bitzer, *Billy Bitzer, His Story* (New York: Farrah, Straus and Giroux, 1973), p. 25.

19. Martin Heidegger, "The Age of the World Picture," in *The Question Concerning Technology and Other Essays*, trans. William Lovitt (New York: Harper and Row, 1977), p. 129.

20. Méliès's Star Film Company adopted the motto when it still intended to produce actualities. See Paul Hammond, *Marvelous Méliès* (London: Gordon Fraser, 1974), p. 30.

21. See the description of the panorama by Quatremère de Quincy from 1832 reprinted in Jacques and Marie André *Une Saison Lumière a Montpellier* (Perpignan, France: Institute Jean Vigo, 1987), p. 173.

22. See the description of the diorama in Helmut and Alison Gernsheim, *L. J. M. Daguerre: The History of the Diorama and the Daguerreotype* (New York: Dover Publications, 1968), pp. 15–17.

23. See Jonathan Crary, *Techniques of the Observer: On Vision and Modernity in the Nineteenth Century* (Cambridge: MIT Press, 1990), especially pp. 116–36.

24. Edison 1901 film catalogue, in Musser et al., *Motion Picture Catalogs*.

25. See G. Michele Coissac, *Histoire du Cinématographe de ses Origines a nos Jours* (Paris: Librairie Gauthier-Villars, 1925), p. 196.

26. Musser, *The Emergence of Cinema*, p. 429.

27. Crary, pp. 129–36.

28. Biograph 1902 film catalogue, in Musser et al., *Motion Picture Catalogs*.

29. Wolfgang Schivelbusch, *The Railway Journey: Trains and Travel in the Nineteenth Century* (New York: Urizen Press, 1979), p. 66, emphasis in original.

30. Film scholars who have made use of Schivelbusch include Mary Ann Doane, " 'When the direction of the force acting on the body changes': The Moving Image," in *Femmes Fatales: Feminism, Film Theory, Psychoanalysis* (New York: Routledge, 1991); Lauren Rabinovitz, "Temptations of Pleasure: Nickelodeons, Amusement Parks, and the Sights of Female Sexuality," *Camera Obscura* 23 (1990): 71–90; Musser, "The Travel Genre"; Kirby, "The Railroad"; and Tom Gunning, "An Aesthetic of Astonishment: Early Film and the [In]Credulous Spectator," in *Viewing Positions: Ways of Seeing Films*, ed. Linda Williams (New Brunswick, N.J.: Rutgers University Press, 1995).

31. Ann Friedberg, *Window Shopping* (Berkeley: University of California Press, 1993), and Guiliana Bruno, *Street Walking on a Ruined Map* (Princeton, N.J.: Princeton University Press, 1993).

32. Schivelbusch, pp. 118–25.

33. Edison 1902 film catalogue, in Musser et al., *Motion Picture Catalogs.*

34. I believe these early fantasies relate strongly to what Philippe Dubois has examined as the devouring and terroristic aspect of the closeup in early cinema, which he relates to the movement of the train toward the camera in Lumière's *L'Entrée d'un Train en Gare de La Ciotat.* See Dubois, "Le gros plan primitif: a propos de *l'Entrée d'un Train en Gare de La Ciotat* (L. Lumière)," in *Revue Belge du Cinéma*, no. 10 (winter 1984–85): 19–34, especially pp. 14, 21–22, 27–28.

35. Edison 1903 film catalogue, in Musser et al., *Motion Picture Catalogs*, p. 13.

36. Ibid.

37. See Gunning, "An Aesthetic of Astonishment."

38. The key essay is "The Work of Art in the Age of Mechanical Reproduction," in *Illuminations*, trans. Harry Zohn (New York: Schoken Books, 1969), pp. 217–52. The most insightful commentary on Benjamin's relation to cinema is Miriam Hansen, "Benjamin, Cinema and Experience: The Blue Flower in the Land of Technology," *New German Critique* no. 40 (winter 1987): 179–224.

39. Bruno, p. 82.

40. For instance, a Biograph 1902 film catalogue advertised the film *Home Life of a Hungarian Family* by saying, "nothing more novel than this picture could be shown to an American audience. The view was taken in the doorway of a peasant's hovel" (Biograph 1902 film catalogue, in Musser et al., *Motion Picture Catalogs*, p. 237). See also the Selig Polyscope catalogue describing *Solomon Island Dance*: "a wild and jerky dance which has the cannibalistic touch in every step" (in Musser et al., *Motion Picture Catalogs*). This film is undoubtedly related to an earlier group of films such as Biograph's *A Hard Wash* and Edison's *A Morning Wash*, both from 1896, which involve the racist joke of washing an African American baby to see if it would come white. See Charles Musser, *The Emergence of Cinema*, p. 148.

PART II

(INTER)DISCIPLINARY PERSPECTIVES ON THE TRAVEL CULTURE

~

White Knee Socks Versus Photojournalist Vests: Distinguishing Between Travelers and Tourists

MARIELLE RISSE

> There is an infallible test for detecting a tourist in any metropolis in the world—simply look for a man standing in front of a cutlery or luggage shop with his mouth ajar, gazing vacantly in at the manicure sets, razor strops, and collar boxes and jingling the change in his pockets.
>
> —S. J. Perelman

THE FIRST TRAVEL books I read were Gerald Durrell's descriptions of his animal-collecting trips to South America and Africa; I went through them settled in a deep, comfortable chair or stretched out on a towel at the beach. Once I began reading travel books as a scholarly pursuit, I had to read sitting up straight at a desk so that I had a pencil ready to make notes in the margin. I knew as I read that I might need to come back, find this passage again, and quote this sentence; so I jotted comments to help me remember. "Fact" scrawled across the bottom of a page reminded me that the author was making a point about distinguishing fact and fiction in travel books. "DD" stood for "double-decker," an author discussing reading travel books while traveling. "T vs. t" in the borders marked the place where the issue of travelers and tourists was discussed; not "t/t" or "t & t" or even "tt." I didn't realize that this might be important until I started to write this essay. The "vs." signifies how the distinction is presented: no sliding scale or variety of options; either you are in or you are out.

People who dispense definitions of "tourists" reflect the worst qualities of country club denizens deciding on new members. There is a pervasive feeling that the definers have passed the Rubicon themselves and refuse to remain in the same company of those who may have merely crossed the Amazon, Mississippi, or Nile. A perfect expression of this snobbery is found at the end of Eric Newby's *A Short Walk in the Hindu Kush* (1958). Newby and Hugh Carless are returning to Panjshir after a grueling, three-week climb through the mountains of Nuristan, a small, seldom visited province of Afghanistan. Sick with dysentery, emaciated, and exhausted, they meet up with Wilfred Thesiger, most famous for exploring the Empty Quarter and Iraqi marshes. Thesiger feeds the two men dinner, then, watching them begin to blow up their air mattresses in preparation for sleeping, remarks, "God, you must be a couple of pansies"(248).[1]

Differentiating between travelers and all lower life forms based on (usually arbitrary) levels of physical toughness is one of the five most popular means to solidify the boundary between travelers and tourists. The other four are how much the person knows about the country visited, how much money the person has, where the person is traveling, and when the person is traveling. Each of these five deciding factors shows up throughout travel narratives and writing about travel narratives, most notably in Paul Fussell's *Abroad: British Literary Traveling Between the Wars* (1980). Yet despite the wide range of attempts to divide travelers from tourists, a division between the two groups is difficult, if not impossible, to maintain.

Thesiger's insult to Newby and Carless implies that "real" men (and "real" travelers) do not need cushions or comforts while traveling. "Real" travelers stoically endure unpleasant experiences. Lawrence Durrell, in a London Sunday *Times* article (1959), affirms this attitude more explicitly:

> Let the tourist be cushioned against misadventure; but your true traveler will not feel that he has had his money's worth unless he brings back a few scars like that hole in his trousers which comes from striking Italian matches towards instead of away from oneself. No, the mishaps and disappointments only lend relief to the splendors of the voyage. (qtd. in Durrell, *Spirit of Place* 426)

Mark Cocker in *Loneliness and Time: The Story of British Travel Writing* (1992) states that "travellers thrive on the alien, the unexpected, even the uncomfortable and challenging" (2). Fussell justifies this position by discussing the word's history: "travel is work. Etymologically a traveler is one who suffers *travail*, a word deriving in its turn from Latin *tripalium*, a torture instrument consisting of three stakes designed to rack the body" (39).[2] In *Representing Reality: Readings in Literary Nonfiction* (1989) John Warnock, less gruesomely, makes the same claim:

> [T]he traveler on the "package tour" runs the risk of sacrificing the essence of the experience of travel. The word *travel* has the same root as *travail*, and it implies something other than the experience of consumer satisfaction. It implies effort and risk, and not just physical effort and risk. Travel is action, not passive motion. (3)

The issue then becomes how to define "misadventure," "suffer," and "action." Beryl Markham and Michael Crichton both have elephant adventures in Africa. In the early 1930s, Markham and Baron Blixen come within ten feet of being "crushed like mangos" by a bull elephant that they have been tracking through four miles of rough bush in East Africa (Markham 216). In 1975, when Crichton and his girlfriend visit a wild-game farm in Kenya, he wakes up one night to find an elephant munching grass "just ten feet" from his tent (complete with shower) (Crichton 160). Although the elephant does nothing more troublesome than chew loudly, Crichton titles his chapter "An Elephant Attacks" and fills the encounter with as much suspense as if he had been chased by velociraptors.

Who suffered? Does an elephant with the midnight munchies count as a "misadventure"? Crawling on all fours through an African thicket probably counts as "action," but does unzipping your tent flap and peering out with a flashlight? Yet Crichton's book is called *Travels*; the preface and back cover and all the pages in between discuss "travels."

In *I Should Have Stayed Home* (Rapoport and Castanera) "51 top travel writers, novelists, and journalists tell of their greatest travel disasters," including army ants in Guatemala, washing machines in Paris that won't stop washing, and buses without air conditioning in the Sinai. Helen Gurley Brown, editor of *Cosmopolitan*, waits "in a hundred-mile-long line" for plane tickets in Madras, only to make the horrified discovery she has coach tickets and must get back in line for first class (198). And this after her husband's shaving cream can exploded in his suitcase and they spent three hours cleaning off his hairbrush, pajamas, card case, and so on. (197–98). Stan Sesser suffers because the Nepalese relieve themselves at a scenic overlook of Mount Everest; Barbara Kingsolver is temporarily denied entrance to the Rainbow Room in New York City.

There are so many ways to encounter unpleasantness while traveling that the first argument (those who suffer are travelers) falls apart. People en route whose dinner is overdone, mattress springs sag, plane departs late, and so on, may claim the appellation "traveler" for themselves.

The second attempt to create a distinction is that travelers know the language of the visited country; tourists don't. Fussell states that "[o]ne who has hotel reservations and speaks no French is a tourist" (41). Michel Eyquem de Montaigne is caught in a cruel paradox on this issue. He argues that the traveler knows and attempts to adapt himself to the mores of the country, which Montaigne does assiduously. His secretary reports that "Monsieur de Montaigne, to essay completely the diversity of manners and customs, let himself be served everywhere in the mode of the country, no matter what difficulty this caused him" (20). Montaigne wrote his journal in Italian "for the last six months of his stay in Italy [although] fluent as he was, he could not express himself fully and personally in that language" and was "annoyed to find so great a number of Frenchmen here [in Rome] that he met almost no one in the street who did not greet him in his own language" (xxxi, 72). On the other hand, Gay Davenport, writing the Foreword to the 1983 edition of Montaigne's *Travel Journal*, blandly declares that Montaigne "is, in a surprising modern sense, a tourist, with a tourist's interest in the amenities of the table and the bedroom" (viii).

Alastair Reid takes the opposite route from the one taken by Fussell:

> To alight in a country without knowing a word of the language is a worthwhile lesson. One is reduced, whatever identity or distinction one has achieved elsewhere, to the level of a near-idiot, trying to conjure up a bed in sign language. Instead of eavesdropping drowsily, one is forced to look at the eyes, the gestures, the intent behind the words. One is forced back to a watchful silence. (11)

I would add an additional rejoinder to Fussell. There is a great deal of latitude within the simple phrase "speaks no French." I had studied the language for six years and was still unable to comprehend how to place a phone call in Corsica when I visited the island. Further, one can speak the same language and still have difficulties communicating. I've lived in North Dakota for four years but I still manage to confuse and amuse my students by saying "y'all," "bubbler," and "pop."

The third attempt to create a tourist/traveler dichotomy is the most insidious because it cloaks itself in smug platitudes of concern that people should "see the real place," but is revealed to be simple class prejudice. When Robin Hanbury-Tenison writes that "everyone should travel, and not as a tourist," he's privileging travel without recognizing what privileges must usually be in place in order to travel (17). In 1957, he graduated from Oxford and drove from France to Ceylon [Sri Lanka] in a Willis jeep with Johnny Clements. The journey "was not a race against the clock. . . . Instead we were free to wander at our will, go and see whatever took our fancy" (18). In the description of this journey, as with his later trips crossing South America horizontally and vertically, in the Kalahari Desert, through west Africa and around Indonesia, he mentions the joys of being able to travel freely, without mentioning the monetary considerations that made such trips possible. From the picture of his sumptuous family estate in Ireland to the descriptions of his farm in Cornwall, one may infer he had the financial resources and corresponding leisure to "wander at will."

This careful separating of travelers and tourists by respective wealth is most often stated in terms of "time": travelers can linger, while tourists are on a schedule. Alastair Reid states in a similar manner, "tourists have a home to go to, and a date of departure" (9). In 1877 Amelia Edwards, bemused to discover that a French boat has headed down the Nile before her English vessel, nicely sets out the hierarchy:

> [I]t was a consolation to know that the Frenchmen were going only to Assuan. Such is the *esprit du Nil.* The people in dahabeeyahs despise Cook's tourists; those who are bound for the Second Cataract look down with lofty compassion upon those whose ambition extends only to the First; and travellers who engage their boat by the month hold their heads a trifle higher than those who contract for the trip. We, who were going as far as we liked and for as long as we liked, could afford to be magnanimous. (36)

In *The Sophisticated Traveler: Great Tours and Detours* (1985), A. M. Rosenthal and Arthur Gelb make a direct appeal to financial snobbery. This collection of essays from the *New York Times* includes the details of where the restaurant is (in the best part of town), how much the meal costs (a lot), and where to rent a plane (private), and so on, which one would expect in a tourist guide, but Rosenthal and Gelb scrupulously avoid the word "tourist." They take care to ground the book in the tradition of the Grand Tour, in which "time was of no account and neither was money" (xi). It is acceptable, if not fashionable, to be "on tour"; it is not so to be a tourist. As Ian Ousby explains, "actors, musicians, and lecturers make tours, and soldiers perform tours of duty, but we do not call them 'tourists' when they do so, since the word implies a leisure activity, incompatible with work or even seriousness of purpose" (18).

John Keats provides an echoing response: "candor compels me to say that the culture they [American travelers] enjoy on five dollars a day is *not* the culture of Europe; it is the universal culture of poverty with a foreign accent" (7). There are many respected travelers who would disagree. Laurie Lee left England for Spain in 1934 with nothing but a small knapsack and his violin; William Least Heat-Moon set out in his van across America with $428. Eric Hansen drifted through Southeast Asia in the early 1970s on a series of jobs such as "smuggling Chinese erasers from Tibet to North India" (ix).

Authors of travel books themselves are often very careful to let readers know they are in the company of a bona fide traveler. Aldous Huxley writes in the beginning of *Along the Road* (1925) that "[t]he fact is that very few travellers really like travelling. If they go to the trouble and expense of travelling, it is not so much from curiosity, for fun or because they like to see things beautiful and strange, as out of a kind of snobbery" (9–10). The reader senses instantly that Huxley is one of the "very few" but his admission takes a few pages. First comes another setup: "Your genuine traveller . . . is so much interested in real things that he does not find it necessary to believe in fables. He is insatiably curious, he loves what is unfamiliar for the sake of its unfamiliarity, he takes pleasure in every manifestation of beauty" (16). Then, at last, comes the confession which puts him squarely into the coveted ranks of the "genuine": "With me, travelling is frankly a vice. The temptation to indulge in it is one which I find almost as hard to resist as the temptation to read promiscuously, omnivorously and without purpose" (19–20).

Gabriel García Márquez at first seems to rise above tourist bashing, but quickly states that although he may sometimes act as a tourist because of time constraints, he is truly a traveler.

> I don't know where the shame of being a tourist comes from. I've heard many friends in full touristic swing say that they don't want to mix with other tourists, not realizing that even though they don't mix with them, they are just as much tourists as the others. When I visit a place and haven't enough time to get to know it more than superficially, I unashamedly assume my role as tourist. I like to join the lightning tours in which the guides explain everything you see out of the window—"On your right and left, ladies and gentlemen . . . "—one of the reasons being that then I know once and for all everything I needn't bother to see when I go out later on my own. (*Best of Granta* 3)

Jan Morris's article "Sick of the Tourist Roller-Coaster" is an excellent example of the linguistic and logical knots one can get tied up in when trying to forge the distinction "traveler" for oneself.

> I spend half my life traveling, and mass tourism pursues me wherever I go. *Pursues* you, you may object? Are you not a tourist too? Well, yes. Every traveller is a tourist of sorts, and as a writer about places I can justly be accused of encouraging tourism myself. But in really wishing, like most of us, that the opportunities of travel could be limited to a congenial few, I may be selfish. But I am not hypocritical. It is the volume of tourism, not tourism itself, that is making it a curse rather than a benefit to mankind. (21)

Yes, in fact, she is being hypocritical. By making her life-work the depiction of foreign places, Morris "encourages" tourism, only now to state that she wishes to limit the number of people who may travel. She, as one of the "congenial few," a shockingly self-serving designation, will not have *her* travel restricted.

As Dean MacCannell points out:

> The error of the anti-tourists is they tend to be one-sided and in bad faith. They point out the tawdry side of tourism and the ways it can spoil the human community, while hiding from themselves the essentially touristic nature of their own cultural expeditions to the "true" sights; their own favorite flower market in southern France, for example, or their favorite room in the National Gallery. . . . Anti-tourists are against these other tourists spoiling their own touristic enjoyments which they conceive in moralistic terms as a "right" to have a highly personalized and unimpeded access to culture and the modern social reality. (164)

MacCannell puts "true" in quotation marks because he rejects the premise that there is a difference between what the traveler sees and what the tourist sees. This is the fourth attempt at distinguishing between travelers and tourists. The argument has run as follows: travelers experience real hardships, know the language of the country they are visiting, and have enough money to take their time. Now we hear that travelers only go to "true" places. Tourists, by implication, go to "false" places. But who then decides what is "true" or not?

Fussell, with an arrogance similar to Morris's, relegates locations visited by tourists to a place outside of reality: "Costa del Sol is a pseudo-place . . . [t]he Algarve, in southern Portugal, is a prime pseudo-place . . . Switzerland has always been a pseudo-place" (43). MacCannell uses Goffman's structure of *front* and *back* to argue that there is no hierarchy of "authentic" experiences.

I agree with this viewpoint. I will not jump on the "authenticity" bandwagon, succinctly put as "you didn't see Rome if you didn't see the Tiber at sunrise, eat gelato at Piazzo Novana. . . . " Either you have been to Rome or not. Rome is big; it contains multiples. My father tells a story of when he and I first visited Rome; green Michelin guidebook in hand, we ventured up the steps on Capitoline Hill which lead to Michelangelo's Capitol Square. Ever desiring to improve my eleventh-grade appreciation of history, he read: "at the bottom of the steps on the left you will see a cage with a wolf symbolizing the legend of Rome's founding, as you reach the top of the stairs you observe the ancient equestrian statue of Marcus Aurelius, a favorite of Michelangelo, and then the majestic Capitol Square unfolds with its three signature buildings." We looked with care—no wolf (the cage had not been used in years), no statue (it was off-site being restored), and the buildings were wrapped in scaffolding and green burlap (being restored on-site). Did this mean we had not "seen" Capitol Square?

The last argument put forth by various writers is that the time period in which people are traveling determines whether they are travelers or tourists. Toward the beginning of his book, Fussell presents the argument for the "when the person is traveling" distinction by sketching the historical constraints governing travelers and tourists:

> Before tourism there was travel, and before travel there was exploration. Each is roughly assignable to its own age in modern history: exploration belongs to the Renaissance, travel to the bourgeois age, tourism to our own proletarian moment. But there are obvious overlaps. What we recognize as tourism in its contemporary form was making inroads on travel as early as the mid-nineteenth century, when Thomas Cook got the bright idea of shipping sightseeing groups to the Continent, and though the Renaissance is over, there are still a few explorers. (38)

According to Fussell, then, the dominant option available to people alive now is tourism, as exemplified by Thomas Cook. Cook's travel company officially started on July 5, 1841, when Cook arranged for a train excursion for 570 people from Leicester to Loughborough and back. By 1877 the company had grown so much that when Amelia Edwards, whom we met above, arrives in Sakkarah, Cook's travelers are not simply familiar visitors; they are an economic force. Edwards writes: "[C]oncluding that Cook's party had arrived, every man, boy, and donkey in Bedreshayn and the neighboring village of Mitrahineh had turned out in hot haste and rushed down to the river; so that by the time breakfast was over there were steeds enough in readiness for all the English in Cairo" (47).

Yet Evelyn Waugh's introduction to his collection of travel pieces, *When the Going Was Good*, argues directly against the viewpoint that only tourism is currently possible: "There is no room for tourists in a world of 'displaced persons' " (9). Fussell posits tourism as the standard at the same historical moment Waugh takes away the option.

Lionel Casson further complicates Fussell's idea that tourism is a recent phenomenon by demonstrating in *Travel in the Ancient World* (1974) that there are clear signs of tourism in Egypt starting from circa 1500 B.C., in the form of organized groups of scribes visiting temples to collect souvenirs. Maxine Feifer in *Tourism in History: From Imperial Rome to the Present* states:

> Graffiti on the pyramid bases date back to the thirteenth century B.C.: in 1261 B.C. Ptah-Ewe wrote that he "came to contemplate the shadow of the Pyramids," [and] in 1244 it was scratched into stone that "Hadnakhte, scribe of the treasury, came to make an excursion and amuse himself on the west of Memphis." By the second century A.D. the paws of the Sphinx and the pyramid bases were densely covered with messages. (23)

The first tourist, according to Feifer, is Herodotus, because "he went everywhere, just to gratify his curiosity" (8). Robert Byron calls Alexander the Great a "tourist" at Cyrus's grave (169).

Thus the historical argument put forth by Fussell falls short. To say that "tourism [belongs] to our own proletarian moment" is to ignore a vast history (38). If one defines tourism as a single person or group of people visiting a new (to him/her/them) site for the purpose of contemplation, amusement, or the purchase of objects, the phenomenon has existed for almost twenty-five centuries and continues today.

If tourism, then, continues today and if it is not distinguishable from travel by a person's physical capabilities, linguistic knowledge, money, or location, is there any difference between travelers and tourists? Venturing into the thicket of definitions, I offer this: travelers make all the logistical decisions about their trip; tourists don't. A traveler, thus, is the active creator of the journey. Travelers may not necessarily want to be at that particular rat-infested hotel, but they recognize that the journey itself makes the bad parts, if there are any, worthwhile. This covers Redmond O'Hanlon in Borneo, Wilfred Thesiger in the Empty Quarter, Annie Taylor in Tibet, Lewis Gannett in America, without stooping to distinctions based on ruggedness, linguistics, class, location, or time period. Tourists, as I use the term without negative implications, follow someone else's agenda; they go, see, and learn as the tour guide, in the form of a person or book, sees fit. There is no need to get lost socially, physically, or linguistically as they have a structure in place to do the interpreting, arranging, or decoding for them. After years of traveling around the Mediterranean on his own, Lawrence Durrell decided to join a bus tour of Sicily, which became the basis for *Sicilian Carousel* (1977). He is a tourist, unabashedly following the orders of the guide, and if nothing else, this lovely book, full of mystical reminiscences and beautifully worked descriptions of Syracuse, Messina, and Palermo, should silence all lofty sneers about bus tours.

I believe W. Scott Olsen has the best idea. He writes in "A Tourist's Petition" that he hopes

> that someday we will all be Tourists. I do not mean to say that every one of us will in some fashion need to visit the places on our personal maps still labeled *terra incognita*, camera straps slung over our necks. Rather, it is my hope that we will recognize that coming home after a day at work is, in its essence, the same thing as walking a wilderness road for the first time. When I go home this evening, the light will have changed. . . . Tourism, in the good sense I want it to mean, does not begin with the first outbound plane ticket,

> or the second. Each day creates a new *terra incognita* out of the whole universe, each morning a new and unexplored venue for the Tourist. To be a Tourist in the way I mean is to learn a new way of seeing freshness, a way to value even the smallest and most perfunctory actions of our days. (73, 74)

Substituting "traveler" for "tourist" in the above passage would not change the meaning; the two terms are interchangeable, as I hope they soon will be in general usage.

NOTES

1. Newby offers a subtle, but delicious, rejoinder. The only picture of the "Great Explorer" in Newby's book has Thesiger lying in bed looking petulant, with blankets tucked in around him.

2. Turning to etymologies for support is a risky business. Maxine Feifer, in *Tourism in History*, claims that " 'tour' derives from 'tower' "; that "the trip is circular" and the traveler "ends up back where he started" (2). Ernest Weekly's *Etymological Dictionary of Modern English* (1967) lists:

> tour. F. (OF *tour*), from *tourner*, to turn (q.v.). In 17 cent. Esp. of the *grand tour*, through France, Germany, Switzerland and Italy, as conclusion of gentleman's education. Hence *tourist* (c. 1800). F. *tour* has also sense of feat, trick, etc., as in *tour de force*.

BIBLIOGRAPHY

The Best of Granta Travel. London: Viking, 1992.

Bryson, Bill. *The Lost Continent: Travels in Small Town America.* 1989. New York: HarperCollins, 1990.

——. *Neither Here nor There.* New York: Avon Books, 1992.

Byron, Robert. *The Road to Oxiana.* 1937. New York: Oxford University Press, 1982.

Casson, Lionel. *Travel in the Ancient World.* Toronto: Hakkert, 1974.

Cocker, Mark. *Loneliness and Time: The Story of British Travel Writing.* New York: Pantheon Books, 1992.

Crichton, Michael. *Travels.* New York: Ballantine Books, 1988.

Durrell, Lawrence. *Sicilian Carousel.* 1976. New York: Viking Press, 1977.

——. *Spirit of Place: Letters and Essays on Travel.* New Haven: Leete's Island Books, 1969.

Edwards, Amelia. *A Thousand Miles up the Nile.* 1877. London: George Routeledge, 1891.

Feifer, Maxine. *Tourism in History: From Imperial Rome to the Present.* Briarcliff, NY: Stein and Day, 1986.

Fussell, Paul. *Abroad: British Literary Traveling between the Wars.* New York: Oxford University Press, 1980.

Hanbury-Tenison, Robin. *Worlds Apart: An Explorer's Life.* Boston: Little, Brown, 1984.

Hansen, Eric. *Motoring with Mohammed: Journeys to Yemen and the Red Sea.* 1991. New York: Vintage Departures, 1992.

Heat-Moon, William Least. *Blue Highways: A Journey into America.* 1982. Boston: Houghton Mifflin Company, 1991.

Huxley, Aldous. *Along the Road: Notes and Essays of a Tourist.* New York: George H. Doran, 1925.

Keats, John. *See Europe Next Time You Go There.* Boston: Little, Brown, 1968.

Lee, Laurie. *As I Walked Out One Midsummer Morning.* 1969. New York: Penguin, 1971.

MacCannell, Dean. *The Tourist: A New Theory of the Leisure Class.* New York: Schocken Books, 1976.

Maghut, Muhammad al-. "Tourist." Trans. May Jayyusi and John Heath-Stubbs. *The Bedford Introduction to Literature.* Ed. Michael Meyer. Boston: Bedford Books, 1990. 883–884.

Markham, Beryl. *West with the Night.* 1942. New York: North Point Press, 1993.

Meyer, Michael. *The Bedford Introduction to Literature.* Boston: Bedford Books, 1990.

Montaigne, Michel. *Montaigne's Travel Journal.* Trans. Donald Frame. San Francisco: North Point Press, 1983.

Morris, Jan. "Sick of the Tourist Roller-Coaster." *The Independent* 9 Dec. 1987: 21.

Newby, Eric. *A Short Walk in the Hindu Kush.* 1958. London: Picador, 1974.

Olsen, W. Scott. "A Tourist's Petition." *North Dakota Quarterly* Winter 1996: 67–75.

Ousby, Ian. *The Englishman's England: Taste, Travel and the Rise of Tourism.* Cambridge: Cambridge University Press, 1990.

Perelman, S. J. "*But I Wouldn't Want to Live There!*" Eds. Michael Cader and Lisa Cader. Philadelphia: Running Press, 1993.

Rapoport, Roger, and Marguerita Castanera, eds. *I Should Have Stayed Home: The Worst Trips of Great Writers.* Berkeley: Book Passage Press, 1994.

Reid, Alastair. *Whereabouts: Notes on Being a Foreigner.* San Francisco: North Point Press, 1987.

Rosenthal, A. M., and Arthur Gelb. *The Sophisticated Traveler: Great Tours and Detours.* New York: Villard, 1985.

Warnock, John. *Representing Reality: Readings in Literary Nonfiction.* New York: St. Martin's Press, 1989.

Waugh, Evelyn. *When the Going Was Good.* 1934. Boston: Little, Brown, 1984.

Weekly, Ernest. *An Etymological Dictionary of Modern English.* Vol. 2. 1921. New York: Dover, 1967.

Childhood and Travel Literature

DAVID ESPEY

CHILDREN ARE conspicuously absent from travel literature. Literary travel is an adult activity, and travel writers are solitary figures. If they have children, they rarely take them along for the trip. In popular culture, the subject of travel with children yields farces like Chevy Chase's *Family Vacation* movies—not really about travel, but rather a low form of tourism.

Real travel, as travel writers continually remind us, is no vacation. They constantly defend themselves against the accusation that travel and travel writing, since they traffic in the world of leisure and holidays, are not serious. "Travel is work," Paul Fussell argues in his essay "The Stationary Tourist." "Etymologically a traveler is one who suffers *travail*" (235).

Children would render impossible the work of serious travel writers like Jonathan Raban, the late Bruce Chatwin, or Paul Theroux. Picture Raban going down the Mississippi in his fragile boat with child in tow, or Chatwin in the wilds of Patagonia or the Australian outback. They could not function as writing travelers without complete freedom and solitude. In *The Happy Isles of Oceania* (1992), Theroux recounts how the family-minded Pacific Islanders call to him, "Where is your wife?" when they see him alone in his one-man kayak.

Most wives of travel writers are at home with the children. Perhaps that is one reason why there are fewer women travel writers than men. Mary Morris, who has written travel books about Mexico and a trans-Siberian rail journey, postponed marriage and childbearing and escaped the fate of her mother. In an essay entitled "Women and Journeys: Inner and Outer," Morris describes how her mother "used to buy globes and maps and plan dream journeys she'd never take while her 'real life' was ensconced in the PTA, the Girl Scouts, suburban lawn parties, and barbecues" (26).

Children are part of that very world of home from which the travel writer must escape—the world of domestic obligation, the routine, the family, and the familiar.

That world defines childhood; children are creatures of home rather than the open road. In literature, a child traveling alone is often a pitiable figure—lost or abandoned, an orphan, a refugee, a runaway. The journey from home marks the coming of age. Travel, Freud maintained, was essentially an escape from the father. Leaving home and taking to the road constitutes a farewell to paternal authority, freedom from the protective but confining environment of home, an embarkation on a rite of passage to adulthood. The childhood memoir, or the Bildungsroman, generally ends when the child leaves home on some sort of journey—to the city, to the university, to sea, abroad. Travel in this sense marks the end of childhood and begins the transformation of child into adult.

Despite the natural opposition between the world of travel and the world of childhood, the traveler is in many ways a child, an innocent abroad. Travel writers enact again and again the archetypal journey of the child's leaving home. Moreover, the traveler in seeking to escape home is often seeking—paradoxically—to rediscover qualities of childhood. Travel may be work, but it also has many elements of play.

Travelers are often in the position of children, like students learning a new language. Unfamiliar with foreign customs, currency, or terrain, they can be gullible and easily led, dependent upon the kindness of strangers, and vulnerable to parasites and touts who hang around train stations and hotels. But if traveling can summon up childlike fears and feelings of vulnerability, it can also bring back childhood impressionability and freshness of perception. The foreign and the unfamiliar open up the senses; colors are livelier, smells more pungent, tastes sharper. Like a child, one discovers challenge and delight in accomplishing simple tasks like making oneself understood, ordering a meal, or finding the way back to the hotel. Ignorance of a foreign culture opens the imagination to hearsay, superstition, fantasy, creative misunderstanding. One of the charms of travel is that it recreates the conditions of innocence and a sense of wonder.

Since the chance for genuine travel is rare for children, childhood is a time of vicarious travel—through reading and fantasy. The seeds of the desire to travel are sown in childhood. The very act of reading is—for a child especially—a mode of travel. In *Abroad*, Fussell remarks on travel writing: "To speak of 'literary traveling' is almost a tautology, so intimately are literature and travel implicated with each other. Any child senses this, and any adult recalling his childhood remembers moments when reading was revealed to be traveling" (212).

Perhaps books about journeys exercise such power over children precisely because the possibilities of real travel are so limited for them. Jonathan Raban, growing up in rural England, saw his childhood "only as constriction." His voyage down the Mississippi, recounted in *Old Glory* (1981), owes its inspiration to a childhood reading of *Huckleberry Finn*: "The picture on its cover, crudely drawn and colored, supplied me with the raw material for an exquisite and recurrent daydream. . . . Going down the river turned into an obsessive ritual" (11, 16).

Raban's adventure epitomizes Freud's notion of travel as escape from the father. Raban recalls fleeing the oppressive presence of his own unsympathetic father by going to a small river near his English home:

> At the river, I was free to dream of what it might be like not to be a child; and all I could imagine was that there would be no father, no constraints. . . . When I tried to make the River Wensum stretch as wide as the Mississippi, I suppose I was attempting to stretch it until it corresponded with the amazing breadth of the freedom I thought I was going to enjoy as a grown-up. (140–41)

When Raban finally lives out his childhood dream of going down the Mississippi, he travels alone, but he carries a child in his imagination. The trip itself is a return to the idyll he imagined, a pastoral world created from *Huckleberry Finn.*

He continually measures the real Mississippi against the idealized one from his childhood vision. When he first confronts the river in Minnesota, he notes that "it wasn't the amazing blue of the cover of my old copy of *Huckleberry Finn*" (31). As he writes about his trip down the Mississippi, Raban combines impressions of the river with his boyhood expectations. The two genres which he mixes—travel narrative and childhood memoir—have common literary roots in the pastoral tradition. Both are forms of autobiography and both became especially popular in the nineteenth century, following the romantic reaction to industrialism.

Travel books, Fussell argues, are "subspecies of memoir" and "displaced pastoral romances" (*Abroad* 209). He locates the golden age of travel in the middle of the nineteenth century and sees the same flight from modern industrial society repeated in the 1920s, when British writers were escaping the ugliness of postwar England to the warmer and sunnier world of the Mediterranean. The very essence of travel writing, he argues, is the journey away from the unattractive present to the romanticized past. Literary travel constitutes "an implicit rejection of industrialism and everything implied by the concept 'modern northern Europe.' . . . One travels to experience the past . . . [and] literary accounts of journeys take us very deeply into the center of instinctive imaginative life" (210).

Like the travel book, the autobiography of childhood can be a spiritual quest, a literary journey back to a past when instinct and imagination were at the heart of an existence colored by nostalgia and the mists of memory. In his survey of childhood autobiography, *When the Grass Was Taller* (1984), Richard Coe finds that the literary form of the childhood memoir crystallized around the mid-nineteenth century, about the same time that the travel book was in its heyday; "the Childhood," as he calls the form, arose as a genre after the French Revolution and the Industrial Revolution, "each in its own way hard at work destroying the past." The Childhood has common roots with the travel narrative in its use of a pastoral tradition, "in nostalgia for the simplicities of a vanished Garden of Eden" (241).

This kind of literary return to the idealized and instinctual realm of childhood parallels many journeys of modern travel writers away from the industrial world to the pastoral. D. H. Lawrence, in his travel books about Italy, the Mediterranean, the American Southwest, and Mexico, represents as dramatically as any modern travel writer the quest for the pastoral ideal of an illusory golden age. In his oft-quoted statement on the basic human desire to travel, Lawrence invokes the mythical childhood of man: "We do not travel in order to go from one hotel to another, and see a few side-shows. We travel, perhaps, with a secret and absurd hope of setting foot on the Hesperides, of running up a little creek and landing in the Garden of Eden" (343).

Lawrence did as much as any writer to make the travel book a record of an inner as well as an outer journey, the traveler's introspective search propelled by a dislike of modern industrial civilization and a desire to find an unspoiled world. It is the kind of quest undertaken in various manners by such different writers as Robert Louis Stevenson, W. H. Hudson, Paul Bowles, or Peter Matthiessen.

For many writers, these inner and outer journeys are atavistic in nature. Bruce Chatwin links a yearning for a mythic past to his own childhood as he explores the basic human urge to travel in *The Songlines* (1987), his narrative about the Australian Aborigines. Chatwin argues that our desire to travel is instinctive, because humans first evolved as travelers—as hunters who walked across grasslands—and that nomadic cultures, like the Aborigines, are purer in spirit than settled, city-building civilizations.

Chatwin not only idealizes the primitive; he traces a universal human desire for travel to man's origins as a walker on the savannahs of Africa. This idealization of the primitive places Chatwin in a two-hundred-year-old tradition of travel writing. Fussell traces the traveler's fascination with the primitive to the 1700s: "Contributing to the rise of tourism in the nineteenth century was the bourgeois vogue of romantic primitivism. From James 'Ossian' McPherson in the late eighteenth century to D. H. Lawrence in the early twentieth, intellectuals and others discovered special virtue in primitive peoples and places" ("Tourist" 234).

This special virtue often attaches to the traveler's childhood as well, which serves to link the traveler and the primitive. The picture of an idealized primitive family on the cover of *The Songlines* comes from a book Chatwin read as a child; he identified himself strongly with the small boy in this first family.

Paul Theroux is more skeptical of the pastoral ideal. In *The Happy Isles of Oceania*, he explores the South Pacific, a traditional site for Edenic visions, and remarks, "As soon as a place gets a reputation for being paradise, it goes to hell" (370). Theroux generally reveals less than other travel writers about his own inner journey, but in the opening line of his very first travel book, *The Great Railway Bazaar* (1975), he acknowledges the childhood origins of his desire to travel. "Ever since childhood, when I lived within earshot of the Boston and Maine [railroad], I have seldom heard a train go by and not wished I was on it."

The only book by Theroux in which children accompany the traveler is significantly a work of fiction rather than nonfiction—*The Mosquito Coast* (1982), a contemporary version of *The Swiss Family Robinson*, the classic account of the family as travelers. Theroux's own trip to Latin America, the subject of his travel book *The Old Patagonian Express* (1979), provided many of the details of landscape and culture for the novel. *The Mosquito Coast* is the story of a failed attempt to return to the Edenic childhood of man. Allie Fox, the protagonist and vehement critic of contemporary American civilization, escapes to the jungles of Central America to establish a family commune free of the evils of modern society. Fox, a brilliant inventor, carries a machine into this primitive world—an ice-making apparatus called "Fat Boy," a kind of demonic mechanical child which brings about the destruction of his jungle paradise. The fact that the novel's narrator is a disillusioned child (Fox's son) heightens the irony of this antipastoral odyssey.

Graham Greene is another writer opposed in temperament to an idyllic vision of childhood and travel. In his travel book about West Africa, *Journey Without Maps* (1936), Greene focuses on the hardship, monotony, and squalor of a trip through Liberia. Despite the general gloom of this world, however, he sees a value in it all because its childhood associations rejuvenate him.

> Oh, one wanted to protest, one doesn't believe, of course, in "the visionary gleam," in the trailing glory, but there was something in that early terror and bareness of one's needs, a harp strumming behind a hut, a witch on the nursery landing, a handful of kola nuts, a masked dancer. . . . The sense of taste was finer, the sense of pleasure keener, the sense of terror deeper and purer. . . . I was discovering in myself a thing I thought I had never possessed: a love of life. (208, 277)

His journey expands beyond a sense of self-renewal; he evokes a collective childhood of man. Greene speaks of travel as a kind of psychoanalysis, a seeking out of "the past from which one has emerged." The masked dancers of Liberia strike him as familiar rather than exotic. "One had the sensation of having come home, for here one was finding associations with a personal and racial childhood, one was being scared by the same old witches" (109).

Greene's attraction to the play element of Liberian culture—the dance, the masks, the music—figures strongly in his connection of Africa to childhood. A similar attraction to play marks the English travel writers who left their country after World War I; as Fussell notes in *Abroad*, these writers were fleeing not merely the dreariness of industrial England, but the joyless existence, the shocking brutality, and the harsh memories of the Great War. Wartime society, with its constant demands of duty and sacrifice, is among other things a world of relentless work. The end of war provides a release for the repressed play impulse. English writers fled by the scores to the warmer climes of the Mediterranean, as if on permanent holiday.

Play, like travel, is underestimated as a significant human activity, because it is not considered as serious as work. In arguing for the seriousness of play (the distinctive activity of children), Richard Coe distinguishes between what he calls the "real" and the "alternative" dimensions of human activity. Activity in the "real" or "work" dimension is materially productive and helps sustain man's existence as an animal. Activity in the "alternative" or "play" dimension is not materially productive; it is gratuitous.

In this analysis, travel belongs to the "alternative" dimension. Travel, like play, is done for its own sake. And travel is no less serious for being considered play. "In fact," says Coe, " 'play' is the most supremely serious of all human activities, because it alone either constructs, reveals, or refers back to a system of values which transcends the drab and stultifying restrictiveness of deterministic utilitarianism" (252).

Thus the child and the traveler are players, in the sense that they act in an "alternative" dimension, one apart from the common daily routines of work. The activity they perform by virtue of being child or traveler is play—free, imaginative, spontaneous, but useful in an aesthetic rather than a narrowly utilitarian way.

Mary Morris avoided the conventional utilitarian role of housewife that prevented her mother from traveling. In her journey from China to eastern Europe, the subject of her 1991 book entitled *Wall to Wall*, Morris travels in search of a world made vivid to her through stories which her grandmother told to her as a child. Her train ride across Siberia becomes an odyssey back to her ancestral home, the Ukraine of her grandmother's childhood. Her own sense of home in the Chicago suburbs becomes inseparable from her grandmother's childhood in the Ukraine: "In all her [grandmother's] stories, made-up and real alike, the meek triumphed, wrongs were made right, the beautiful, the great survived. It was a child's world, one I came back to again and again" (7).

Like most travel writers, Morris is traveling alone; the search for home becomes the search for a deep human bond. Denied the possibility of visiting her grandmother's village because of the nuclear accident at Chernobyl, Morris shifts her yearning to the child within her—both symbolically and literally, since she realizes on the journey that she is pregnant.

The longing to visit the archetypal home becomes a longing to have a child, to end the loneliness that marks the journey of the solitary traveler. She sees a family of travelers, each child wearing a backpack, and her desire becomes clear to her: "I knew then that I wanted to have a child to journey with, to see the world" (168).

The child within is herself as well, the childhood of her past, her memory. Her grandmother had recounted a tale of being buried alive in the Ukraine to escape the pogroms of the Cossacks. Morris identifies the image of the buried child as a symbol of her quest, the very motive for her trip. "In my own way I had buried a child of my own. Not the one I was going to have, but the one I had been" (239).

The return to the home of one's childhood, the place that is strongest or earliest in memory, is a kind of ultimate journey, a mythic return which completes the cycle begun by the departure from home. Like the literature of travel, childhood autobiography is grounded in a strong sense of place. The former is a journey outward, away from home, toward the discovery of place; the latter is a return to home as a place rediscovered in memory.

In an essay entitled "Autobiographical Memory and Sense of Place," Rockwell Gray writes:

> My pleasure or displeasure in a particular landscape or interior carries within it roots deep in my first years of life. As we do not see landscape and the natural world without instruction from art—without the perceptual frames and visual conventions regnant in our culture—neither do we respond to any place without the informing presence of many remembered places and experiences layered palimpsest-like in consciousness. (56)

Childhood affects travel literature precisely in this way; it is a palimpsest of memory, desire, and impression—an earlier manuscript which lies beneath the travel narrative and guides it. Childhood is the temporal dimension of a space that was home. Rooted in collective origins as migratory animals, myths of primal innocence, and the memory of earlier years, the travel impulse in these writers leads away from one home while at the same time it seeks another, more fundamental sense of home. And wherever the outer journey may lead, the inner journey draws continually on the presence of the child within.

REFERENCES

Chatwin, Bruce. *The Songlines.* New York: Viking, 1987.
Coe, Richard. *When the Grass Was Taller.* New Haven: Yale University Press, 1984.
Fussell, Paul. *Abroad.* New York: Oxford University Press, 1980.
———. "The Stationary Tourist." In *The Random House Reader.* Ed. Frederic Crews. New York: Random House, 1981. 233–44.
Gray, Rockwell. "Autobiographical Memory and Sense of Place," *Essays on the Essay.* Ed. Alexander Butrym. Athens: University of Georgia Press, 1989. 53–70.
Greene, Graham. *Journey Without Maps.* Garden City, N.Y.: Doubleday, 1936.
Lawrence, D. H. *Phoenix: The Posthumous Papers of D. H. Lawrence.* Ed. Edward P. McDonald. London: Heineman, 1936. 343.
Morris, Mary. *Wall to Wall.* New York: Viking, 1991.
———. "Women and Journeys: Inner and Outer," *Temperamental Journeys: Essays on the Literature of Modern Travel.* Ed. Michael Kowaleski. Athens: University of Georgia Press, 1992. 25–32.
Raban, Jonathan. *Old Glory.* New York: Simon and Schuster, 1981.
Theroux, Paul. *The Great Railway Bazaar.* Boston: Houghton Mifflin, 1975.
———. *The Happy Isles of Oceania.* New York: Putnam, 1992.
———. *The Mosquito Coast.* Boston: Houghton Mifflin, 1982.
———. *The Old Patagonian Express.* Boston: Houghton Mifflin, 1979.

~

Popular Science on the Road: Adventures in Island Biogeography

MICHAEL BRYSON

DAVID QUAMMEN'S newest book, *The Song of the Dodo: Island Biogeography in an Age of Extinctions* (1996), merges the genres of travel narrative, scientific history, and nature writing and is a recent example of what I like to call "science on the road." Quammen, a veteran science journalist, takes his readers on a traveling adventure of truly global proportions—we visit Hawaii, Tasmania, Madagascar, Malaysia, the Manaus "Free Zone" in the Amazon rainforest, the Galàpagos Islands, the Baja peninsula of California, Guam, and countless other islands (and islandlike patches of landscape) around the world. *The Song of the Dodo* is thus not only an engaging narrative, but also a well-researched primer on evolutionary theory as well as a detailed introduction to a wide range of current ecological problems—landscape fragmentation, insularization of species, small-population jeopardies, extinction, and ecosystem decay. As we visit various island ecosystems around the world, we come face-to-face with unusual (and, in the case of the Komodo dragon, frightening!) animal species, talk with a number of engaging field scientists, and meet many local inhabitants whose knowledge of the natural world complements and often eclipses that of the professionals. By interweaving the history of island biogeography—the study of the facts and patterns of species distribution—with a modern-day journalist's ten-year odyssey, Quammen educates us in the theory and practice of evolutionary ecology, and sounds a timely warning about the disturbing rate at which so many of the earth's species are disappearing.

Quammen's overall argument is fairly straightforward: "islands give clarity to evolution," he notes (Quammen 19), something Charles Darwin and Alfred Russel Wallace came to realize in the mid-nineteenth century. Islands thus function as microcosms of evolutionary processes: biogeographers have long noted the extraordinary profusion and variety of life that develops on islands. Plants and animals often assume shapes, proportions, and behaviors that are nothing short of fantastic, and these developments happen more quickly on islands than elsewhere.

In addition, this accelerated rate of evolution goes hand in hand with extinction, and the rate of both these processes, scientists have shown, is directly related to area—the smaller the island, the faster evolution and extinction proceed. Finally (and here's why we need to pay attention to island biogeography, according to Quammen), humans have been hacking the world up into little pieces quite efficiently the last few hundred years, turning once large ecosystems like the prairies of North America's Great Plains or the rainforests of South America's Amazon River basin into places resembling islands in terms of their size and isolation. We are in an age of extinctions, Quammen strives to convince us, because we are fragmenting the earth's ecosystems into ever smaller islands.

As a scientific travel narrative, *The Song of the Dodo* is part of a genre with a long and fascinating history. These narratives, particularly in the nineteenth century, fulfill the dual function of entertaining homebound readers with exciting tales of exotic locales and serving as an all-important repository of scientific information. Charles Darwin's travelogue, *The Voyage of the "Beagle"* (originally published in 1839 as *Journal of Researches into the Geology and Natural History of the Various Countries Visited by H.M.S. Beagle . . . from 1832 to 1836*), a highly popular account of his trip to South America and the Galàpagos Islands, is a key exemplar, as well as a historical starting point for Quammen's late twentieth-century travels. But simply observing that the scientific travel genre serves these two functions begs the important question of how they interrelate. Instead, as one who is interested in the strategies writers employ to communicate complex scientific information to a general readership, I suggest looking at how the excitement, the surprise, and the wonder generated by the travel aspects of a text contribute to its didactic function, its ability to provide a scientific education. Along these lines, I analyze the relationship between travel and science in *The Song of the Dodo* and argue that Quammen's narrative persona—a wry, curious, humble, and ostensibly naive adventurer—is the key textual link between our enjoyment of the travel adventure and our understanding of island biogeography. The voice of *The Song of the Dodo*, by establishing a tangible, accessible, and unapologetically subjective point of view, provides readers with a lens through which to view the day-to-day dynamics of other species and cultures, as well as a humorous, challenging, and eminently entertaining tutor in the abstract world of ecological science.

EVOKING A SENSE OF WONDER

The literature of travel and exploration typically contains elements of wonder, various and shifting rhetorical responses to what literary critic Stephen Greenblatt calls "the shock of the unfamiliar, the provocation of an intense curiosity" (Greenblatt 2). In his analysis of fifteenth- and sixteenth-century European travel and exploration writings, Greenblatt argues that "[w]onder is . . . the central figure in the initial European response to the New World, the decisive emotional and intellectual experience in the presence of radical difference" (14). But what is this experience, precisely? How does it manifest itself in specific instances?

We can begin to answer these questions by a brief look at a few more-recent examples, for the paradigm of wonder also characterizes much of the travel literature of the last two hundred years. Consider William Bartram, an eighteenth-century naturalist who ventured through what is now South Carolina, Georgia, and Florida and who published his well-received and influential *Travels* in 1791. Describing the "astonishing native wild scenes of landscape" when he comes upon a small lake and meadow at the edge of a "great savanna" (Bartram 166), the deeply religious botanist exclaims:

> [H]ow is the mind agitated and bewildered, at being thus, as it were, placed on the borders of a new world! On the first view of such an amazing display of the wisdom and power of the supreme author of nature, the mind for a moment seems suspended, and impressed with awe." (166–67)

Bartram thus sees in the abundance, beauty, and variety of nature the handiwork of a masterful, all-powerful God—his faith is part and parcel of his sense of wonder. Additionally, the contrast between the workings of Bartram's "mind" (i.e., rational, controlled reflection and observation) and his feelings of awe, agitation, and bewilderment represents an archetypal eighteenth-century response to nature—the apprehension of the sublime. Bartram's narrative is an American expression of English philosopher Edmund Burke's well-known theories about the human response to nature (published in Burke's *A Philosophical Enquiry into the Origin of Our Ideas of the Sublime and Beautiful*, 1757). Burke painstakingly categorizes various aspects of nature as either sublime or beautiful and describes how these two qualities exert distinct effects upon the human psyche.[1] His ideas shaped European and American attitudes in the eighteenth century about the relationship between humanity and nature and find direct expression in the writings of Thomas Jefferson, the consummate voice of the American Enlightenment.[2]

American travelers in the nineteenth century also gave eloquent expression to their feelings of wonder in response to the natural world. Margaret Fuller, a journalist, social commentator, and feminist, writes of her experiences traveling through the region of the Great Lakes in her classic narrative, *Summer on the Lakes, in 1843* (1844). Like Bartram, Fuller harbors "a genuine admiration, and a humble adoration of the Being who was the architect" of nature (Fuller 9). Yet her description of her first encounter with Niagara Falls illustrates how the sense of wonder can be ephemeral and unpredictable, can occur at unlikely times and in unexpected places. Strangely, the view of the falls themselves, choked by tourists even in the more innocent times of 1843, leaves Fuller unmoved: "I expected to be overwhelmed, . . . but, somehow or other, I thought only of comparing the effect on my mind with what I had read and heard" (8). But later, while viewing the expanse of water and rumbling rapids upriver from the precipice, Fuller, profoundly moved, marvels at the "natural grandeur of the scene," where "mutability and unchangeableness were united" (9).

In later works of American exploration literature, where the discourses of science and travel coexist quite frequently, wonder is often expressed within a framework of empirical observation and analysis, as in the journals of geologist, ethnologist, and explorer John Wesley Powell. Powell's most widely read text, *The Exploration of the Colorado River and Its Canyons* (originally published in 1875 and revised in 1895), describes his 1869 and 1870 scientific expeditions down the Colorado and through the hitherto unexplored Grand Canyon. In one telling passage, Powell moves from a detailed and relatively detached geologic description to an emotionally charged expression of wonder and amazement:

> In some places, when the flow [of lava] occurred the canyon was probably about the same depth that it is now, for we can see where the basalt has rolled out on the sands, and—what seems curious to me—the sands are not melted or metamorphosed to any appreciable extent. In places the bed of the river is of sandstone or limestone, in other places of lava, showing that it has all been cut out again where the sandstones and limestones appear; but there is a little yet left where the bed is of lava.
>
> What a conflict of water and fire there must have been here! Just imagine a river of molten rock running down into a river of melted snow. What a seething and boiling of the waters; what clouds of steam rolled into the heavens! (Powell 274)

In the latter paragraph, Powell shifts from a careful reconstruction of the geologic history of the canyon—the rational voice of science, if you will—to a narrative enabled by his imagination and inspired by the landscape he has so precisely analyzed—the voice of awed wonder. Yet the tone of the final sentences is foreshadowed by Powell's previous statement, "what seems curious to me," a small point which nevertheless suggests that wonder is the possession of not just the imagination, but also scientific speculation.

These brief examples, then, give us a hint of how wonder—as a theme as well as a rhetorical device—is a variable but key element in the literature of travel and exploration in America. In *The Song of the Dodo*, we are brought up to the present time—David Quammen has spent the late 1980s and early 1990s traveling, interviewing ecologists and island biogeographers, touring various islands in search of living and extinct wonders. But for him the situation is decidedly different from that of earlier travelers—relatively little of the world is unexplored, and not much more is left untouched by the forces of mobile market capitalism. As an explorer he seldom, if ever, blazes new paths, but follows in the footsteps of others, such as Alfred Russel Wallace, who developed the theory of natural selection in the mid-nineteenth century simultaneously with Charles Darwin (Wallace, not Darwin, takes center stage in Quammen's historical account of the discovery). Quammen's rhetorical task, then, is not so much to express the wide-eyed, awestruck wonder at the natural world articulated in previous centuries, but rather to draw us in as readers, to capture our attention and emotions as a means of achieving his primary objective: educating us about evolution, ecology, and island biogeography (all of which, as we learn, overlap).

Quammen plays to our sense of (and hunger for) wonder by discussing a bewildering number of species—whether prevalent, endangered, or extinct. He seeks contact with some of the stranger creatures that exist on earth, such as the once mysterious and now probably extinct thylacine, a flesh-eating marsupial also known as the Tasmanian wolf. Some of these encounters are all the more powerful because they are laced with danger, as when Quammen meets up with wild Komodo dragons in Komodo National Park:

> We watch the komodo go. Exactly how big is it? I couldn't say. If not for the likelihood that I've been deluded by its aura of power and strength, I would tell you twelve feet, maybe fourteen, roughly four hundred pounds. But I won't tell you that, because nine feet and two hundred pounds is about the maximum that Walter Auffenberg [an expert on komodos] will allow me. Nine feet and two hundred, then—but for God's sake the beast is *galloping up a cliff*! (172, emphasis his).

He tells us of seeming improbabilities, such as hippos, deer, and elephants which swim considerable distances and consequently colonize new, formerly isolated territories (152–54). And he lets us know about the evolutionary significance of ratites, those large flightless birds like the ostrich, the best-known example of the group. The infamous dodo—a bird that was not dumb, but merely "ecologically naive," Quammen argues—was a ratite native to the island of Mauritius and was driven to extinction by 1690. For Quammen the dodo is

> the best emblem of this general truth: that insular evolution [evolution occurring in an isolated geographical area, such as an island] often involves transforming an adventurous, high-flying ancestor species into a grounded descendent, no longer capable of going anywhere but extinct. It's our reminder that insular evolution, for all its wondrousness, tends to be a one-way tunnel toward doom. (147)

Quammen's evocation of wonder here is double-edged: in the process of portraying the sheer power of evolutionary forces, how natural selection in a geographically isolated area can produce animals of immense, fantastic size, he emphasizes how such selective forces sometimes can leave a given species vulnerable to unexpected pressures. On Mauritius, such pressures began with the arrival of human beings on the formerly uninhabited island (first explored by the Portuguese in 1507). This is not to say that flightlessness itself is always an evolutionary disadvantage, as could be inferred from the above quote—the ostrich, for instance, has survived human contact rather admirably. More important, the dodo example shows us that extinction is more than just a natural evolutionary phenomenon, but also a consequence of "humanity achiev[ing] ubiquity and dominance on Earth" (263). Consequently, the unfortunate (and surprisingly complex) story of how the dodo became increasingly rare and finally extinct incites our wonder. Even as we learn the how and the why of the dodo's disappearance, we are compelled to speculate how a similar chain of events might be prevented in the future.

WHERE POPULAR SCIENCE AND TRAVEL LITERATURE MEET

Quammen's travel narrative is part of another literary tradition as well—popular science. *The Song of the Dodo* interweaves several important themes present in environmentally minded popular science writing the last thirty years or so, encompassing the major subjects of works such as Jonathan Weiner's *The Beak of the Finch: A Story of Evolution in Our Time* (1994), Paul and Anne Erlich's *Extinction: The Causes and Consequences of the Disappearance of Species* (1981), and Rachel Carson's landmark book *Silent Spring* (1962). These texts address the process of evolution, the patterns and implications of extinction, and the fundamental workings of ecological science (with varying emphasis). In addition, they critically evaluate humanity's past and present relationship with the environment and other species. Quammen's *The Song of the Dodo* is clearly part of this important subfield of popular scientific writing, but Quammen does something the above authors do not: he sounds his warning call about species extinction within the context of a travel narrative. I argue that this textual relationship, as embodied in Quammen's narrative persona, is important to our understanding of *The Song of the Dodo*. Specifically, the image of Quammen-as-traveler positively reinforces the role of Quammen-as-educator.

But first, a bit more context. Mary Louise Pratt, author of *Imperial Eyes: Travel Writing and Transculturation* (1992), argues that eighteenth- and nineteenth-century travel and exploration texts are important expressions of European ideology besides being repositories of information. Many earlier travel narratives, such as the journals and letters of Columbus, have long been characterized as the literature of "conquest," for such narratives make rather explicit claims about territorial appropriation.[3] In an interesting analytical move, Pratt distinguishes these narratives of conquest from much of the European travel literature of the eighteenth and nineteenth centuries, literature she calls "anti-conquest" (Pratt 7). Narratives such as Mungo Park's *Travels in the Interior Districts of Africa* (1799) and Alexander Humboldt's *Ansichten der Natur* (*Views of Nature*, 1808) are not explicit representations of the appropriation of lands and the subjugation of peoples by a heroic, larger-than-life discoverer/colonizer. Rather, in this process of "anti-conquest," the explorer-naturalist narrative persona is often (though not always) passive, detached, and unheroic to the point of near invisibility (60). Thus, Park's narrative seems to focus mainly upon Mungo Park-as-character, a "sentimental" stranger in a strange land, while Humboldt's voice is that of the authoritative yet emotionally distant scientist. Nevertheless, Pratt contends, texts like those of Park and Humboldt naturalize the "bourgeois European's own global presence and authority" (28). By creating order out of a seemingly disordered territory, by making the European traveler a comfortable, amusing, informative, utterly *familiar* figure in the natural and cultural landscape, these texts correlate with and even underscore the forces of European colonialism. In other words, it is precisely *because* their strategies of representation "secure innocence" for the traveler (and, by extension, the reader) that "they assert . . . [the] hegemony" of European culture (7).[4]

While I in large part agree with Pratt's important analysis of travel literature's relationship to imperialist ideology, I want to differentiate the textual workings of *The Song of the Dodo* from those of the eighteenth- and nineteenth-century travel narratives she studies. Quammen's traveler persona is neither a brash conqueror of other lands nor a passive, detached, uncritical scientist. The text, by extension, cannot be labeled conquest nor anti-conquest, strictly speaking. Quammen's attitude is by and large a revision of the traditional explorer's survey-and-conquer ethos. While considering an organized search for giant tortoises on the isolated island of Aldabra, Quammen muses:

> I can content myself with having seen *G. gigantea* in a botanical garden in Mauritius. The wild tortoises of the Indian Ocean have been harried enough. Let them have their refuge, their privacy, on that one little desolate atoll. If Aldabra is the epitome of isolation, I figure, then what better way to highlight that fact than by staying away from it myself? (127)

Here Quammen establishes and reinforces a contemporary environmental ethos. His traveler persona is one who can recognize limits to the process of exploration, who realizes that at this point in history there are places on earth better left unvisited by yet another curious writer. Such a sensibility works to draw in our sympathies as readers and virtual travelers, as we grapple with the implications of Quammen's decision.

Along similar lines, Quammen-as-traveler is not one who implicitly assumes that he (or American and/or scientific culture) is superior to the people (or ways of life) he encounters elsewhere. While he does spend considerable time interviewing and discussing the work of prominent professional ecologists (most of whom are transplanted Americans) studying the ecosystems of other countries, Quammen supplements these vignettes with stories of and by local experts native to the area. The greatly moving tale of Bedo, a Malaysian teenager who trained himself to be the foremost authority on the forest reserve of Analamazaotra in the eastern part of Madagascar, is a prime example. Analamazaotra is a reserve created to protect the indri, the largest of the earth's surviving lemurs, a rare and peculiar tree-dweller. As a youth, Bedo assisted several professional scientists, learned sophisticated scientific procedures and several languages readily, and continually amazed even expert ecologists with his knowledge of the forest flora and fauna. These scientists tried to recruit Bedo for formal training, but Bedo rejected some of the Westerners' methods, such as the practice of capturing animals to inspect them closely. By the time he was approaching adulthood, Bedo had carved out an independent niche in the local economy. He established a profitable reputation as the preeminent guide to the forest, someone "admired not just by tourists but by . . . eminent foreign biologists who had either done fieldwork at Analamazaotra or at least stopped there to see and hear the indri" (524).

Quammen's story of Bedo—a complex young man alternately admired, envied, appreciated, and patronized, and who was unwilling to adopt the career path of professional scientist—does not end happily, for Bedo was mysteriously murdered before his twentieth birthday. Quammen, touched by the tragedy, exercises his journalist's skills in pursuit of solid information concerning the indri expert's untimely death, but comes up empty. The tragedy of Bedo as related by Quammen is significant, I think, for several reasons. First, it represents a point of contrast with eighteenth century travel discourse: rather than render Bedo in caricature, a modern-day version of Rousseau's "noble savage," Quammen depicts Bedo as a complex, multidimensional, *fully human* human being. Second, the vignette demonstrates the importance of involving oneself in the culture through which one travels. Rather than simply remain a passive, detached observer of events and interviewer of authoritative scientists, Quammen-as-traveler juxtaposes the pronouncements of professionals with the expertise of Bedo and implicates himself in the story as well. In doing so, he highlights compassion and empathy as important characteristics of the contemporary travel narrative. Far from being uninvolved in the lives of those he writes about, Quammen, unwilling to hide behind a guise of objectivity, implicitly emphasizes the subjectivity—that is, the emotions, biases, and limitations—of his traveler persona.

Whether this is a sincere expression of David Quammen's personal character (as I like to believe) or a cleverly manipulative rhetorical device is ultimately immaterial. More important, Quammen uses the very same technique in the construction of his complementary narrative persona, Quammen-as-educator. The respectful, empathetic attitude Quammen evinces as a twentieth-century traveler translates into a patient, thoughtful, and persuasive teacher figure. Stepping rather nimbly from one role to the other, Quammen guides us concept by concept through the basics and complexities of island biogeography, all the while emphasizing where we've been and where we're going. For example, approximately two hundred pages into his book, Quammen asks, "You know something about adaptive radiation because you know something about the tenrecs of Madagascar, yes?" (217). Here he is getting ready to launch into a discussion of adaptive radiation, or the process by which "species originating from a common ancestor [diversify] to fill a wide variety of ecological niches" (217). His question is a reminder, an effort to jog our memory about a previously discussed concrete example. But to the reader who, like me, has read those 217 pages of *The Song of the Dodo* in short bursts of concentration (rather than all at once and with perfect retention), Quammen's gentle question is an innocuous, even *teacherly* reminder: if you don't remember that the tenrecs of Madagascar are long-snouted, spiny-backed, sharp-clawed, nocturnal mammals that eat insects, go to the index and look them up. Review, review! Get the concrete details before the abstract theory!

Indeed, this repeated emphasis of what I'll paraphrase as "OK, we've talked about that, so now let's tackle this" underscores the theme of learning as a figurative journey, one that parallels Quammen's physical trip across the globe. Thus, it's important that we consider both the literal *and* metaphoric aspects of Quammen's journey. In this context, the otherwise unnoteworthy phrase "where we're headed" takes on a dual significance. Consider Quammen's discussion of the types of speciation: he notes that allopatric speciation (the development of new species under conditions of geographic separation)

> is the rule. Sympatric speciation [speciation which occurs in the same area, i.e. without the benefit of geographic separation] is either a rare exception or an illusion, depending on which argumentative biologist you consult. And the prerequisite to allopatric speciation . . . is geographical isolation.
>
> I suspect you can see where we're headed. We're headed toward understanding the whole planet as a world of islands, and evolution itself as a consequence of insularity. (130)

It is this very specific understanding of the earth "as a world of islands" with which Quammen begins and ends our figurative journey, a circular (rather than linear) movement which suggests that our education is never finished, but ongoing. The recognition that human activity is fragmenting the world's ecosystems into islands, isolated and vulnerable, is not an abstract exercise in memorizing statistics or comprehending theoretical equations. This recognition, rather, is gradual—place by place, species by species, we (along with Quammen) come to appreciate how the inexorable forces we euphemistically call "development" and "progress" are linked to evolution and extinction.

HUMOR AND METAPHOR = GOOD "SCIENCE ON THE ROAD"

Much more could be said about various aspects of Quammen's rhetoric: the way he stresses connections among key ideas, linking the concrete to the abstract and tying together basic concepts; the detailed glimpses he gives us into the everyday practices of field scientists, showing how resourceful men and women do creative science in challenging environments; or his relation of the history of island biogeography, most notably how the findings and theories of Darwin and Wallace served to undermine scientists' belief in the divine creation of the earth.

Instead, I will conclude by concentrating on just two vital components of travel/popular science writing: humor and metaphor. I freely admit to a personal bias toward humor in just about any kind of writing—one of my favorite travel narratives is Bill Bryson's *The Lost Continent*, an expatriate's witty and often hilarious account of his journey across America in a Ford Pinto (and no, it's not my favorite book because of the author's last name!). Humor in popular science writing, too, is a stimulating additive—the power of Stephen Jay Gould's writing is certainly enhanced by his ability to make us chuckle in the midst of a detailed argument or explanation. As for metaphor—popular-science writers typically embrace figurative language as a necessary tool of the trade, but must use metaphor as carefully and precisely as possible in order to avoid misleading the general reader who routinely accepts analogies on good faith. On both of these points—a vibrant sense of humor and the intelligent, effective use of metaphor—Quammen's narrative excels; more important to my discussion, these elements further cement the complementarity of Quammen's narrative personas.

The Song of the Dodo is a genuinely funny book—when, for example, you consult the glossary and look up the term "biogeography," you find this definition: "Come on, you've read the book." However, Quammen employs his wit sparingly and purposefully, rather than gratuitously, as when he discusses the distribution of the Galàpagos finches.

> Consider the sheer mathematical fact that every one of those thirteen finch species either is or is not resident on each of seventeen major islands, and you get a sense of the potential complexity. And to make matters worse, there are subspecies. If I were so foolish as to expect you to contemplate these particulars, I would pack them all into an elaborately annoying chart, with the islands along a horizontal axis, the species along a vertical axis, and alphabetical subspecies in gridwork boxes to indicate the presence of different subspecies. You'd have the whole pattern at your fingertips, but your eyes would drop shut like an electric garage door. (222–23)

Ignore, for the moment, the metaphor in the last sentence; we'll get to that technique presently. This passage is typical of Quammen's propensity for drawing a line between the formal discourse of science (i.e., technical prose) and his comparatively informal rhetoric. Elsewhere Quammen jokes about the incomprehensibility of the mathematics employed by theoretical ecologists (whose work he often praises, by the way), all the while assuring the reader that *he* won't indulge in such quantitative overkill. In the above excerpt, Quammen stresses that he is not "so foolish" as to adopt the schematic format and objective stance of the technical writer; nor will he bury us in overwhelming particulars. By giving us a laugh at the expense of formal scientific writing, Quammen uses humor to draw us into his analysis, to increase our comfort level with the material at hand. Finally, there's a point that's easy to miss: Quammen's expression of reluctance to have us "contemplate these particulars" is harmlessly insincere, for throughout his book he does little else but build up to general points through the accumulation of carefully selected details and particular examples! Of *course* he doesn't want us to worry about particulars—meanwhile, we're absorbing them like a dry plant takes in mid-July rainwater.

While the measured use of humor highlights and defines, rather than obscures, the persona of the narrator, the use of metaphor is particularly crucial to our understanding of island biogeographical concepts. The stodgy old view, I might suggest, is that metaphors are the stuff of poetry and have no place in science. Good science avoids notoriously imprecise and potentially misleading linguistic traps like metaphors because . . . well, because that just isn't good science. Recently, however, scholars from various disciplines have discussed the fundamental role metaphor has played, for better or worse, in the rhetoric and methods of science. Indeed, many claim that metaphor is a vital (and unavoidable) intellectual tool at *all* levels of scientific discourse, not simply in the specialized genre of popular science. As physicist Roger Jones argues in his book, *Physics as Metaphor* (1982), "the metaphoric act transcends language and vitalizes creativity in science. . . . [S]cientists . . . conjure like the poet and the shaman[;] . . . their theories are metaphors which ultimately are inseparable from physical reality" (Jones 4–5).

Quammen liberally uses a wide range of figurative tropes, including analogy, paradox, and that favorite of poetry teachers everywhere, synecdoche. Let's look at one salient example: an extended metaphor in which Quammen illustrates the fundamental yet rather slippery evolutionary concepts of the "founder principle" and "genetic drift" by referring to a "drawerful of socks" (219). Quammen-as-teacher invites us to imagine alleles (defined in the glossary as "one of several possible forms of a given gene") as socks, an analogy he calls (with tongue in cheek, I hope) a "pedestrian example" (219). Without summarizing the metaphor here, I'll simply note that Quammen rather cleverly explains (1) how a "population" of socks (constituted by different colors) can change over time depending on which ones get packed for a trip, which colors are more popular in a large group of people, and so on; and (2) how these changes apply to the proportional prevalence of genes in a natural population of organisms. Moreover, Quammen is aware of and deliberately points out the limitations of his metaphor: "There is no *precise* analogy from the realm of socks, but only because suitcases are incapable of meiosis" (221, emphasis mine). And finally, he adds the coup de grâce: Quammen reminds us, albeit rather subtly, that the expression/concept "genetic drift" (the formal name given to the process by which the gene pool of an isolated population becomes different over time from the gene pool of its larger parent population) *is itself a metaphor.* Alleles don't literally drift through space and shift position on a chromosome; rather, the frequency with which certain alleles are present in a defined population changes. Drift, as a metaphor, connotes a gradual shift as well as a change in status—a piece of wood that drifts onto a beach changes position but also condition (from wet and heavy to dry and light). Quammen alerts us to the fact that metaphors can turn up in unexpected places in scientific discourse, and thus they require our thoughtful and critical attention.

Through his careful and creative use of metaphor and humor, as well as his effective blending of two functionally distinct narrative personas, David Quammen guides us through the ins and outs of island biogeography while appealing to our imagination, our sense of wonder. Quammen-as-traveler, who partakes of a revised explorer's ethos (one centered upon empathy and understanding rather than objectivity and conquest), complements Quammen-as-educator, who teaches us the lessons of science in the context of a literal *and* figurative journey. *The Song of the Dodo* thus exemplifies how the literature of travel and the discourse of popular science co-exist not only comfortably, but also productively. Just as "islands give clarity to evolution" (19), so Quammen's narrative provides a clear view of the development of the long and heterogeneous tradition of science on the road.

ACKNOWLEDGMENTS

I would like to thank Dr. Carol Traynor Williams for her many helpful suggestions in response to an earlier draft of this essay.

NOTES

1. Some of the aspects of nature Burke classifies as sublime include darkness, vastness, magnitude, and suddenness, qualities which produce two kinds of "passion": astonishment and horror (primarily), as well as admiration, reverence, and respect (Burke 57, 73). The beautiful, by contrast, is "that quality or those qualities in bodies by which they cause love, or some passion similar to it" (91).

2. As a key example, see Jefferson's description of Virginia's Natural Bridge in *Notes on the State of Virginia* (1787): "It is impossible for the emotions, arising from the sublime, to be felt beyond what they are here: so beautiful an arch, so elevated, so light, and springing, as it were, up to heaven, the rapture of the Spectator is really indiscribable! [*sic*]" (Jefferson 25).

3. See Tzvetan Todorov's *The Conquest of America: The Question of the Other* (1984) for a thorough and nuanced analysis of the literature of conquest, particularly the writings of Columbus.

4. I feel obligated to note that a one-paragraph summary cannot do justice to the intricacies and forcefulness of Pratt's argument. Interested readers should spend some time working through *Imperial Eyes*, particularly pages 1–60.

REFERENCES

Bartram, William. *Travels.* 1791. Ed. Mark Van Doren. New York: Dover, 1928.

Bryson, Bill. *The Lost Continent: Travels in Small Town America.* New York: HarperCollins, 1990.

Burke, Edmund. *A Philosophical Enquiry into the Origin of Our Ideas of the Sublime and Beautiful.* 1757. Ed. J. T. Boulton. London: Routledge and Kegan Paul, 1958.

Carson, Rachel. *Silent Spring.* Boston: Houghton Mifflin, 1962.

Darwin, Charles. *Journal of Researches into the Geology and Natural History of the Various Countries Visited by H.M.S. Beagle . . . from 1832 to 1836.* London: Henry Colburn, 1839.

Erlich, Paul, and Anne Erlich. *Extinction: The Causes and Consequences of the Disappearance of Species.* New York: Random House, 1981.

Fuller, Margaret. *Summer on the Lakes, in 1843.* Reprint of the 1844 edition. Urbana: University of Illinois Press, 1991.

Greenblatt, Stephen. *Marvelous Possessions: The Wonders of the New World.* Chicago: University of Chicago Press, 1991.

Humboldt, Alexander. *Ansichten der Natur* (*Views of Nature*). 1808. Trans. E. C. Otte and Henry G. Bohn. London: Henry G. Bohn, 1850.

Jefferson, Thomas. *Notes on the State of Virginia.* 1787. Ed. William Peden. New York: Norton, 1954.

Jones, Roger S. *Physics as Metaphor.* Minneapolis: University of Minnesota Press, 1982.

Park, Mungo. *Travels in the Interior Districts of Africa.* 1799. Edinburgh: Adam and Charles Black, 1860.

Powell, John Wesley. *The Exploration of the Colorado River and Its Canyons.* Reprint of the 1895 edition. New York: Dover, 1961.

Pratt, Mary Louise. *Imperial Eyes: Travel Writing and Transculturation.* New York: Routledge, 1992.

Quammen, David. *The Song of the Dodo: Island Biogeography in an Age of Extinctions.* New York: Scribner, 1996.

Todorov, Tzvetan. *The Conquest of America: The Question of the Other.* 1984. Trans. R. Howard. New York: Harper and Row, 1987.

Weiner, Jonathan. *The Beak of the Finch: A Story of Evolution in Our Time.* New York: Knopf, 1994.

~

Mapmaking: The Poet as Travel Writer

BEATRIZ BADIKIAN

ALL POETS are travelers. Whether literally or metaphorically, we journey through words to discover new worlds. And we journey through the world to create new words. To trace our "own personal" maps we move through the world with words and through words in the world. During these journeys we also become travel writers of sorts.

Although in her introduction to *Maiden Voyages*, Mary Morris reminds us that "[s]ince women, for so many years, were denied the journey, they were left with only one plot in their lives—to await the stranger" (xv), her anthology is replete with the writings of women who did not await "the stranger;" women who instead went out to look for the stranger or strangers, for the other women, for themselves. Theirs was an internal journey as well as an external search. Like them, we, today, still look for that cohesiveness, that unification of mind and body. We labor in order to make sense of our lives, which have been, until recently, controlled by others. We search for congruence and meaning, justice and happiness through our stories and poems. Morris agrees when she comments that most male travel writers "explored a world that is essentially external and revealed only glimpses of who and what they are, whom they long for, whom they miss," but "for many women, the inner landscape is as important as the outer, the beholder as significant as the beheld. . . . There is a dialogue between what is happening within and without" (xvii).

The women included in *Maiden Voyages* are travelers who write about their experiences and the consequences of those journeys, external as well as internal. Writing in the eighteenth century, Lady Montagu tells about the women in Constantinople who hide in safety behind the veil—an antecedent to Frantz Fanon's *Wretched of the Earth*, where he relates the stories of the Algerian women fighting for independence, whose veils turn out to be extremely useful. Montagu admires the fact that the Turkish women can do what they please beneath and behind all those layers of clothes, garments that provide them with cover and safety to pursue lovers without being recognized, to pursue an independent life that she herself, a European woman, cannot enjoy. On the other hand, Flora Tristan, in her writings about her travels through Peru in the nineteenth century, laments the fate of men who sacrifice everything for power and glory, even their present happiness for future honors, and conversely admires the *limenas*, the women of Lima who "are so free and exercise so much power." She describes them as taller than men, with easy pregnancies and irresistibly attractive without being beautiful. They come and go as they please, keep their names after marriage, gamble, smoke, ride in breeches, swim, and play the guitar. Echoing Montagu's descriptions, Tristan analyzes the *limenas'* unique style of dress, the *saya y manto*, which she sees as central to their social and sexual freedom. These dresses consist of a long, tight, pleated skirt and a black, hooded garment that completely covers the head and upper body except for one eye (Pratt 167).

Through their travels and, more important, because of the people they meet and learn from, these women discover their own personal strengths and go on to live lives filled with struggle as well as personal fulfillment, during a time when "it was frowned upon for women to travel without escort, chaperon, or husband" (Morris xv). These are unconventional women living unconventional lives, who, nevertheless, "approach their journeys with wit, intelligence, compassion, and empathy for the lives of others" (Morris xx). Now, sometimes, "we [women] feel a little like exiles; a woman feels like that when she does not live up to the image of her required by the times, when she does not interpret it, and hence searches for paths, for other 'countries' where life for her will be different from that in her own country, in the homeland given her by her mother's womb" (as quoted in Cisneros 39), proclaims Maria Isabel Barrerro in *The Three Marias: New Portuguese Letters.* Women in exile, whether literally or metaphorically, become the driving paradigm of many of our contemporary poets: women poets who search for other countries because this one is inhospitable.

Like their sisters earlier, contemporary women poets' writings postulate a dialectic between the outer world that surrounds us and the inner landscape that is inside us. Furthermore, women travelers, as Mary Morris points out, form a bond with other women travelers and "confide" in each other, telling "one another the secrets of their cycles, their children, their husbands, their lovers, the difficulties of their lives" (xviii). In Sandra Cisneros's poem "Letter to Ilona from the South of France" (41) from her collection *My Wicked, Wicked Ways*, the poet speaks of a night spent in a field of poppies where she has, surprisingly, felt joy and freedom despite her usual fear of the dark. The poet, in her attempt to explain this unusual phenomenon, finds that only another woman can "understand / my first sky full of stars— / you who are a woman." The epistolary form this poem takes echoes earlier works where women write to women in search of understanding, validation, or simply an empathic ear. The poem begins with a declaration: "Ilona, I have been thinking / and thinking of you since I went away, / dragging you with me across the south of France / and into Spain." The outer landscape of nighttime and poppies offers the poet the opportunity to liberate her inner self from previous fears and taste "the liberty of darkness." In the conclusion, the poet declares her joy at being able "[t]o wander darkness like a man." Traditionally, men have been the travelers as well as the travel writers for whom danger was not ever present compared to the multiple possibilities that women face every moment of the day. In this poem, the speaker rewrites that tradition, reverses the trend, and reinscribes herself as a new subject who can do what she was not able to do before, not only as an individual but as a member of a group, namely as a woman.

"Paris, December 24th," a poem in my collection *Mapmaker* which I dedicated to my friend Olga, also places itself within the tradition of the epistolary form (14–15). The speaker finds herself alone, in a strange city, at a special time of the year: Christmas Eve. In an attempt to establish some form of human connection, she writes a letter to a dear friend back in Chicago. The speaker is reminded of this friend because she is in exile just like the people who populate the Paris of the underground—literally speaking—that she frequents: the refugees and exiles who have come to Paris escaping "terror, torture, poverty" and who live and work in the subway stations where the speaker of the poem and writer of the letter finds solace and comradeship. This friend appears to be the only one who can empathize with the speaker: a woman from the same country of origin who has left her home in search of freedom and survival, now engaged in another struggle for growth and understanding. While "Paris / is a Pandora's box, cruel, hard and / multitudinous; a forbidden fruit I'd / like to taste someday," the speaker, at this juncture in her life, needs to "return, rest, continue / the task, plant roots, grow, sow and / harvest." In this dialogue between the outer world of Paris and the inner world of the speaker's growth process, it appears that the latter wins over the former. However, it is important to note that the outer world contributes to the speaker's realizations and resolutions because this stop in the journey is "one more link in this chain" (14–15).

Christmas is traditionally associated with family and home. In keeping with the unconventionality of the women referred to earlier, the speaker proclaims that this is her "first Christmas Eve far from / everyone and everything." This conscious decision situates her alongside the women travel writers who have gone on a journey rather than staying home to await the stranger, to paraphrase the late John Gardner's dictum regarding literary plots. Like the speaker in the Cisneros poem, who marvels at the possibility of being able to wander in the dark, in a strange place, free from the fear of danger, the speaker in "Paris" chooses to leave home at a very special time of the year in search of knowledge, maturity, even perhaps herself.

This search is not new. However, as Morris points out, "flights and evasion, the need to escape domestic constraints and routine, to get away and at the same time to conquer—this form of flight from the home is more typical of the male experience" (xv). But in keeping with contemporary women's quests and unconventional behavior, in Cisneros's poem "Moon in Hydra," from the same collection, the speaker narrates a different story.

Women fled.
Tired of the myth
they had to live.
They no longer wait
for their Theseus
to rescue, then
abandon them.
Instead,
they take
the first boat out
to Athens.
Live alone. (57)

The poet recalls the ancient myth of Theseus and Ariadne, which, repeated for thousands of years, has finally left a Hydra empty of women who have gone to Athens, escaping the routine of domesticity. The islanders theorize that the smoke rising from the Athenian shore is pollution from cars and factories, but the poet speculates it is the women's "ancient rage. / Women who grew tired / beneath the weight of years / that would not buckle, / break nor bend." And so, living alone, away from the home that bound them to domestic concerns, offers them the opportunity to free themselves of the oppression that weighs heavily and refuses to subside.

Embarked on the search for justice and equality, internal as well as external congruence, the women poets denounce racism and sexism. Ana Castillo's poem "In My Country" presents us with a utopian country where "men do not play at leaders," where she does not "hesitate to sit / alone in the park, to go / to the corner store at night . . . to wear / anything that shows my breasts" (73). The poem confronts us with a long list of demands for our real country disguised behind an imaginary one the poet creates where there is no violence, no child abuse, no hunger nor prejudice against people of color. Beginning with a series of negatives, the poem shifts: "[t]his is not my world. / In my world, Mesoamerica / was a magnificent Quetzal, / Africa and its inhabitants / were left alone. Arab women / don't cover their faces or / allow their sexual parts to be / torn out. In my world, / no one is prey" (74). The expectations of the poet turn to the world, a world where there is clean air and where poetry is "heard / without recoiling . . . sweet / as harvest, sharp as tin, strong / as the northern wind, and all had / a coat warm enough to bear it" (75).

As an "other," a Chicana who must live with the daily reminders of racism, Castillo's speaker searches for an outer world that will satisfy her personal, inner desire for equality and justice. Her need to confront these prejudices is echoed by Lorna Dee Cervantes in her "Poem for the Young White Man Who Asked Me How I, an Intelligent, Well-Read Person Could Believe in the War Between Races." Cervantes's speaker responds to a "white" audience, specifically addressing its questions and misconceptions. The utopic device is also present in this poem, as when the poet proclaims "[i]n my land there are no distinctions. / The barbed wire politics of oppression / have been torn down long ago . . . In my land / people write poems about love . . . [t]here are no boundaries. / There is no hunger." After such "wishful thinking," she confronts the audience with the reality of this land, where "everywhere crosses are burning, / sharp-shooting goose-steppers round every corner" (35). Cervantes's speaker travels the outer world that surrounds her, where she is "marked by the color of my skin" and where "bullets are discrete and designed to kill slowly." She is very aware of the fact that "[o]utside my door / there is a real enemy / who hates me" but wishes to "dance on rooftops, / to whisper delicate lines about joy / and the blessings of human understanding." The sharp contrast between her inner and outer landscape "bring[s] me slaps on the face" (36). She needs to reconcile and bring together these two distinct terrains of her reality in order to survive.

The dialectics of her existence are made even more evident at the conclusion of the poem because "[e]very day I am deluged with reminders / that this is not / my land / and this is my land" (36–37). This conflict must be resolved. The struggle to reach some form of coexistence between the desired and the real world must continue even though the speaker asserts, "I do not believe in the war between races / but in this country / there is war" (37). Cervantes has traveled and lived the reality of people of color in the United States, and now she denounces it, instigated by the naive questions of a "young white man."

As we have learned from cultural critics such as bell hooks, those who live in the margins are better equipped to describe the center. The women of color poets who live on the borders of mainstream society confront it and question it, calling attention to its inconsistencies, demanding changes. Our struggle takes us around the world, literally and metaphorically. Our weapons are nothing more and nothing less than words. Brandishing the words we created outside, we discover and conquer our interior landscape, forever embarked on the search for justice and equality. I would like to end with a poem of mine that inspired the title of this chapter: "Mapmaker."

> I am Eratosthenes' heir, the librarian
> who measured earth. He took an obelisk,
> a well, the sun, and made a triangle:
> geometry simple and accurate.
>
> A cartographer of sorts—I measure
> earth with words. I have drawn roads
> and made them impassable. I have laid
> railroad tracks to serve as escape
> routes. I have surveyed rivers and
> seas by touch and taste. And yet,
> I ignore my point of departure or
> destination, only know the lands
> that lie in between.
>
> Growing up under an obelisk's shadow I
> heard the story of genocide, of World
> War II, read geography, poems,
> swallowed them whole and learned—but

this journey never ceases.
Mapmaking is a life-long task.

REFERENCES

Badikian, Beatriz. *Mapmaker.* Chicago: Red Triangle Books, 1994.
Castillo, Ana. *My Father Was a Toltec.* Novato, Calif.: West End Press, 1988.
Cervantes, Lorna Dee. *Emplumada.* Pittsburgh: University of Pittsburgh Press, 1981.
Cisneros, Sandra. *My Wicked, Wicked Ways.* Bloomington: Third Woman Press, 1987.
Morris, Mary, ed. *Maiden Voyages: Writings of Women Travelers.* New York: Random House, 1993.
Pratt, Mary Louise. *Imperial Eyes: Travel Writing and Transculturation.* New York: Routledge Press, 1992.

Identity in John Lloyd Stephens's *Incidents of Travel in Central America, Chiapas, and Yucatan*

WILLIAM E. LENZ

AS EARLY AS 1815, the *North American Review* declared that a sumptuous variety of narratives of travel and exploration were being devoured by its readers and that their appetite for more narratives was apparently insatiable. In a review of the *Journal of a Cruise Made to the Pacifick Ocean, by Captain David Porter* . . . , the writer argues that even though there had been "so many expeditions by different nations, so many scientifick voyages, and such copious accounts published of the islands and coasts of the Pacifick Ocean; yet the distance, the grandeur, the beauty of those countries, the magnificent serenity of the climate, the wonderful productions of animate and inanimate nature, and the still uncivilized state of mankind in that part of the globe, make us open every new description of them with avidity" (247–48). Nineteenth-century Americans had a fundamental desire to travel, a cultural need that expressed itself in actual exploration or migration or, in more settled lives, in imaginative travel through the act of reading. Though most Americans could not travel to the Arctic Circle, many could read John Franklin's *Narrative of a Second Expedition to the shores of the Polar Sea.* Those who did voyage out often kept journals which found a ready market when worked up into travel books. John Franklin and David Porter are but two of a host of American travelers who published their accounts; part of the process of travel was to report home, in letters, in a journal, or in more literary reflections. A very abbreviated list of well-known American travel writers would include Washington Irving, James Fenimore Cooper, Nathaniel Hawthorne, Sophia Peabody, Charles Fenno Hoffman, Margaret Fuller, Richard Henry Dana, Herman Melville, Henry David Thoreau, and of course Mark Twain.

John Lloyd Stephens is a typical nineteenth-century American traveler, a New York lawyer who was sent abroad for his health in 1834. Uniquely, his journey took him from Rome, Naples, and Sicily, to Mycenae, Smyrna, Ephesus, Constantinople, Odessa, Moscow, St Petersburg, Warsaw, Vienna, Paris, and on to Alexandria, Cairo,

Luxor, Mount Sinai, Aqaba, Petra, and Jerusalem. Letters which he sent to his friend Charles Fenno Hoffman were immediately published in Hoffman's *American Monthly Magazine* as "Scenes in the Levant" in four installments (1835–36) "by an American." Upon his return to New York, Stephens wrote his first book, *Incidents of Travel in Egypt, Arabia Petraea, and the Holyland* (1837), followed by *Incidents of Travel in Greece, Turkey, Russia, and Poland* (1838), *Incidents of Travel in Central America, Chiapas, and Yucatan* (1841), and *Incidents of Travel in Yucatan* (1843). The lawyer evolved into the professional traveler and travel writer.

John Lloyd Stephens's *Incidents of Travel in Central America, Chiapas, and Yucatan* went through twelve printings and sold twenty thousand copies in three months (Ackerman 6). As Stephens constructs identity, he reveals nineteenth-century cultural concerns: he offers himself as a normative member of American society who leads the reader through the exotic landscape of the Republic of Central America, a landscape characterized by civil war, lost cities, fanatical soldiers, fascinating women, and unusual opportunities for self-promotion. Reviewing Stephens's narrative, Edgar Allan Poe asserted that "no one can deny his personal merits as a traveller, his enthusiasms, boldness, acuteness, courage in danger—perseverance under difficulty. His narration is also exceedingly pleasant, frank, unembarrassed and direct without pretensions or attempt at effect" (quoted in Ackerman 7). Stephens allows modern readers to understand the cultural anxieties of nineteenth-century American society on both a private and a public level; he presents himself as a simple citizen who creates a public persona as he puts on his "official" diplomatic coat. His confident cultural superiority in the era of manifest destiny leads Stephens to believe he can inscribe himself in the historical landscape as the archetypal modern American man.

In the book's opening sentence, Stephens immediately constructs himself as an ordinary American asked to complete an extraordinary task: "Being intrusted by the President with a Special Confidential Mission to Central America, on Wednesday, the third of October, 1839, I embarked on board the British brig Mary Ann, Hampton, master, for the Bay of Honduras" (Stephens 1:9). His language defines him as a cultured, sophisticated, urbane man of learning and leisure. The details of his departure anchor his text in a common reality we recognize as our own, while the "special confidential mission" launches Stephens into a public sphere distanced from the average citizen-reader. Throughout his narrative, Stephens moves back and forth between the private and the public self. Welcomed by Colonel M'Donald at Government House in British Belize, Stephens performs the public role of national representative, "and albeit unused to taking the President and the people upon my shoulders, I answered as well as I could" with a toast to Her Majesty (1:22). Despite the self-deprecating humor, Stephens reminds the reader of the imminent danger to which he is exposed; Colonel M'Donald draws him aside to warn him that "if danger threatened me, I must assemble the Europeans, hang out my flag, and send word" to Colonel M'Donald for military assistance (1:22).

Essentially alone in an exotic foreign environment, Stephens sees himself as one of the Europeans, a modern man defined by bonds of culture, language, and aspiration. In a "distracted country," it is important to identify one's allies: the

British officer represents the order and safety of civilization, values that a New York lawyer can understand. These values Stephens opposes to the decadence and decay of the declining Spanish empire in Central America and to the animal fanaticism of the indigenous Indians. The civil war which he must navigate and which threatens Stephens personally and publicly he presents as the result of Spanish imperialism declining into indolence and as a result of the anger of exploited Indians stirred up by Catholic priests. Stephens defines himself against these "others": he is not a sixteenth-century Spaniard driven mad by the lust for gold; nor is he a "mestitzo" clinging to the shreds of military empire; nor is he an Indian motivated by primal urges and superstitions; nor is he a Catholic guided by modern inquisitors and controlled by a priestly network.

As he leaves Belize,

> flags were run up at the government staff, the fort, the courthouse, and the government schooner, and a gun was fired from the fort. As I crossed the bay, a salute of thirteen guns was fired; passing the fort, the soldiers presented arms, the government schooner lowered and raised her ensign, and when I mounted the deck of the steamboat, the captain, with hat in hand, told me that he had instructions to place her under my orders, and to stop wherever I pleased.
>
> The reader will perhaps ask how I bore all these honours. I had visited many cities, but it was the first time that flags and cannon announced to the world that I was going away. I was a novice, but I endeavoured to behave as if I had been brought up to it; and, to tell the truth, my heart beat, and I felt proud; for these were honours paid to my country, and not to me. . . .
>
> Verily, thought I, if these are the fruits of official appointments, it is not strange that men are found willing to accept them. (23–24)

Here we see the ease with which Stephens the private citizen becomes Stephens the public performer. The flags, the salutes, the authority all converge to encourage Stephens to recognize his own public identity: he has the power to stop his steamboat, to cause a thirteen-gun salute—and to feel himself as the embodiment of American nationalism. But with a public persona come additional problems.

Having stopped at a settlement of Carib Indians, Stephens goes on a tour of these exotic people. He notes that they were "living apart . . . not mingling their blood with that of their conquerors" (1:28), that they were "descendants of cannibals, the fiercest of all the Indian tribes" (1:29). Stephens defines himself against these people, as superior to these people. Although he approves of their fierce independence, an American trait he can identify in these "others," especially against the decadent Spanish conquistadors, he establishes his cultural superiority as he describes their primitive conditions. They live in "houses or huts . . . built of poles about an inch thick, set upright in the ground, tied together with bark strings, and thatched with coroon leaves" (1:28). He takes great delight in describing "one old woman" who "received us with an idiotic laugh; her figure was shrunken; her face shrivelled, weazened, and wicked; and she looked as though, in her youth, she had gloried in dancing at a feast of human flesh" (1:29). Stephens thrills at his own proximity to an excitingly savage cannibal. Even if she is not a real cannibal, her "idiotic laugh" insures that we, like Stephens, associate her with forces of barbarism. To Stephens, she and the other Indians are primitive, their newly acquired Catholic religious faith like that of children, for they are "strict observers of the forms prescribed" (1:29). They suspect the Irish padre of not being orthodox because he does not speak Spanish; like true children, however, "when they saw him in his gown and surplice, with the burning incense, all distrust vanished" (1:29). Stephens enjoys his superiority, helping the priest with his baptisms by aiding in translation and eventually becoming entangled himself in the slapstick proceedings in Spanish, French, English, and Latin to the extent of becoming the godfather of an Indian baby; it is humorous because he sees himself as superior to the Indians. "In all probability," he writes, "I shall never have much to do with its training; and I can only hope that in due season it will multiply the name and make it respectable among the Caribs" (1:31–32). Stephens enjoys imagining his name in the Indian's lineage just as he enjoys imagining the old woman as a dancer at a cannibal feast. His pleasure is dependent on his position of confident cultural superiority.

In Central America, however, identity is extremely fluid. The suddenness with which Stephens's name becomes attached to a Carib Indian baby at the impromptu baptism demonstrates the rapid redefinitions to which the self is susceptible. Stephens and his English companion Frederick Catherwood plunge into the interior of the "distracted country, . . . each armed with a brace of pistols and a large hunting-knife" (1:40). Here they appear as conventional American explorers, armed to the teeth like Daniel Boone and Davy Crockett. In the village of Comotan, however, they are arrested and incarcerated by a band of "twenty-five or thirty men . . . the alcalde, alguazils, soldiers, Indians, and Mestitzoes, ragged and ferocious-looking fellows, and armed with staves of office, swords, clubs, muskets, and machetes, and carrying blazing pine sticks" (1:80). Drunk and aggressive, this mob demands to see Stephens's passport, his proof of identity and his license to travel. The officer leading the mob declares Stephens's passport to be invalid; in fact, he finds all sorts of things wrong with the passport. They refuse to recognize Stephens's official identity as special minister to Central America, they insist that the seal of General Cascara affixed to it only guarantees safe travel in Chiquimula and not in Guatemala, they argue that Stephens's large-format passport is not the correct shape and size and so is probably a forgery, and they therefore place Stephens under arrest and demand that he surrender his passport at once. In New York, in London, or even in Belize, a passport is a visible symbol of national sovereignty that offers an individual traveler the security of certain international rights. But in war-torn Central America, a passport is a tenuous symbol of both national and individual identity and may not authenticate or protect the self. "If we had been longer in the country," Stephens writes, "we should have been more alarmed; but as yet we did not know the sanguinary character of the people, and the whole proceeding was so outrageous and insulting that it roused our indignation more than our fears" (1:82). Stephens coolly tucks the passport into his vest and dares the young officer to take it by force, standing his ground with his hands on his pistols, backed by Catherwood and his servant, Augustin. The servant urges Stephens to fire on the unruly mob: "We had eleven charges, all sure; we were excited, and, if the young man himself had laid his hands upon me, I think I should have knocked him down at least" (1:82). Identity is unstable, and the ignorance, aggressiveness, and barbarity of the mob threaten to overwhelm it; in reality John Lloyd Stephens is, after all, no Daniel Boone. Before any violence erupts, however, a new military officer arrives, "of a better class, wearing a glazed hat and round-about jacket" (1:82), asks to see Stephens's passport, and reads it aloud to the mob. The effect is immediate—the mob, apparently illiterate, suddenly backs down. Nonetheless, they decide to keep Stephens under arrest, allowing him to write a letter to General Cascara in order to verify his official status. Stephens pictures these natives as primitive, illiterate children; at the bottom of his letter Stephens presses "a new American half dollar" into sealing wax: "The eagle spread his wings, and the stars glittered in the torchlight. All gathered round to examine it . . . and I have no doubt that the big seal did much in our behalf" (1:83–84). After the threat has been overcome, as he writes his narrative in the security of New York City, he constructs himself as superior to them all, able to impress them with a parlor trick seal as if they had been five-year-olds.

To avoid a repetition of his incarceration, at Copan the careful Stephens attempts to establish his official identity immediately with the local important personages, Don Jose Maria and Don Miguel, showing them "a large bundle of papers, sealed credentials to the government and private letters of introduction in Spanish to prominent men in Guatimala [*sic*], describing me as 'Encargado de los Negocios de los Estados Unidos del Norte' " (1:123). But in a land torn by civil war, the consequences of mistaking identity can prove fatal. They need something more tangible. "I again went into proof of character," Stephens writes.

> Don Miguel read my letters of recommendation, and re-read the letter of General Cascara. . . . [T]he shade of suspicion still lingered; for a finale, I opened my trunk, and put on a diplomatic coat, with a profusion of large eagle buttons. . . . Don Jose Maria could not withstand the buttons on my coat; the cloth was the finest he had ever seen; and Don Miguel, and his wife, and [his son] Bartalo realized fully that they had in their hut an illustrious incognito. (1:127–28)

The diplomatic coat functions as a visible symbol of Stephens's official public identity, one that is immediately recognizable by illiterate soldier, downtrodden mestizo, or fanatical Indian.

But violence always lurks beneath the surface of Central American life, violence which threatens the private and the public self. In the city of Mixco, Stephens attends a festival to celebrate the village's patron saint. There is feasting, dancing, and general merriment. The scene suggests comfort, security, and safety. As Stephens describes it, "We were in our hammocks . . . when we heard a noise in the street, a loud tramping past the door, and a clash of swords" (1:257). Chico, his host's son, had been walking with his friends when he was challenged by a bully. Chico and the bully drew their swords to settle this matter of personal and family honor. Chico had his right hand severed "through the back above the knuckles, and the four fingers hung merely by the fleshy part of the thumb" (1:259). "[T]o me, a stranger, it was horrible to see a fine young man mutilated for life in a street-brawl" (1:259). In the midst of a religious festival, in an apparently civilized community, violence erupts. It is senseless violence, characterizing Spanish American society, that Stephens implicitly contrasts with the safe American democratic life he shares with his comfortable readers. The violent nature of the white mestizos troubles Stephens; it is part of the malaise that is destroying Central America: "All this time the uproar continued, shifting its location, with occasional reports of firearms; an aunt was wringing her hands because her son was out, and we had reason to fear a tragical night. We went to bed, but for a long time the noise in the street, the groans of poor Chico, and the sobbing of his mother and sister kept us from sleeping" (1:260).

Stephens personalizes this violence and suggests three paragraphs later that it stems from a source deep in the heart of Spanish Central America. "Sunday though it was," he writes, "the occupations for the day were a cockfight in the morning and a bullfight in the afternoon" (1:261). Central American society is built upon violence, Stephens argues associatively, is preoccupied with violence, and takes pleasure in violence: "In less time than had been taken to gaff them, one [gamecock] was lying on the ground with its tongue hanging out, and the blood running from its mouth, dead. The eagerness and vehemence, noise and uproar, wrangling, betting, swearing, and scuffling of the crowd, exhibited a dark picture of human nature and a sanguinary people" (1:261). Stephens's language has itself become emotional, mirroring in its staccato delivery the excitement these activities stimulate in him.

Violence in Spanish Central America is also linked by Stephens to religion, specifically, to the extreme emotionalism inspired by Catholicism. Take the case of Vice-President Flores of Guatemala, a liberal, who levied a state tax upon a convent:

> the friars of the convent excited the populace against him, as an enemy to religion. . . . [T]he friars urged on the mob, who became so excited with religious phrensy [*sic*], that, after kneeling before the figure of the Savior, exclaiming, "We adore thee, oh Lord, we venerate thee," they rose up with the ferocious cry, " . . . for thy honour and glory this blasphemer, this heretic, must die!" They dragged him from the pulpit across the floor of the church, and in the cloisters threw him into the hands of the fanatic and furious horde, when the women, like unchained furies, with their fists, sticks, and stones, beat him to death. (1:196–97)

The Catholic Church Stephens portrays as institutionalizing violence. Women are the agents of this uncontrolled violence.

To Stephens, women are, like the Indians, a symbolic "other," fascinating yet potentially threatening. In the first days of his travels, Stephens describes the "primitive costumes" of local women; the dress of one woman

> was . . . somewhat in the style of the oldfashioned shortgown and petticoat, only the shortgown and whatever else is worn under it were wanting, and their place supplied by a string of beads, with a large cross at the end . . . ; and women and girls in such extremes of undress, that a string of beads seemed quite a covering for modesty.
>
> Mr. C. [Catherwood] and I were in a rather awkward predicament for the night. . . . I was dozing, when I opened my eyes, and saw a girl about seventeen sitting sideway upon [a bed near mine], smoking a cigar. She had a piece of striped cotton cloth tied around her waist, and falling below her knees; the rest of her dress was the same which Nature bestows alike upon the belle of fashionable life and the poorest girl. (1:56)

Stephens is attracted to the primitive sensuality of these women, as Melville was in Polynesia, to the easy physicality of their deportment, but their behavior is also mysterious and disturbing. They seem to beckon, to tempt, to entice him. But to what? Are they intending to embrace him or beat him? Like Melville, he is caught in a cultural dilemma: how can he, a man raised in another culture, be certain, based upon appearances, that he understands the reality of these foreign women? If he throws off the restraints of American culture to enjoy these women, will he open himself to the destruction of his cultural and individual identity?

Stephens betrays as well a cultural concern with race. He portrays himself as liberal, sitting down to breakfast between "two colored gentlemen. Some of my countrymen, perhaps, would have hesitated . . . but I did not" (1:12). Nevertheless, he seems to quote uncritically the comments of a teacher in Belize that, "though she had many clever black girls under her charge, her white scholars were always the most quick and capable" (1:16–17), and he remarks "that the whitest women were the prettiest" (1:177). He is drawn to American women who have "gone native," such as the Pennsylvania woman who happily married a don of Guatemala; she seems to offer Stephens a way to think about crossing a racial boundary, one that becomes entangled in his preconceptions of race, gender, and religion. She enjoys the festivities which mix indigenous Indian customs with Catholic pageantry, and she takes Stephens to see a young woman's farewell to the world before becoming a Catholic nun. Stephens visits the convent of La Concepcion "for the purpose of embracing a nun, or rather *the* nun, who had taken the black veil" (1:222).

> At length our turn came; my fair companion embraced her, and, after many farewell words, recommended me as her countryman. I never had much practice in embracing nuns; in fact, it was the first time I ever attempted such a thing; but it came as natural as if I had been brought up to it. My right arm encircled her neck, her right arm mine; I rested my head upon her shoulder, and she hers upon mine; but a friend's grandmother never received a more respectful embrace. "Stolen joys are always dearest;" there were too many looking on. (1:223)

That Stephens seems to fantasize about a more sensual embrace with this young nun should come as no surprise, for at the fete of La Concepcion Stephens had been compulsively attracted to the church pews of devout women: "The floor was strewed with pine leaves, and covered with kneeling women, with black mantas drawn close over the top of the head, and held together under the chin. I never saw a more beautiful spectacle than these rows of kneeling women, with faces pure and lofty in expression, lighted up by the enthusiasm of religion" (1:211). The religious enthusiasm of these women functions like a strong perfume, intoxicating Stephens with its exotic pungency. That the women are kneeling reinforces their stereotypic submissiveness; it appeals to one extreme of American culture's gender stereotype of femininity. At the other extreme are the "natives" with bare breasts, or the old female Carib Indian who Stephens imagines having danced at a cannibal feast.

He is attracted by the exotic and the sensual, yet he is careful to maintain a cultural distance. At Guanacaste, for example, Stephens goes as far as is possible for him with the belle of the town: "her mouth and eyes were beautiful; and her manner was . . . so much like the frank and fascinating welcome which a young lady at home might extend to a friend after a long absence, that if the table had not been between us I could have taken her in my arms and kissed her" (1:390). "The mother . . . said the place was dull, but that her daughter would try to make it agreeable; and her daughter said nothing, but looked unutterable things" (1:390). With undoubtedly "unutterable" thoughts in his head, Stephens retires to the bed he has been assigned yet feels "uneasy." "At the head was a lovely pillow with a pink muslin covering, and over it a thin white pillowcase with a bewitching ruffle. Whose cheek had rested on that pillow? I pulled off my coat, walked up and down the room, and waked up one of the boys. It was as I supposed. I lay down, but could not sleep" (1:391). This symbolic copulation is as close as Stephens gets to consummating his exotic fantasies.

To extrapolate, Stephens finds the exotic attractive. He is drawn to the sensuality of native women, their passionate religion, their dominance by Catholicism, and he flirts with the forbiddenness of interracial sexuality. These episodes confirm his masculinity, his personal identity, and his superior nationality. Ultimately, in their "otherness," these women assure him of his Americanness. They are sirens to be escaped.

But it is at the Mayan ruins of Copan that Stephens reveals most fully his representative American identity. "It is impossible to describe the interest with which I explored these ruins. The ground was entirely new; there were no guide-books or guides; the whole was a virgin soil . . . all created an interest higher, if possible, than I had ever felt among the ruins of the Old World" (1:119–20). First, he writes his name in "a quarried block" (1:147), inscribing his American identity onto the multilayered cultural artifact, impressing his identity onto it as easily and as confidently as he had pressed his half dollar into the sealing wax on his letter, proving that he had been there, explored Copan, had savored it, embraced it, possessed it. At Mayan Copan as at Mexican Conata (2:246), Stephens feels he is entitled to write his name in the monument; it validates his personal identity and is a projection of national identity. When at the Volcano El Agua he reads a series of inscriptions, including one dated 1834 and carved by a Philadelphian, he communicates a shock of recognition (1:273–75). Central America becomes, through the acts of exploring and inscribing, an imaginative extension of the United States. As Stephens writes his name in stone, as he reads the Philadelphian's name, as he writes his narrative, and as we read his narrative, Americans possess Central America and absorb its history.

And then, in a quintessentially American gesture, Stephens decides "To buy Copan! remove the monuments of a by-gone people from the desolate region in which they were buried, set them up in the 'great commercial emporium' [that is to say, in New York City], and found an institution to be the nucleus of a great national museum of American antiquities!" (1:115). Like the Elgin marbles carted off by the British, the Mayan ruins, Stephens declares, "belonged of right to us" (1:115). The pattern of attempting to purchase Mayan ruins Stephens repeats in Quirigua and again in Palenque, while at the volcano of Masaya he indulges an American fantasy of the success he would have if only the volcano were in the United States, "with a good hotel on top, a railing round to keep children from falling in, a zigzag staircase down the sides, and a glass of iced lemonade at the bottom" (2:13). P. T. Barnum would be proud.

What the violence, fanaticism, sensuality, exoticism, and ruin of Central America teach Stephens is a lesson in individual and national identity: he is not a violent mestizo, an ignorant Indian, a fanatical Catholic, or an expatriate losing touch with his homeland and language. He learns over and over again that he is an American by birth and by culture, despite the continual pressures of other cultures to absorb, reshape, or destroy him. At Aquachapa, he writes, "The captain introduced me by the title of Señor Ministro del Norte America. . . . The fact is, although I was not able to get into regular business, I was practising diplomacy on my own account all the time; and in order to define at once and clearly our relative positions, I undertook to do the honours of the town, and invited General Figoroa and all his officers to breakfast" (2:78). Identity is defined in the immediate moment, in each situation at once as an assertion of self. Identity is consciously constructed by extending an invitation to breakfast, by making an offer to purchase, or by putting on a diplomatic coat. Stephens will not live to see a Barnumesque museum of Indian antiquities rise in New York, nor will he sell tickets to volcanic eruptions, nor will he marry a señorita and entertain tourists at Palenque; nonetheless, in *Incidents of Travel* Stephens will successfully introduce Americans to the exotic worlds of Mesoamerica as a natural extension of personal and national desire.

REFERENCES

Ackerman, Karl, ed. *Incidents of Travel in Central America, Chiapas, and Yucatan.* By John Lloyd Stephens. Washington and London: Smithsonian Institution Press, 1993.

Review of *Journal of a Cruise Made to the Pacifick Ocean, by Captain David Porter, in the United States Frigate Essex, in the Years 1812, 1813, and 1814. . . . North American Review* 2, 1 (1815): 247–74.

Stephens, John Lloyd. *Incidents of Travel in Central America, Chiapas, and Yucatan.* 2 vols. 1841. 12th ed. New York: Harper & Brothers, 1871.

~

D. H. Lawrence in Taos: High Pilgrimage, Low Pilgrimage

JOHN W. PRESLEY

> When I first came into the presence of D. H. Lawrence's paintings, I immediately saw and felt how they charged the air with colour.
>
> —Harry T. Moore

ALTHOUGH THEY may know that D. H. Lawrence lived and worked for eleven months in Taos in 1924–25 and even know that his ashes were placed in a "chapel" there in 1934, tourists and pilgrims to New Mexico may be startled by the various ways in which Lawrence is remembered and presented to the traveler. As Anthony Burgess says in his Lawrence study, *Flame into Being*,

> Anyone wishing to contact the ghost of Lawrence in Taos will find his books and books about him in the shops, as well as a display of some of his paintings at La Fonda, on the Taos plaza (the mildly erotic ones may be viewed only on request). The Lawrence ranch is still there, the log cabin in which he lived with Frieda intact, and the small chapel where his remains are interred is kept in order for tourists. Brett's home has been turned into a restaurant called Whitey's. (258)

D. H. Lawrence's Kiowa ranch, which one can reach by going fifteen miles northeast of Taos, then five miles up a gravel road, was home to Lawrence in 1924–25. *Birnbaum's Santa Fe and Taos* has a short historical paragraph on the Lawrence ranch:

> The small house was a gift to Lawrence from Mabel Dodge Luhan, the wealthy sponsor of Taos's artistic and literary community, who tried (unsuccessfully) to persuade the author to settle in the area. After his death, Lawrence's wife,

> Frieda, returned to their New Mexico home and lived here for many years. Now a writer's retreat (under a program sponsored by the University of New Mexico), the property includes a shrine and a simple shed-like building. (63)

Lawrence first came to Taos at the insistence of Mabel Dodge Sterne (later Luhan) who offered him first an adobe house on her property. "She had read *Sea and Sardinia*, had determined that Lawrence's descriptive powers should be employed in word-painting her beloved Taos" (Moore 342). Lawrence tried to discourage her enthusiasm, but enquired "most practically about costs." On August 10, 1922, he set sail for San Francisco and Taos.

Lawrence spent about eighty weeks in and around Taos, though he arrived on September 11, 1922, and left on September 10, 1925. He made several trips to Mexico during these three years and, in fact, lived mostly on the mountain ranch twenty miles away when he was "in Taos," as far away from "that center of twittering malice" as possible while still enjoying the largesse of Mabel Dodge Sterne—he called her property in Taos "Mabeltown." As Harry T. Moore describes Lawrence's arrival, "they all drove away together over the desert, Mrs. Luhan from the first feeling hostile toward Frieda and prehensile towards Lawrence [Mabel had later written of their first meeting: 'The womb in me roused to reach out and take him!']" (Moore 354–55).

For his part, Lawrence described Mabel Dodge Luhan in a letter to his mother-in-law:

> You have asked about Mabel Dodge: American, rich, only child, from Buffalo on Lake Erie, bankers, 42 years old, has had three husbands—one Evans (dead), one Dodge (divorced), and one Maurice Sterne (a Jew, Russian, painter, also divorced). Now she has an Indian, Tony, stout chap. She has lived much in Europe—Paris, Nice, Florence—is a little famous in New York and little loved, very intelligent as a woman, a "culture-carrier," likes to play the patroness, hates the white world and loves the Indian out of hate, is very "generous," wants to be "good" and is very wicked, has a terrible will-to-power, you know—she wants to be a witch and at the same time a Mary of Bethany at Jesus's feet—a big, white crow, a cooing raven of ill omen, a white buffalo. (translated and quoted in Moore 354)

Despite his views on the artists of Taos, Lawrence made several friends there, and the stories of the years spent in Mexico and Taos, of the clash of eccentric personalities, make for fascinating reading. The number of memoirs written about Lawrence in these years attests to Lawrence's influence on the writers and painters of Taos, as a number of critical studies point to the influence of Mexico and New Mexico on Lawrence's work. Among the former are Mabel Dodge Luhan's *Lorenzo in Taos* (1932), poet and translator Witter Bynner's *Journey with Genius* (1953), painter Knud Merrild's *A Poet and Two Painters* (1938), Joseph Foster's *D. H. Lawrence in Taos* (1972), and Lady Dorothy Brett's *Lawrence and Brett* (1933).

Among the latter, David Cavitch's *D. H. Lawrence and the New World* (1969) is typical in that it focuses entirely on Lawrence's writing.

In March 1924, when Lawrence returned to New Mexico from a short stay in London, he spent five weeks in Taos before going up to the ranch on Lobo Mountain, where he spent some six months finishing the novella *St. Mawr.* The ranch, which Lawrence renamed Kiowa ranch, was presented, oddly enough, to Frieda by Mabel Dodge Luhan. In return, Frieda gave her the original holograph manuscript of *Sons and Lovers.* (Mabel later used the manuscript as partial payment of a psychoanalyst's bill; the manuscript is now at the University of California.)

It was to *her* Kiowa ranch that Frieda Lawrence returned, after the death of Lawrence in 1930 at Vence, France. Lawrence's body was interred in France, beneath a phoenix patterned in colored pebbles on a gravestone designed by Dominique Matteucci. But in 1935, Frieda's third husband, Angelo Ravagli, went to Vence at Frieda's request and had the body disinterred, then cremated at Marseilles. After many difficulties, with the help of Alfred Stieglitz and Lady Dorothy Brett (also part of the Taos colony), the ashes were brought to New Mexico (and apparently left on the station platform at Lamy, in the confusion).

Frieda and Ravagli had built a chapel for the ashes, at Kiowa ranch. Mabel Dodge Luhan had decided, however, "that the ashes didn't belong to Frieda but to the world, as represented by its self-appointed spokeswoman, Mrs. Luhan. . . . At the time the ashes arrived, Mrs. Luhan decided to steal them, but someone warned Frieda" (Moore 388, 511–12). As a result, Lawrence's ashes are embedded—mixed into—the concrete altar in the chapel, according to Frieda Lawrence, but the story varies with the teller.

Brenda Maddox, in *D. H. Lawrence: The Story of a Marriage* (1994), reveals that in 1956, while drinking with a relative of Maria Huxley just before he returned to Italy for the last time, Ravagli confessed that Lawrence's ashes were actually scattered in Vence. Fearing the difficulties and expenses of importing human remains into the United States, Ravagli crossed the Atlantic with an empty urn, he said (501). Alfred Stieglitz, who claimed "Angelo really has no idea of what happened," has even *another* version of how the ashes were lost and "returned." Stieglitz's other theories, some quite disgusting, are listed for the reader in Janet Byrne's *A Genius for Living: The Life of Frieda Lawrence* (Stieglitz 1995, 366). Taoseños feared that Angelo was planning to make the chapel a tourist attraction; these contradictory stories no doubt in fact do draw some of the curious to New Mexico.

University of New Mexico offices are in the house that Angelo and Frieda built, but the caretaker, Albert Bearce, seldom answers the doorbell—unless you engage him in surprise conversation, as I did, when he stepped out of his car after taking his dog to the veterinarian. The small cabin the Lawrences lived in, and the even smaller cabin in which Brett lived, are not open to the public.

Beverly Lowry, writing in the *New York Times Magazine* in October 1989 ("Lawrence: Keepers of the Flame"), presents a very jaded view of the high pilgrimage to Taos.

> The shrine—at the end of a steep walk up the mountain—looks something like one of those do-it-yourself storage sheds. . . . The altar is a square box, painted hard-gloss silver. . . . [T]he wrought-iron lamp hanging over the altar might have come from the Taos J. C. Penney . . . [T]here was a broom in one corner that needed using. . . . [T]he only vision I could conjure up was Frieda, dumping the leftover chips of Lawrence into the soft concrete. (87)

Visitors are directed to the Lawrence chapel—"shrine" as some call it—by a highway sign near San Cristobal. There is a gradual climb for five miles along a gravel road that leads from the valley floor, through juniper to ponderosa pine forest. The ranch is about 8,500 feet above sea level, after the pilgrim passes through a private cattle ranch. Kiowa is now owned by the University of New Mexico and operated as a "research/recreation facility." The caretakers are careful not to encourage visitors to linger.

Inside the chapel, which Mabel Dodge Luhan said looked like a "station toilet," are the "altar," a phoenix, a set of exhumation and cremation certificates placed there by Frieda Lawrence, and the guest book. An "agricultural wheel" forms a rustic rose window at the rear of the chapel. Outside, a simple white stone marks Frieda's grave.

The very steep, zigzag climb to the chapel puts some visitors into a semireligious mood: the phoenix above the altar is adorned with coins, cards, feathers, stones, pens, and blank pieces of paper. The visitors' book contains signatures from around the world—Sweden, Japan, and even from Eastwood, Lawrence's birthplace. Like pilgrims, some visitors attest to Lawrence's prescience and his work's power to change lives. Some recount Lawrentian evenings with lovers. Some complain about the University's maintenance of the road up the mountain and the condition of the shrine—there has been a problem with nesting birds since the day Angelo Ravagli built it.

The Taos area is rich in Lawrence artifacts, but some are curiously difficult to find, such as the furniture Lawrence made and painted, the woodblock print he designed for the cover of *Laughing Horse* magazine, the many objects he and Frieda created and presented to Taos friends and visitors. Typical of these "ephemera" are some paintings done for Mabel Luhan.

The tourist will find little to alert him or her to the paintings' presence. The *Birnbaum* guide describes the Luhan house very briefly. "The Mabel Dodge Luhan house is adjacent to the Taos Pueblo reservation. An original 3-room adobe 18th century house was expanded by Luhan (Mabel, as the operators refer to her), and she lived here until her death in 1962. There is now a newer guesthouse with 10 rooms, in addition to the nine guest rooms in the main house which 'often hosts art and writing workshops during the year' " (71).

Lawrence painted many household objects for Mabel. She describes at great length in *Lorenzo in Taos* the painting of a "brand new pine-wood toilet." She wanted it painted a green that "would have faded into the landscape and been unnoticeable." But Lawrence painted it a cream color, with "an enormous design. In the center, coil on coil, and swaying upwards, was a great, green snake wrapped around the stem of a sunflower. . . . [O]n either side of it, he painted a black butterfly as large as a plate, a white dove, a dark brown bullfrog, and a rooster."

As he and Frieda and Brett painted furniture and doors, Lawrence's favorite symbol, the Phoenix, appeared frequently. Mabel writes: "I had heard him talk often enough about the Phoenix. He identified himself with it. It was himself he wanted to place there—his sign manual on that house." Clearly, Lawrence's work was never entirely pleasing to his *patrona*.

After Lawrence had painted the phoenix on the top of one door to Mabel's guest house, he and Brett painted the bottom half with a Garden of Eden scene, "an apple tree with red apples on it, a *huge* serpent, and a brown Adam and Eve on either side of the tree." Lawrence was careful to "put a smile on the serpent," and Brett gave "a good fat tummy" to Eve, whom Lawrence called, according to Mabel, "the dirty little bitch with her sly, wistful tricks." Mabel identified herself with Eve, so it is easy to imagine how unhappy she was with this chubby Eve on her door (Luhan 173–75).

After Mabel Dodge Luhan's death in 1962, the seventeen-room, 8,440-square-foot. "Big House" she built at the edge of the Taos Pueblo passed first into her son's hands, then those of a granddaughter, Bonnie Bell. After several years of vacancy, Dennis Hopper bought the estate; the actor lived in the smaller "Tony House" and rented the Big House to a group of silversmiths. In 1977, an academic group bought the house, planning a conference and seminar center. The brochure advertising the Mabel Dodge Luhan home as a bed-and-breakfast "with engaging evening salons featuring local artisans" lists the many features of the house, "from colorful bathroom windows painted by D. H. Lawrence to carefully crafted traditional breakfasts." Two of the bedrooms, "Tony's Room" and the solarium, share the use of what the brochure calls "The D. H. Lawrence Bathroom."

Several anecdotes attest to Lawrence's unease in the presence of Mabel's exhibitionism (both physical and psychological), but these windows are an odd response: local lore has it that Lawrence painted the windows to Mabel's bath when he realized she had no drapes or blinds over the windows.

Still bright despite years of neglect in a damp bathroom shared by what must by now be hundreds of guests, Lawrence's window paintings show both his primitive approach to design and the effect of New Mexico on his sensibilities. Stars and suns are drawn in a very simple, stylized fashion, and the petroglyph-like animal figure surrounded by geometric designs and arrowheads shows Lawrence's reaction to now omnipresent Southwestern art motifs. Many of the figures he drew in New Mexico to decorate furniture and gifts were barnyard animals; the hen or cock drawn on one of Mabel's bathroom windows is typical of these primitive figures.

Other paintings of Lawrence's are easier to find and represent a startling contrast to these "hidden" Lawrence paintings. La Fonda de Taos is described in *Birnbaum's* as a

> timeworn grande dame . . . [once] the place of choice for movie stars, well-known writers, and other visiting glitterati. These days, though it's in sad need of renovation, the landmark exudes a certain quaint charm. . . . [T]he main attraction is a small gallery (which the desk clerk will open for a nominal

> charge) that contains a group of "naughty" paintings by novelist D. H. Lawrence. These scandalized people in Great Britain when they were first exhibited there in 1929, but today they are merely proof that Lawrence was far more talented with a pen than with a paintbrush. (70–71)

The hotel is owned by Saki Karavas, described in tourist guides as "the Greek-American hotel owner whose eccentricities shed light on the Taos of another era." His role as a link to the past of Taos and to the Lawrence circle is real and is embodied in his hotel and in his collections.

> The hotel's lobby walls are covered with gaudy pictures of bullfighters, black velvet portraits, and florid sunsets that are appropriately tacky complements to the eye-popping red leather furniture. For a nominal fee you can enter, through the glass door of Saki's private office, Taos's Bohemian past. This inner sanctum houses a gallery of photos of the then-young Saki with painter Dorothy Brett, Mabel Dodge, art collector and oil heiress Millicent Rogers, and the whole Roaring Twenties Taos crowd. If Saki is around, he'll happily tell you stories about all of them. This alone would attract the curious, but the office also contains D. H. Lawrence's scandalous oil paintings of nudes (in 1929 Scotland Yard confiscated them from a London exhibition); Saki obtained them from Lawrence's widow, Frieda. Some are better than others, most are bad—but all are signed either "Lorenzo" or "D. H." (*Birnbaum's* 144)

Those drawn in by the sign outside, "This is the Only Showing of the D. H. Lawrence Controversial Paintings since his Exhibition Was Permanently Banned by Scotland Yard When his Show Opened at the Warren Galleries, London, in 1929," are amazed or sometimes bewildered to find the collection crowded onto the walls of Karavas's tiny office. My wife and I spent two afternoons in Taos with Karavas, visiting with him and a friend, viewing the Lawrence collection, and watching a videotape of a British documentary made in 1991. Called *Lost Lawrence*, the videotape collects images of as many of the paintings in the Warren exhibition as could be found and describes critical reaction to a restaging—with photographs—of the Warren exhibition, in London.

Despite the use of the term "lost Lawrence paintings," Lawrence scholars have long been at least *aware* of the Karavas collection. Four of the plates in Marianna Torgovnick's *The Visual Arts, Pictorialism, and the Novel* are taken from this collection; note 54 to Chapter 1 indicates that "many of the originals may be seen at the La Fonda Hotel in Taos, New Mexico."

The year 1903 began what Harry T. Moore calls Lawrence's "apprenticeship." Lawrence the student-artist copied or adapted the work of other painters, producing many still-lifes, flower-pieces, and some landscape scenes. Moore says that though Lawrence painted and drew throughout his life, only the paintings from 1926–29 ("the last phase") and the early exercises are of interest (in Levy 17–18, 25–26).

D. H. Lawrence was clearly knowledgeable about the visual arts and wrote critically about them, usually in letters or in personal essays—not critical reviews. He preferred painting to sculpture and he enjoyed the Italian High Renaissance artists most, especially Titian. He also enjoyed the work of Rembrandt, Velasquez, Van Dyck, and Turner. He especially liked Rubens and William Blake—not surprisingly.

As a young man, Lawrence liked much of the Victorian and Edwardian popular art and "traditional" art. He was tutored in geometrical drawing as a young man by a local potter, George Leighton Parker, and he copied illustrations from magazines. Jessie Chambers reported that Lawrence spent much of his free time painting, usually copying other artists as faithfully as he could, preferring flowers and landscapes. His letters during this period mention his copying exercises and frequently allude to artists, art, and his gallery visits. He offers opinions on Watts, Sargent, Millais, and Watteau, among others (Torgovnick 46–53).

His great enthusiasm in his youth was for a painting now found clichéd and sentimental: Maurice Greiffenhagen's *An Idyll*, painted in 1891. Lawrence copied the pastoral lovers, the woman "swooning" into her lover's arms, four times.

Lawrence's "flaming and often quite vicious disdain" for the Bloomsbury group is well known: Chapter 18 of *Lady Chatterley's Lover* is a thinly disguised account of Lawrence's own visit to the studio of Duncan Grant, and many of the *Women in Love* characters are based on Bloomsbury members (Torgovnick 56–57).

Late in the 1920s, he painted the twenty-five works that made up the ill-fated 1929 Warren Gallery exhibition. All twenty-five were reproduced in *The Paintings of D. H. Lawrence.* These late works were variously dispersed, some purchased, some given as gifts to Lawrence's friends. In 1956, Frieda Lawrence owned nine of the paintings: *Red Willow Trees, Rape of the Sabine Women, Flight Back into Paradise, Boccaccio Story, Fight with an Amazon, Fawns and Nymphs, Close-up (Kiss), Dance Sketch,* and *Summer Dawn.* After Frieda's death, eight of the paintings—*Boccaccio Story* is "lost"—were bought from Frieda's third husband, Angelo Ravagli, by Saki Karavas (Levy). Besides these eight paintings in the Karavas collection, there are many other early and later Lawrence works in private collections and in universities around the world.

After Lawrence had finished the final version of *Lady Chatterley's Lover*, in Switzerland in 1928, he took pleasure in what Moore calls the last phase of his painting, with the watercolor *Fire Dance*, which was finished after his arrival at the Villa Mirenda, in Italy. "Two naked men—rather nice, I think—not particularly natural." Later, he wrote to Aldous Huxley, "I painted a charming picture of a man pissing" (qtd. in Moore 442). He mentions several more paintings; these formed the base of his exhibition in 1929 at Dorothy Warren's gallery in London. There was, for Lawrence, an even more interesting possibility: that some firm would publish a portfolio of reproductions of the paintings.

Frieda wrote in a letter to Mabel Dodge Luhan, from Villa Mirenda on May 4, 1927, that the painting was going well. "Maria Huxley says they are 'grand'! And so they are. And the first conception of one is very thrilling when Lawrence gets his paints and his glass bits, puts his overalls on, takes a bit of charcoal from the kitchen, is quite still and suddenly darts at the canvas, goes on for a few hours. I sit and watch and then it's there and we both feel dead tired" (qtd. in Luhan 324).

In fact, as Lawrence was writing the introduction to the portfolio, the furor over his poetry collection *Pansies* (and of course *Lady Chatterley's Lover*) was reaching a peak, with the British government attempting to suppress the poems, as it had suppressed *The Rainbow*, fifteen years before. The *Pansies* manuscript and the paintings manuscript were seized by Home Secretary Sir William Joynson-Hicks, a "religious zealot," who was in fact searching Lawrence's mail for copies of *Chatterley*. The Obscene Publications Act allowed any metropolitan police magistrate or any two justices of the peace, "on sworn information," to issue a search warrant and seize any "obscene" book or picture. Further, the Post Office Act of 1908 decreed that the ostmaster-general "must refuse to take part in the conveyance of any indecent matter." It was the postmaster-general, apparently, who made the first determination of *prima facie* indecency (Moore 462, 464).

On July 5, 1929, the London police seized thirteen of Lawrence's paintings from the Warren exhibition and stored them in the basement of the Marlborough Street police court; rumor had it that they were to be burned. (The police had also seized George Grosz's *Ecce Homo*, but had left some Blake reproductions when it was explained to them that Blake was dead, and they had left the *Hunting of the Snark*, once Dorothy Warren explained that the Louis Arragon translation was a children's book, even if written in the filthy French language.) The police had apparently acted on either citizen complaints or descriptions in the press that had mentioned the pubic hair visible in the paintings. Nine days later, Lawrence wrote to Warren that she should compromise with the police: "There is something sacred to me about my pictures, and I will not have them burnt, for all the liberty of England . . . to change an English law" (Moore 475).

During the "trial of the pictures," Lawrence remained in Baden-Baden; seven months away from his death by tuberculosis, he contented himself with savaging his critics in poems and essays. In London on August 8, the trial began, heard by an eighty-two-year-old magistrate, whose first decision was to ban testimony from the artists Augustus John, Glyn Philpot, and William Rothenstein. He did, however, listen to testimony from one Herbert G. Muskett, who as a literary expert had testified at the trial of *The Rainbow*; in the guise of an art critic, Muskett declared the paintings "gross, coarse, hideous, unlovely, and obscene." In fact, though, the magistrate never declared the pictures obscene; when defense counsel St. John Hutchinson offered to agree that the paintings would be withdrawn from the gallery exhibition and never again shown in England, the magistrate ordered the gallery owners to send the paintings back to their owner (Moore 473–74, 479).

Before the paintings were shipped by Serafina Ravagli from Vence to Taos in 1936, Martha Gordon Crotch exhibited them in her "tearoom"—she called it a gallery—where for a while Frieda held court as tourists and scholars "eager to buy the Paris edition of *Lady Chatterley's Lover*, which was sold at a front table," filed in (Byrne 359). And before their installation in the room Ravagli built for them in the Los Prados house, Lawrence's paintings were shown once more, at the "prominent Los Angeles gallery Stendhal," where not a single canvas was sold. (Therefore,

Karavas's claim that "this is the only showing . . . since his exhibition was permanently banned by Scotland Yard" isn't precisely accurate.) Frieda brought the paintings back to Taos, strapped to the top of a La Salle (Byrne 373–74).

Saki Karavas's collection of Lawrence artifacts includes eight of the Warren Gallery paintings, plus the original of Knud Merrild's famous portrait of Lawrence (Merrild lived with the Lawrences at Del Monte ranch during the winter of 1922–23), at least one Lawrence landscape which has never to my knowledge been discussed or reproduced, and a collaborative painting done by Lawrence, Brett, Frieda, and possibly Mabel. Mabel mentions the "rather thin pictures of the desert" that Brett painted when she wasn't doing Lawrence's typing, and the collaborative painting of "the ranch with the desert below, and all the animals on the place, and themselves flying along on horses." She continues, "They had fun together and I envied them, because they liked to *do* things" (Luhan 212).

Two of the paintings in the Karavas collection are rather atypical, in Torgovnick's terms. *Rape of the Sabine Women* presents an image perhaps of Lawrence himself, the only figure presented "individually and frontally." The colors are darker; the abduction seems lifeless, the Lawrence figure disgusted. The forms of the abductors and abductees are indistinguishable. Lawrence once called this painting "A Study in Arses." Torgovnick concludes, "inevitably, the painting suggests less the subject painted earlier by Poussin than the state of sexuality in contemporary society as Lawrence perceived it" (58–59).

The other, *Flight Back into Paradise*, is atypical since it is the only Lawrence painting in which the "pressures of modernism" are dealt with directly. In this painting, the Eve figure is fleeing a futurist-like city. The city seems to slither into the foreground as a tape-like snare around her legs. The two sinister-appearing male figures are identified by Lawrence, in a letter, as Adam and the angel at the gate. The figures of the two humans are distorted, after the modernist fashion, and the strongly painted lines that suggest form and movement are a futurist device. The easy, comfortable sexuality of Lawrence's *The Holy Family* (c. 1926), for example, is gone: in *Flight Back into Paradise*, Adam "glares" at Eve and the "menacing red smokestacks [are] acknowledged by Lawrence as modernity's 'tribute' to the phallus it everywhere else tried to deny" (Torgovnick 59).

"Lawrence's own work as a painter has prompted mixed evaluations. All agree that he had a gift for color, but lacked adequate training in formal composition" (Torgovnick 56). It is also clear, from his letters and critical comments, that he felt the instinctive sources of painting were obscured by highly realized formal qualities in art. "Lawrence's paintings recapitulate the same concerns and preoccupations evident in his fictions" (Torgovnick 57). The somewhat flattened perspectives are reminiscent of Manet, the softened primary colors of Blake and certain postimpressionists, but in *Dance Sketch* and *A Holy Family*, for example, there is little influence of modern art. *Boccaccio Story* mischievously presents four nuns giggling at the sight of a man naked from the waist down (it may have been *Boccaccio Story* which caused the police's seizure and threats to burn these paintings in 1929; the chief reason for their being classified as obscene was apparently the exhibition of pubic hair). *Red Willow Trees* shows the forms of men and women imitating the forms of the bending willows, illustrating the Laurentian idea that humanity is only one of the forms in which nature expresses the life force. "The paintings are almost entirely *ahistorical*, with their generalized settings suggesting no particular time and place."

John Russell's essay "D. H. Lawrence and Painting" argues that Lawrence used painters whose work he approved, such as Cezanne, as figures of himself. Russell also claims that Lawrence used the 1929 exhibition to "set up a definitive confrontation, on a new ground of his own choosing, with the authorities who had treated him as a common criminal" (241). The essay attempts to show why "it is worthwhile to think about D. H. Lawrence in the context of D. H. Lawrence" (243).

Similarly, it has been argued that specific schools or movements in the arts influenced Lawrence's thinking and style. Jack Lindsay's essay "The Impact of Modernism on Lawrence" shows how the futurists' view of the alienating and dehumanizing forces of the modern world helped shape Lawrence's own views, even his use of mechanical imagery and how he appropriated some of the futurists' views for an artist-character like Loerke, or even Gudrun, in *Women in Love.* One may argue that his use of these ideas places him centrally in ideological arguments about modern art (discussed in Levy 44).

Harry T. Moore says he first saw the paintings from the Warren Gallery exhibition in 1932 at Martha Gordon Crotch's pottery shop at Vence. He did not see them in 1933 when he visited Frieda and Angelo Ravagli at Kiowa ranch, but during the 1940s and 1950s they were exhibited in the Ravaglis' El Prado home, just outside Taos. (In fact, *Flight Back into Paradise* hung over the dining table.)

Moore argues that "Lawrence might have been a remarkable painter if he had given his life to the medium of representational art rather than to writing" (qtd. in Levy 18). Since he did not, of course, the paintings are interesting for other reasons. "The pictures have in them features recognizably Laurencean: the eye that was responsible for refracting landscapes through the novels, poems, and travel books is the eye that was similarly active in these pictures" (Moore, qtd. in Levy 18). Moore admires "the feeling for colour . . . the rhythms the artist has stroked into the paints . . . such form as he has devised" (qtd. in Levy 21). Moore illustrates how, even in the early paintings, Lawrence's coloring of a copy from Giotto shows the "quickness" of his best writing (qtd. in Levy 26). Moore is at pains to point out, from the "expertness" of his introduction to the Mandrake Press volume to the choice of painting for Paul Morel's profession, Lawrence was familiar with art, even though "he always remained an amateur, a Sunday painter" (qtd. in Levy 26).

Moore, perhaps alone of the Lawrence critics and biographers, made every effort to see every picture Lawrence created. (It was one of Moore's major disappointments that in the 1940s he was unable to purchase a volume of anatomical sketches by Lawrence, a volume which has since disappeared. That volume might be very valuable in understanding Lawrence's paradoxical refusal to draw from live models.) Moore resolutely avoids the technical in his discussion of the paintings, preferring to read in them the biographical and broadly thematic elements that connect the paintings to Lawrence's other work and that make them "a pleasant addition, if not to modern art, at least to Lawrence's achievement" (qtd. in Levy 34).

Responses to Lawrence's paintings remain mixed, even at the photographic recreation of the Warren exhibition in 1991. In *Lost Lawrence*, a video documentary made to commemorate the exhibition, Sara Kent, art critic for *Time Out*, said that she had "no enthusiasm" for what she considered "curios" and that if the paintings were hung at the British Museum, "they'd be in the basement." George Melley called them "poor pictures" and said, "they should stay where they are, which is a place of pilgrimage anyway . . . [the pictures are] part of the pilgrimage to the shrine" (in the documentary, *Lost Lawrence*) Even Anthony Burgess, in *Flame into Being*, his very readable critical biography of Lawrence, writes, "My personal view of the pictures of Lawrence that I have seen is not very favorable. . . . The colors are bright, the subjects life-enhancing, the flesh tones unconvincing, the anatomy vile" (247).

Sara Kent's remarks about the paintings and the British Museum are not without cause; since shortly after he bought the Lawrence paintings, Saki Karavas has tried to repatriate them to Britain. His early efforts to sell them to British museums or collectors were stymied by the question of their status with U.K. Customs: were they still regarded as obscene? In 1966, Karavas wrote Roy Jenkins, then home secretary, offering to give the Lawrence paintings to the United Kingdom in return for the Elgin marbles' return to Greece; Jenkins said that he would refer the matter of the paintings' obscenity to the Office of Customs and Excise. On February 5, 1990, Neil Kinnock's office (in the person of Charles Clark, an assistant) wrote to Karavas to indicate that while the office wished to repatriate the paintings to England, neither their status nor that of the Elgin marbles was "appropriate for *quid pro quo* bargains." Finally, in 1991 Home Secretary John Patton reported that the Office of Customs and Excise had "given a written undertaking that the 1929 ban was now without force." But so far, the fears of some Taos citizens that the paintings would be sold have not been realized, though the University of Texas did offer to accept—not buy—them. (This rather recapitulates their earlier negotiation with Frieda Lawrence for the paintings and manuscripts.)

Karavas will not disclose the original price he paid for the paintings. He says that as Angelo Ravagli was preparing to return to his family in Italy, the two met on the street in Taos, where "Angie" remarked that "they were having trouble with the bankers." The trouble may have been Ravagli's or "they" may have referred to Amalie de Schulthess, who bought the manuscript of *Chatterley* and one of the paintings, *Boccaccio Story* (according to Karavas), and who clearly wanted all of them.

Whatever the price Karavas paid, he has continued to exhibit the paintings at La Fonda and live modestly—though the word "playboy" continues to appear in Lawrence biographies that describe him. Seventy-two years old when I interviewed him in 1995, he lives in one small room of the hotel, his office and room packed with Taos memorabilia, including paintings by his mother, paintings by Brett, signed editions of *Lady Chatterley's Lover*, an edition of *Memoirs of the Foreign Legion* signed by Maurice Magnus with an inscription to Karavas by Frieda Lawrence, and letters from David Garnett, Karavas's close ("best") friend.

One clipping on his desk that Karavas acknowledges with only a wistful grin is from the Sydney, Australia, *Sunday Telegraph*. At the time of the 1991 recreation of the Warren Gallery exhibit, the *Telegraph* estimated the value of the Karavas collection at over $48 million. One's faith in the accuracy of their estimate is tempered, however, by their identification of Karavas not as a Taos hotelkeeper, but as a "South American collector."

Beverly Lowry's article in the October 1, 1989, *New York Times Magazine*, "Lawrence: Keepers of the Flame," paints a very skeptical view of the Taos Lawrence artifacts, but her article is aimed at the tourist who might wish to make the trip to New Mexico. Lowry did not meet Saki Karavas, but she did meet Johnny Chapman, the desk clerk, who explained why Karavas's shoes were lined up in his office, opposite the Lawrence paintings (so the janitor could shine them overnight). It was also Chapman who delivered Taos's judgment on the whole drama: "Angie had the last laugh. He went back to Italy after Frieda died, a rich man. . . . Shows you who the smart guy was. The one who ended up with the money" (65).

The last laugh may be Karavas's, if the paintings are as valuable as he believes. As we walked with Karavas and a friend, retired matador Miguel Larrea, to a cafe on Taos Plaza, it is clear that while some in Taos still regard him as a *patron*, others are confused about his connection to Taos's glory days. The teenager operating the cash register at the gift shop in the Mabel Dodge Luhan house confided that she had "heard that Saki was a distant relative of Mabel's."

Of course, the net effect of the way Karavas presents his collection to the public is to celebrate the "salacious" aspects of Lawrence's work, capitalizing on the public conception of that work—even if some of the tourists who wander into his office can't quite figure out which of the works are supposed to be the "obscene Lawrence," since standards have shifted so much since 1929. Saki Karavas is not the only person to blame for capitalizing on this long-held, long-inaccurate view of Lawrence. "It is unfortunate that the name D. H. Lawrence should, in the common mind, be associated with only one book, and that one far from his best," says Anthony Burgess, who continues to compare the legacy of *Lady Chatterley's Lover* for Lawrence with the legacy of *Clockwork Orange* for his own career. "Sex can be written about scientifically, and then it becomes an aspect of biology. Write about it in human terms, and you can produce only the dysphemisms, or dysglot, of pornography or the euphemisms, or euglot, of a legitimate erotic work such as *The Rainbow* or *Women in Love*." Since Lawrence chose his subjects—for writing and for painting—to shock the bourgeoisie, "if Lawrence is primarily the author of *Lady C*, it is mainly his own fault" (267–68).

Each of these Taos presentations of the D. H. Lawrence myth serves to present the myth to separate and distinct audiences for their consumption and approval. The one is a form of high pilgrimage, with many of the trappings associated with pilgrimage; another presents Lawrence's work quite literally as a minor distraction subsumed in, for its audience, a greater edifice of a greater myth. The third presentation of Lawrence's work might be viewed as exploitation, but I believe it is more correctly seen as fitting Lawrence into "the prevalent ideology, or those notions and useful schemata by which our society imagines itself . . . the fastest way to generate automatic, immediate meaning" (Evans 161). Saki Karavas's presentation of his Lawrence paintings is precisely what the theories of Habermas and the

Frankfurt School and Hans Robert Jauss's reception theory would predict: a complex aesthetic experience is presented well within "the horizon of expectations of the public," not as an experience the consumer works at comprehending, but as "pure distraction" and well within "the prevalent ideology." For Saki Karavas's intended consumer, D. H. Lawrence is a pornographer, even if the works on the wall of Karavas's office no longer seem lascivious to either the British Post Office or the postmodern tourist.

REFERENCES

Birnbaum's Santa Fe and Taos. New York: HarperCollins, 1995.

Burgess, Anthony. *Flame into Being.* New York: Arbor House, 1985.

Byrne, Janet. *A Genius for Living: The Life of Frieda Lawrence.* New York: HarperCollins, 1995.

Evans, Christine Ann. "On the Valuation of Detective Fiction." *Journal of Popular Culture* 28.2 (1994): 159–67.

Lawrence, D. H. *The Paintings of D. H. Lawrence.* London: Mandrake Press, 1929.

Levy, Mervyn. *Paintings of D. H. Lawrence.* New York: Viking, 1964.

Lowry, Beverly. "Lawrence: Keepers of the Flame." *New York Times Magazine* 1 Oct. 1989: 65, 86–87.

Luhan, Mabel Dodge. *Lorenzo in Taos.* New York: Knopf, 1932.

Maddox, Brenda. *D. H. Lawrence: The Story of a Marriage.* New York: Simon and Schuster, 1994.

Moore, Harry T. *The Priest of Love.* Carbondale: Southern Illinois University Press, 1974.

Russell, John. "D. H. Lawrence and Painting." *D. H. Lawrence: Novelist, Poet, Prophet.* Ed. Stephen Spender. New York: Harper and Row, 1973.

Torgovnick, Marianna. *The Visual Arts, Pictorialism, and the Novel.* Princeton: Princeton University Press, 1985.

Lawrence and Beauvoir at Tua-Tah: European Views of the Heart of the World

TAMARA TEALE

IT IS WELL KNOWN that D. H. Lawrence visited Taos town and pueblo, less so that Simone de Beauvoir made a brief stop in 1946. Both intellectual travelers have left us images of indigenous people as unreasonable and, perhaps, obsessive in denying Caucasians access to sacred places. In fact, the question of the sacred and religious privacy is at the heart of Lawrence's and Beauvoir's experiences at Tua-Tah, the Tiwa name for Taos pueblo. It is easy to find fault with travelers of eras less enlightened than we believe ours to be, but a close look at the self-serving and irresponsible aspects of Lawrence and Beauvoir as travelers is not a misapplication of our present critical consciousness. When we examine tourist behavior, we honor the indigenous people we visit. As travelers, writers, and cultural thinkers we can attempt to make the future better for native people, especially now that we are in the thick of mass travel.

In his essay "New Mexico," Lawrence is quite eloquent about the "*greatness* of beauty" of the landscape and the deep religiosity of the people (142–43), and there's little doubt that he genuinely took part in fighting the Bursum Bill[1] then in Congress, which would have granted title to squatters on pueblo land; nonetheless, there is evidence that Lawrence expressed his touristic experiences at the expense of native people. Lawrence expressed apprehension in racial terms, writing to Mabel Dodge Luhan from Sri Lanka: "I still of course mistrust Taos very much, chiefly on account of the artists. I feel I never want to see an artist again while I live. The Indians, yes: if one is sure that they are not jeering at one. I find all dark people have a fixed desire to jeer at us: these people here—they jeer behind your back" (qtd. in Luhan 19). Mabel Dodge Luhan continually wrote encouraging him to visit Taos; finally, he responded from Sydney, Australia: "I do hope I shall get from your Indians something that this wearily external white world can't give, and which the east is just betraying all the time" (qtd. in Luhan 23). But the thought that indigenous people may be jeering at him occupies his mind long after arrival at Taos town.

In one incident, recorded in the "Taos" essay, Lawrence is with "Dr. West," a New Yorker who has "settled in one of the villages." Lawrence says West is "well enough known" in the villages; however, when they approach the Catholic church, attended by many indigenous people, they are denied admittance. Lawrence records the scene as follows:

> Mass was being said inside the church, and she [Dr. West] would have liked to go in. She is well enough known, too. But two Indians were at the church door, and one put his elbow in front of her.
>
> You Catholic?"
>
> "No, I'm not."
>
> "Then you can't come in."
>
> The same almost jeering triumph in giving the white man—or the white woman—a kick. It is the same the whole world over, between dark-skin and white. Dr. West, of course, thinks everything Indian wonderful. But she wasn't used to being rebuffed, and she didn't like it. But she found excuses.
>
> "Of course," she said, "they're quite right to exclude the white people, if the white people can't behave themselves. It seems there were some Americans, boys and girls, in the church yesterday, insulting the images of the saints, shrieking, laughing, and saying they looked like monkeys. So now *no* white people are allowed inside the church."
>
> I listened, and said nothing. I had heard the same story at Buddhist temples in Ceylon. For my own part, I have long since passed the stage when I want to crowd up and stare at anybody's spectacle, white man's or dark man's. (102, Lawrence's emphasis)[2]

In this episode, Lawrence attributes the concrete explanation for excluding whites to Dr. West. With what Lawrence knew of the native people's fight against the Bursum Bill and their ongoing battle to regain sacred land (see note 1), it seems he could have taken this opportunity to make an appropriate statement about sacrilege instead of commenting on his own status as outsider.

Another incident in which a native person comes off badly with no material explanation given is also recounted in Lawrence's essay "Taos." One day a maypole was to be erected in the plaza; Lawrence recalls "[o]ne of the white boys took the bossing of the show," but "the Indians were none too ready to obey, and their own dark-faced boss gave counter orders." Lawrence saw it as "the old, amusing contradiction between the white and the dark races" with himself as an "outsider at both ends of the game," neither of the "dark" race nor the white. An "American girl came with a camera" and took a snapshot of the ceremony, while a Tua-Tah man "went to her abruptly, in his quiet, insidious way," took the camera from her, and took out the film. Lawrence reproduces the interaction in the following way:

> "You give me that Kodak. You ain't allowed take no snaps here. You pay fine—one dollar."
>
> She was frightened, but she clung to her camera.

> "You're not going to take my Kodak from me," she said.
>
> "I'm going to take that film out. And you pay one dollar fine, see?"
>
> The girl relinquished the camera; the Indian took out the film.
>
> "Now you pay me one dollar, or I don't give you back the Kodak."
>
> Rather sullenly, she took out her purse and gave the two silver half-dollars. The Indian returned the camera, pocketed the money, and turned aside with a sort of triumph. Done it over one specimen of the white race.
>
> There were not very many Indians helping to put up the pole.
>
> "I never see so few boys helping put up the pole," said Tony Romero to me. (101–2)

Lawrence gives no explanation of this incident that would suggest the Tua-Tah tourist guides were acting responsibly in protecting the photographic recording of a native ceremony. What is curious about these incidents is that Lawrence makes no mention of the pressures the citizens of Tua-Tah were under because of the Bursum Bill fight, nor does he mention religious persecution under the Religious Crimes Act of 1921 and the actions of the Bureau of Indian Affairs commissioner, Charles Burke, in attempting to suppress religious freedom, described by R. C. Gordon-McCutchan in *The Taos Indians and the Battle for Blue Lake.* And in another essay, "Indians and an Englishman," Lawrence describes being chased away from a kiva by a young Apache on the Jicarilla reservation; he gives no specific reason for such seemingly strident protection of the ceremonial structure. It's as though, after all is said and done, Lawrence wants to be alone with his fine sensitivity, his supreme and ideal consciousness. He wants to see the kiva alone despite religious laws.

The type of travel writing I propose for European and Euro-American tourists would include at least a sketch of the current political-juridical events which affect the pueblo visited rather than having separate book genres: one book for politics and another for landscape or, say, pottery aesthetics. R. C. Gordon-McCutchan gives a thorough historical and political background for Lawrence's and Beauvoir's era of travel by documenting the battle for Blue Lake from 1906 to 1970. He writes that Charles Burke took the opportunity to "give wide circulation to lurid reports of immorality and debauchery at Indian ceremonials" at Blue Lake, and Burke "claimed that native religion was largely responsible for the Indian failure to assimilate into the cultural mainstream." Gordon-McCutchan explains that for Burke "pagan worship" must be destroyed so that native people can "rise above their 'savage' state" (16). Because of the religious and political struggles faced by Tua-Tah pueblo since the Burke era of the 1920s, religious privacy continues to be the natives' central concern and one which shapes Caucasian travel experience at Tua-Tah.

Lawrence finishes the "Taos" essay by again referring to himself as outsider. He observes that the Tua-Tah dancers didn't seem to mind "that white crowd of inquisitives." They danced in front of the "impassive white faces," the tourists with "indomitable curiosity" (103). The contradiction of tourism is that Lawrence is often eloquent in his praise of Tua-Tah, which he knew was "the heart of the world" for the Tiwa people. Lawrence calls Tua-Tah a place with "true nodality," "one of the choice spots of the earth" (100).

Similarly, Simone de Beauvoir doesn't understand Tua-Tah religious restrictions. She couldn't see Tua-Tah on its own terms but as a village she recognized in its European form. She wrote, "all this was nearer to our villages. . . . We found an ancient rural civilisation, several thousand years old, that has perpetuated itself in Europe and also in these privileged territories where the Americans have not murdered the past" (150–51). As charmed as Beauvoir was, three times she lets us know her irritation with restrictions on tourists' movements. She intends to slip away from the tour group and wander on her own. Beauvoir left her car at the entrance to Tua-Tah and read the posted notice, which she paraphrases: "white people were forbidden to wander inside the enclosure after five o'clock in the afternoon, and one must pay half a dollar to park one's car on the square. One may not take photographs without permission of the governor and one must report to him on arrival" (151). Today, the Eight Northern Indian Pueblos Council publishes an official visitor's guide in which each pueblo lists its regulations.[3] Such measures are not only a statement of religious values but are also an effort to head off any cultural misunderstanding.

Beauvoir and her companion found the governor's representative "arguing with a group of tourists parking their cars and [he] asked us where ours was." She recalls that "[h]e seemed annoyed by our leaving it outside, pretending that it was rash" (151). It is hard to tell what irritates Beauvoir other than what she perceives is the Tua-Tah man's greed for the fifty-cent parking fee: "We would not prevent him from getting his half dollar and he was disappointed that we had no camera":

> The other tourists had them and paid their due. The representative of the governor guided them to the best vantage points.
>
> We slipped away from the group and climbed a low stone wall. . . . We sat on the edge of a well from which two poles protruded, but women waved their arms in our direction and shook their heads; one of them approached us: "Go away or the governor will expel you." We got up and found that the well was a *khiva*, a place sacred above all others, where no European, were he even the best friend of the Indians, had the right to linger.
>
> As we hurried off the governor ran to the spot with flying robes: we had transgressed the boundaries permitted to white people. (151–52, Beauvoir's emphasis)

The need to "slip away from the group" seems to be an elite tourist move; one wishes to avoid the loathsome crowd, avoid being told what to look at, avoid "trooping about in a gang" as Lawrence's character Birkin says in *Women in Love.* In addition, there are benefits from slipping away: one can feel the thrill of seeing the forbidden. The irony is that someone must troop about in a gang in order to make slipping away thrilling for the few.

Near the spot to which the governor's representative has led them, Beauvoir and her companion encounter "a braided Indian" finishing a watercolor; "he took us to his house, which was light and airy," and "showed us pictures in which the traditions of Indian art were studiously forgotten" (152). We have no idea what the man's art work consisted of; Beauvoir may have been looking at a blend of modern and traditional. She might have given us more details of what she believed "Indian art" should be, except that Beauvoir is not open to having her expectations countered; she's not looking at what is there. She "fled without buying anything and crossed the stream" that separates the north part of Tua-Tah from the south buildings (152).

A third time, she is annoyed with having her expectations thwarted:

> As we were walking up a winding street a man on a terrace signalled to us to go back; and there once again was the governor, running up out of breath: here too it was forbidden to walk. It appeared that only the main square was allowed. I had been told that in many villages the Indians surround themselves with forbidden zones so as to preserve the mystery and attraction, their chief sources of wealth: they live largely on the money they extort from tourists, but perhaps they have some respect for certain taboos. Those who know them best say that no one can really boast of knowing them. Whether commercial ruses or religious prejudices, these restrictions annoyed us. We visited out of politeness a house where they sold pottery, bead necklaces and bad paintings, and bought a few post cards. We should have to come back in invisible guise after five o'clock when the *pueblo* reverted to solitude. But even this greeting, at once fierce and commercial, did not spoil its beauty. (152, Beauvoir's emphasis)

Again, Beauvoir mentions the ultimate "slipping away," to return in "invisible guise after five" to see the secret life of the pueblo as though what she was allowed to see was not enough or somehow not real, or as though the pueblo plaza is a staging area for mass tourism with a behind-the-scenes tour for sophisticated travelers. She sees the parking fee as extortion where another might see tourist dollars paying for legal fees which Tua-Tah may have incurred in defense of the Blue Lake region, repair of the road from Taos town, maintenance of buildings, care of cattle, or upkeep of fences. Most obviously, Beauvoir sees religious "restrictions" as a function of tourism: preserving "the mystery" does indeed attract tourists, but the Tiwa people would be religious regardless of tourism. Beauvoir did not know the effects of her unwitting lack of knowledge about indigenous culture. Uninformed tourists have the collective power to flatten cultural difference; their expectations can condition "Indians" to behave in stereotypical ways. Indigenous people take measures against the distortion of tourists' misconceptions, often through official visitor's guides such as that for the eight northern pueblos.

Finally, for travelers who know better, Beauvoir's repeated misspelling—or her British translator's—of pueblo San *Ildefonso* as "Idelfonso" does not help her credibility (152, 156, 157). At a Santa Fe reception, on Canyon Road, Beauvoir listened to the conversation if it touched on the familiar subjects of European-style labor unionization and class struggle but did not get the name of the "society for the protection of the Indians" (153) to which many of the artists in Santa Fe belonged: the Association on American Indian Affairs (Gordon-McCutchan 41). Such misspellings and lack of attention to detail are hard to forgive.

To do Beauvoir justice without entirely letting her off the hook, I can see that given the intense level of commercial development in New Mexico, it's no wonder that she did not "see" Tua-Tah: She suspected another American showbiz coup. In an article, "From Desert to Disney World: The Santa Fe Railway and the Fred Harvey Company Display the Indian Southwest," anthropologist Marta Weigle makes the point that guided tours through the pueblos were part of a network of commercialized places that shaped and contained tourist experience. Weigle writes that in 1903, a New Mexico newspaper article, "The Tourism Industry," stated that "good Indian legends can be grown in almost any locality with a little care and attention, and it adds an interest to a very ordinary cliff to know that a persecuted and necessarily beautiful maiden leaped thence to her death" (117). Weigle mentions another bit of advertising fluff, employing metaphors appropriated from Asia Minor: "Travelers passing the Pueblo villages of the Southwest in the eighties [1880s] were invited to recall the villages of ancient Egypt and Nubia, Ninevah and Babylon, rather than to study the remains of American aboriginal life"; and the native people were "like the descendants of Rebecca of Bible fame" (117).[4] No wonder Beauvoir believed that the religious restrictions at Tua-Tah appeared artificial. To "see" the pueblo, however, one must take the time to understand that the necessity of controlling tourists' movements at the pueblo is very different from commercial staging and control.

When he looked past "all that film stuff," Lawrence was able to make distinctions between some concept of native culture and the tourist attractions. But he could not have done that without the consciousness-raising events of the battle for Blue Lake and the Bursum Bill fight. Without Tua-Tah's struggle and the struggle of all the pueblo cultures in the All Pueblo Council, it seems Tua-Tah would have been *totally given over* to tourism exploitation and the domination of a fierce commercial development. Between Lawrence's visit in the mid-1920s and Beauvoir's in 1946, little had changed in the courtroom battles to regain Blue Lake, but tourism developed rapidly and has done so since. Today, private autos of the Fred Harvey Company are gone, and senior citizens arrive by the busloads. As the long wooden poles still mark the entrance to the kivas, and non-Tua-Tah people are restricted from entering, it is more important than ever that tourists educate themselves to honor the indigenous people's homes we visit.

NOTES

1. Lawrence's article against the Bursum Bill, "Certain Americans and an Englishman," appeared in the *New York Times Magazine*, December 24, 1922, 3. In *The Taos Indians and the Battle for Blue Lake*, author R. C. Gordon-McCutchan explains that the Bursum Bill was "a quick and easy way for [Caucasian and Hispanic] squatters to obtain clear title to their stolen Indian land" (including the lake) (17). The Bursum Bill, initiated by the fears of the twelve thousand squatters, was a political reaction of the state of New Mexico to the 1913 case of *United States v. Sandoval*, which gave federal protection to pueblo natives. The text

of the Bursum Bill can be found in Francis Paul Prucha, *Documents of U.S. Indian Policy* (Lincoln: University of Nebraska Press, 1975, pp. 215–18.

2. Unfortunately, many white people have not yet learned respectful conduct. The Zuñi Tribal Council banned non-Indians from witnessing pueblo ceremonies until August 30, 1996 (*News from Indian Country*, vol. 9, no. 24, late December 1995, p. 3A). "The ban will include Sha'lak'o ceremonies," the paper reports. "Non-Indians can still visit the pueblo during the ceremony ban. Councilmen said the ban was necessary because people touch dancers or mock the traditional nightlong dances."

3. The 1994 Eight Northern Pueblos' visitor's guide gives guidance to tourists while protecting native privacy. The guide lists "Courteous Behavior" for travelers: "To avoid any misunderstanding or the violation of our customs, these suggestions should prove helpful"; "photography is a particularly important issue; fees and restrictions vary" (4–5). At Tua-Tah specifically, there is no photography allowed during the Feast of San Geronimo; Tua-Tah may be closed to travelers in February, March, and August for sacred ceremonial observances (48–49).

4. Weigle in part quotes Earl S. Pomery, *In Search of the Golden West: The Tourist in Western America* (Lincoln: University Press of Nebraska Press, 1957), pp. 40–41.

REFERENCES

Beauvoir, Simone de. *America Day by Day*. Trans. Patrick Dudley. London: Gerald Duckworth & Co. Ltd., 1952. (*Amérique au jour le jour*, Paris: Gallimard, 1948.)

Gordon-McCutchan, R. C. *The Taos Indians and the Battle for Blue Lake*. Foreword by Frank Waters. Santa Fe: Red Crane Books, 1991.

Lawrence, D. H. *Phoenix: The Posthumous Papers of D. H. Lawrence*. Ed. Edward D. McDonald. London: Heinemann Ltd., 1932.

Luhan, Mabel Dodge. *Lorenzo in Taos*. New York: Alfred A. Knopf, 1932.

Weigle, Marta. "From Desert to Disney World: The Santa Fe Railway and the Fred Harvey Company Display the Indian Southwest." *Journal of Anthropological Research* 45.1 (Spring 1989): 115–37.

"There's a Great Big Beautiful Tomorrow": Historic Memory and Gender in Walt Disney's Carousel of Progress

LYNN Y. WEINER

THE WALT DISNEY corporation has been a major purveyor of popular history throughout the twentieth century. From cartoons to television shows, feature films to amusement parks, Disney has shaped and reshaped the presentation of the past for an audience of millions. With the creation of enormously successful amusement parks in California and Florida, Disney history became part of tourist itineraries throughout the world. Disney's interpretations of history, however, are not static. A look at one attraction in particular, the Carousel of Progress suggests how Disney has transformed the presentation of the history of women and the family over the past thirty years. Disney's "collective memory" of family life reflects a persistent nostalgia for a pleasant, highly controlled past and an equally well ordered future, in the context of an ever changing present.

The Carousel of Progress is a Walt Disney stage attraction that uses "audio-animatronic" robots to portray the evolution of technology in the American home. The Disney corporation claims that this show has entertained more viewers than any other theatrical presentation in world history (Bierman 223). After its introduction as a General Electric–sponsored attraction at the 1964 New York World's Fair, the show moved to Disneyland in California and then in 1975 to Disney World in Florida. An examination of four versions of the Carousel from 1967 to 1995 indicates how history has been interpreted and reinterpreted by Disney to tens of millions of people.[1] A comparison of each act of the play, looking particularly at the depiction of gender roles, should demonstrate not so much how gender roles have actually changed, but rather how those changes have been constructed as a kind of collective memory of the history of women and the family during the twentieth century.

The Carousel is a combination play, advertisement, and amusement park ride. The audience sit in seats that rotate around a stage to view an affluent white robot family in four different eras: the pre-electric turn of the century, the 1920s, the

1940s, and the most up-to-the-minute "present." The setting is the kitchen and its ever improving wonders, with side glances at other parts of the house. At the end of each act, a catchy musical refrain ("There's a great big beautiful tomorrow . . . ") builds while the seats rotate to the next scene and the next historical era.

Family life has of course transformed dramatically during the course of the last century. Perhaps most significant, women have entered the paid labor force in droves; at the same time, the rise in divorce and single-parent households has made the two-parent family, with a full-time mother at home, anomalous, representing at best a tiny proportion of current American families.[2] Equally buffeted by change has been the nature of historiography since 1964, particularly as the disciplines of women's history and family history have developed. These conceptual approaches barely existed when the Carousel first turned. For example, a topic like the evolution of domestic technology has been subject to increasingly sophisticated analysis, much of it suggesting that "labor-saving" devices don't always save labor (Cowan; Strasser). Hence, a comparison of different versions of the play might suggest the degree to which social change, or at least its historiography, has influenced Disney's construction of the past.[3]

The Walt Disney corporation has enormous influence on the historical consciousness of popular culture in the United States (Watts). As Michael Wallace has suggested, "Walt Disney has taught people more history, in a more memorable way, than they ever learned in school" (158). The Carousel of Progress is a case in point. During the show's first two decades, an estimated one hundred million people sat in the revolving chairs to view the products of General Electric and the shifting depictions of the evolution of family life.[4] The current venue for the show—Disney World in Orlando, Florida—is the world's top tourist destination, hosting over thirty-three million people a year (Jackson 99). Disney's claim for a theatrical record, then, is not surprising.

The Carousel of Progress opened at the New York World's Fair in 1964. Like earlier expositions, the fair showcased technology, consumerism, and industry.[5] At this fair Walt Disney's "imagineers" received corporate funding to create four audio-animatronic displays, following the success a year earlier of the "Enchanted Tiki Room" replete with chattering "birds" at Disneyland. Audio-animatronics was to Disney a form of "animation through electronics"—a kind of three-dimensional cartoon (Jackson 103, 249). Audio-animatronic productions could play forever but the script could change; unlike a conventional play, television drama, or cartoon, these shows do not stay fixed, but are continually revised (or, perhaps more accurately, "reprogrammed"). Audio-animatronics therefore represents a unique genre of popular culture.[6]

It has been suggested that Thornton Wilder's play *Our Town* provided the original model for the structure of this theater piece (Bierman 223). In both *Our Town* and the Carousel, a stage manager, or narrator, directly addresses the audience to describe the characters and their daily lives. In both plays, there is a sense of nostalgia for the past and anticipation of the future. There is only one version, or script, of *Our Town*, however, although we do see Grover's Corners over the passage of time. While the Carousel of Progress has been described as a "robot drama," at the same time it can be seen as a domestic comedy of household technology, with a long-suffering male narrator getting audience laughs as his female partner goofs up.[7]

In all four versions of Carousel, the narrator is John, also known as "Father." Pipe in hand, he affably presides over a family including Sarah ("Mother"), their son James, daughter Jane (who is sometimes known as Patricia), and a dog who transforms from Rover to Sport to Queenie back to Rover. A house guest, variously Cousin or Uncle Orville, is occasionally present, as are Grandma and Grandpa. These characters people the cast, along with a rapidly modernizing collection of kitchen appliances (which sometimes steal the show as they busily whir, clang open and shut, and light on and off).

The character of Mother is especially illustrative of the theme of gender in the Carousel story. Mother appears differently in each version and in each act of the play. She is always a consumer. She is variously a household drudge, flighty housewife, or social activist. While newly developed labor-saving devices are lauded for providing Mother with new "freedoms," these never include the provision of more time so that she can enter the world of waged labor. Mother is alternately clever, incompetent, very competent, long-suffering, annoying, sarcastic, bitter, comically overly talkative, and completely dehumanized. The order in which these characterizations are presented is surprising.

In the first act of the 1960s version, vaguely set "just before the turn of the century," Father boasts of the family's new acquisitions—an icebox, water pump, gas lamps, telephone, stove, "talking machines," and vacuum cleaner. Father lauds these things for saving so much time for Mother:

> *Mother:* With my new washday marvel it takes only five hours to do the wash—imagine!
> *Father:* That's right, folks. . . . Now, mother has time for recreations like . . . Mother (interrupts, sarcastic): Like canning and polishing the stove!
> *Father* (chuckles): Okay, Mother, you just iron the wrinkles out of my *shirts.*
> *Mother* (tolerantly): Yes, dear. ("GE Carousel" 4)

The labor-saving function of the appliances is noted with an ironic twist regarding the continued drudgery of Mother's labor—presumably an irony shared by the audience.

In Act 2, set in the 1920s, the updated kitchen now houses a coffee percolator, waffle iron, refrigerator, and toaster. There are so many appliances, Father notes, that blowing a fuse is a constant danger. Mother has also been given an electric iron and, therefore, Father says, even more leisure time:

> *Father:* Mother has something to do to fill in her evenings. . . . Now, it's no problem at all to get my collars smooth—right, Mother?"
> *Mother* (hot and tired): Yes, dear. ("GE Carousel" 9)

Act 3 takes place in the "electronic era" of the 1940s. In this version, as in all the others, there is no evidence of the war. There are, however, many more new appliances: an electric washing machine, electric range, refrigerator, and dishwasher. But there is something else: clever Mother has figured out how to use her electric food mixer to stir paint as she remodels the basement:

> *Father:* Mother's remodeling my basement workshop . . . into something called a "rumpus room." . . . Be careful now, Mother.
> *Mother:* Don't worry about me, dear . . . (resumes humming)
> *Father:* Mother's pretty ingenious . . . like using her food-mixer for stirring paint?? . . . Well, that's my wife, Sarah. ("GE Carousel" 16–17)

Just like Rosie the Riveter, Mother adapts her domestic sensibility to the business of production (Milkman 341). Then Mother, not to be *too* competent, falls off the ladder.

The final act in the first version is set in the General Electric "Medallion Home" of the 1960s. It's Christmas. Mother now has the annoying habit of interrupting Father in an almost maniacal manner, because she's so excited she can't wait to tell us about her electric range with the self-cleaning oven and her huge choice of appliance colors. Mother has lots of free time now. She is active in the garden club, the literary society, and the ladies' bowling league. "Colormatic" lighting matches the mood of the music emanating from the hi-fi. Grandma and Grandpa, busy sidekicks in the first three acts, have disappeared to their own home in the nearby "Community for Senior Citizens." The play ends in this version with the audience shuttled toward a "Kitchen of Tomorrow" display of General Electric appliances ("GE Carousel" 20–27).

This 1960s version of the family over a span of the twentieth century, like all the later productions, seems to occur outside time and place. There are a few references to innovations beyond the little, contained world of this family (innovations like electric street lights or retirement homes) but none at all to the cataclysms of war, assassination, depression, urban riots, racial struggle, or social change. Time is confused and foggy, with cheerful clichés ("the frantic forties") substituting for disturbing fact. The role of Mother is generally one of beneficiary of labor-saving devices, within the context of her subordination to Father. Her free time is oriented toward the needs of the family. Still, during the 1940s segment she shows some spunk and ingenuity of her own.

The second version examined here is that of the play as it was redesigned for the move from California to Florida's Disney World in 1975. It apparently existed in a similar form as late as the mid-1980s. Mother in these versions has to some degree achieved more autonomy. While she still irons Dad's shirts in the first act, by the second, 1920s scene, instead of ironing Dad's collars Mother spends her free time at a new hobby for her own pleasure: embroidery. Daughter Jane, obviously a kind of roaring twenties "new woman," also wants to enlarge her activities—she argues with Father about finding a job:

> *Daughter:* I don't see any harm in looking for a job, Daddy.
> *Father:* It's a man's world out there, Jane.

Daughter: Well, it won't always be, Father.
Queenie: Arf, arf!
Father: Now cut that out, Queenie. You're supposed to be *man's* best friend. (Fjellman 82)

The 1920s are remembered here differently than they were a decade earlier; the imagineers are aware not only of the changed status of women in the postsuffrage 1920s, but perhaps of a new sensibility about women in general, reflective of the 1970s.

By the "frantic forties" Mother is still remodeling the basement and still using her food mixer to stir the paint. But this time, certainly reflecting the feminist debates of the 1970s, she argues that perhaps she should be compensated for her labors:

Mother: If you hired a man to do this, wouldn't you pay him?
Father: Of course, dear.
Mother: Then I should get equal pay.
Father: Heh! Heh! Heh! We might negotiate something later on.
Mother: When?
A cuckoo clock goes off. The bird sings, "Now is the best time."
Father: You stay out of this. (Fjellman 82–83)

The last act is also changed. Mother's volunteer activities have taken on a more activist slant; she works in her free time on the Clean Waters Committee and has been "commended by the mayor for getting a bond issue passed." Luckily, she had time to do this thanks to her convenient General Electric dishwasher and dryer. Father, picking up some of the responsibility at home, bumbles through meal preparation (Bierman 234–35). If woman's role is expanding, men obviously still are not comfortable in the kitchen.

This version of the mid-1970s through the 1980s reflects the impact of feminism and the widening role of women, on the presentations of both the past and the present. Mother spends more time on her own affairs and less on those of her family. If she's not yet working for wages (as most of her nonmechanical contemporaries are), still she is engaged in activities of civic importance. The products of General Electric free her to follow these various pursuits.

In the most recent version of the Carousel of Progress viewed in 1995, General Electric is no longer the sponsor, and Mother has been transformed yet again. Surprisingly, this transformation does not reflect the legal and economic gains for women of the 1970s and 1980s. Instead, for the Mother of the 1990s these gains seem to have been erased. At the "turn of the century" now, Mother has still been given time by the new labor-saving devices to clean the oven and get the laundry off the line. Somewhat anachronistically, there's a radio playing in the background.

By the 1920s, Mother, provided yet more free time by her new "electric servants," no longer chooses to spend her leisure hours at her hobby of embroidering. Instead, she is making costumes for the rest of the family so they can take part in her ladies' club holiday parade. Mother, by the way, comically "interrupts" even more than she did in the earlier versions. And the daughter, now called Patricia, is no longer interested in finding a job. She is only interested in boys. The somewhat ironic banter between daughter and Father about a man's world has completely disappeared.

The 1940s in this latest version are no longer "frantic" but "fabulous," and time is conflated in an even stranger way than before. Such 1950s phenomena as commuting, the "rat race," and television have already become part of family life. Significantly, the notion that Mother be reimbursed for her work on the rumpus room, evident in the Carousel versions from the 1970s and 1980s, has vanished. Instead, Father chastises Mother for her appeal for help with the basement-remodeling project. There is a decidedly chilly undertone to the interaction between husband and wife in this 1990s version of the 1940s:

> *Mother:* John, this papering is getting out of hand. I could use a little help.
> *Father:* Now, Sarah, didn't I set up that clever automatic paint stirring machine for you? (whirring noise)
> *Mother:* Yes, John, you're a genius. Of course, this will ruin my food mixer. What do you care?
> *Father:* Oh, good old Sarah. Always the last laugh. (loud noise; dog barks)
> *Mother:* Oh, you and your progress! That paint mixer of yours just sloshed paint across my room—my rumpus room!
> *Father:* How do you like that: I always say, if you're going to be married, marry a girl with a sense of humor! ("Performance Notes" 11–12)

Something has happened since 1967. Then, Mother was dubbed "ingenious" for figuring out how to stir paint with the food mixer. During the next productions in the 1970s and 1980s she additionally argued for the need for equal pay for her labor in rehabbing the rumpus room. Now, in the 1990s, it is instead Father who has performed the clever task of inventing a paint stirrer, while Mother rather ineptly does the labor. No Rosie the Riveter is she. The discourse over the worth of female labor for both mother and daughter seems to have completely faded from Disney's collective memory.

The last act, too, is different. Mother in the 1960s script, we recall, kept busy with the garden club and bowling league. The version from the 1970s and 1980s involved her more centrally in civic life, in the Clean Waters Committee and bond issue drive. But by the 1990s there is deafening silence on any work or community commitments. Mother sits in a corner of the kitchen toying with a "new voice activation system" for the oven while Father, as ever a stooge with a stove, happily burns a turkey. The earlier acknowledgment of social change, and of the historiography of change, is gone. Labor-saving devices at this point don't seem to produce much in the way of leisure, self-improvement, or satisfaction for Mother at all. By the 1990s, her activities have been more subordinated to those of her family than at any time in the long history of this drama.

Twenty years ago, the Carousel was criticized for its portrayal of women. A newspaper writer suggested, "The G.E. Carousel was a sexist hymn to all-electric progress in the 20th century. Through the years, dumb old Mom would fall off ladders replacing light bulbs. . . . Dad, of course, would be long-suffering."[8] James Bierman, who analyzed the play as a "robot drama," disagreed with this analysis, arguing that the women of the Carousel had nowhere to go outside the kitchen, not because there was nowhere to go, but because "Disney's women are good for nothing else." Furthermore, he stated, if the play was sexist, it was not from malice but from the deeply rooted male chauvinism in American culture. The play, he argued, "reflects; it does not invent" (229). If the women's liberation movement of the 1970s altered the historical perspective of the audience and imagineers, as Bierman argues, what happened in the 1990s?

It is difficult to get through the Disney or General Electric organizations to speak with the creators themselves and to understand the process through which the scripts have been revised.[9] General Electric, of course, had since the 1920s worked hard at creating a "positive electrical consciousness" that would build a desire in families throughout the country to "make their homes into electrified dwelling places."[10] This was the task given the Disney imagineers, who strove to create a new kind of realism that left the audience feeling good about the sponsor. "What we create," one imagineer has said, "is a 'Disney realism,' sort of Utopian in nature, where we carefully program out all the negative, unwanted elements and program in the positive elements."[11] But like Thornton Wilder's Grover's Corners, Disney's idealized family has dystopian as well as utopian features. It appears that a feminist perspective, acknowledged during the 1970s and 1980s when feminism was part of the national discourse, has been scripted out of the Carousel's world in the more conservative 1990s.

Disney history may be, as the historian Michael Kammen suggests, "shallow entertainment" of a bland and nostalgic past, but it also reflects a powerful collective memory of women and the family (639). For millions of people, it has been an entertaining and memorable, if not always accurate, account of American social history with a whiggish perspective on progress and consumerism. Kammen has written that "Americans will historicize the present in a somewhat facile, somewhat inadvertent way, and they will continue to depoliticize the past as a means of minimizing conflict" (704). Perhaps it is this process that accounts for the popularity of the Carousel's theater. Feminist gains, part of the national experience a decade ago, are erased during a time of political and social backlash. The play presents a history that forgets its own past.

ACKNOWLEDGMENTS

For help with this project, thanks to the Disney Archives, Ben Weiner, Stuart Weiner, Maria Treccapelli, Tom Moher, and Marilyn Perry. An earlier version of this paper was presented at the 1996 Berkshire Conference on the History of Women.

NOTES

1. The primary sources for this chapter are as follows: for the 1967 script—"GE Carousel"; for the 1975 script—Bierman; for the 1980s report of the show—Fjellman and Wallace; for the February 1995 version of the show—"Performance Notes."

2. There is of course a vast literature on this topic. For the rise in working mothers, see Weiner; on the effects of the feminist movement of the 1970s, see Evans.

3. For another interpretation of Disney, see the discussion in Wiener of changing representations of the American West in Disneyland's Frontierland.

4. This estimate was made by Walt Disney Enterprises in 1975; millions more have seen the presentation by the late 1990s (see Bierman 223).

5. The attraction was at first entitled Progress Land and later renamed the General Electric Carousel Theatre of Progress and then the Carousel of Progress (see Jackson 65). On the cultural analysis of world's fairs and expositions, see Nye; Smith; and Sorkin.

6. "Performance Notes" 1. That the Carousel has been edited in this way was acknowledged in the 1995 production; the narrator proclaimed, "Although our Carousel family has experienced a few changes over the years, our show still revolves around the same theme and that's progress." It is hard to get a grip on this "genre"; because of the revisions it is ephemeral, slippery, never fixed. Perhaps the Carousel is more like a museum exhibit, or even a puppet show, than a conventional play.

7. For the "robot drama" definition, see Bierman. Thanks to John Kasson for pointing out the domestic comedy aspect of the play.

8. Michael Seiler, *Los Angeles Times*, 3 July 1974 (cited in Bierman 229).

9. See my correspondence with both General Electric and Walt Disney: Weiner to Archivist, General Electric company, 11 August 1995, and e-mail correspondence between Weiner and Robert Tieman, Walt Disney Archives, Burbank, Calif., 15 June 1995, 19 June 1995, 22 June 1995, and 23 June 1995. Copies of correspondence in my possession.

10. In an earlier theatrical promotion, General Electric had, at the 1933 Century of Progress in Chicago, created a "talking kitchen" exhibit (see Nye 265, 358).

11. Cited in Zukin 222.

REFERENCES

Bierman, James H. "The Walt Disney Robot Dramas." *Yale Review* 66 (1976): 223–36.

Cowan, Ruth Schwartz. *More Work for Mother: The Ironies of Household Technology from the Open Hearth to the Microwave.* New York: Basic, 1983.

Evans, Sara M. *Born for Liberty: A History of Women in America.* New York: Free Press, 1989.

Fjellman, Stephen M. *Vinyl Leaves: Walt Disney World and America.* Boulder: Westview, 1992.

"GE Carousel of Progress." Typescript. Burbank: Walt Disney Archives, 1967.

Jackson, Kathy Merlock. *Walt Disney: A Bio-Bibliography.* Westport: Greenwood, 1993.

Kammen, Michael. *Mystic Chords of Memory: The Transformation of Tradition in American Culture.* New York: Vintage, 1991.

Milkman, Ruth. "Redefining 'Women's Work.' " *Feminist Studies* 8 (1982): 337–72.

Nye, David E. *Electrifying America: Social Meanings of a New Technology, 1880–1940.* Cambridge: MIT Press, 1990.

"Performance Notes of the February 1995 Carousel of Progress." Typescript in author's possession.

Smith, Michael L. "Making Time: Representations of Technology at the 1964 World's Fair." *The Power of Culture: Critical Essays in American History.* Ed. Richard W. Fox and T. J. Jackson Lears. Chicago: University of Chicago Press, 1993.

Sorkin, Michael. "See You in Disneyland." *Variations on a Theme Park: The New American City and the End of Public Space.* Ed. Michael Sorkin. New York: Noonday, 1992.

Strasser, Susan. *Never Done: A History of American Housework.* New York: Pantheon, 1982.

Wallace, Michael. "Mickey Mouse History: Portraying the Past at Disney World." *History Museums in the United States: A Critical Assessment.* Ed. Warren Leon and Roy Rosenzweig. Urbana: University of Illinois Press, 1989.

Watts, Steven. "Walt Disney: Art and Politics in the American Century." *Journal of American History* 82 (1995): 84–110.

Weiner, Lynn Y. *From Working Girl to Working Mother: The Female Labor Force in the United States, 1920–1980.* Chapel Hill: University of North Carolina Press, 1985.

Wiener, Jon. "Tall Tales and True." *The Nation,* 31 January 1994: 133–35.

Wilder, Thornton. *Our Town.* New York: Coward McCann, 1938.

Zukin, Sharon. *Landscapes of Power: From Detroit to Disney World.* Berkeley: University of California Press, 1991.

Route 66: Still Kickin' for Students and International Visitors

TERRI RYBURN-LAMONTE

I WAS FIVE years old when my family moved from Illinois to California along Route 66. It was 1953 and Route 66 was a very busy road, with many families traveling for vacations, as well as to hoped-for plentiful jobs in sunny, magical California. My father built a homemade camper on the back of our pickup truck, complete with a chicken wire top, which held gunnysacks of our clothes and other necessities. He covered the wire with canvas that had roll-up sides, both to protect against the weather and to provide ventilation to my three brothers, me, and the two hunting dogs who filled the back of the truck. He, my mother, and my younger brother occupied the cab of the truck. With children and canvas flapping in the wind, we set off for our big adventure! We camped out along the way, sleeping in and under the truck at whatever pull-offs my father could find. This trip made such an impression on me that I have become a Route 66 enthusiast and, among other things, have taught a course about the road, as well as conducted a survey of international visitors to determine what brought them to America to travel Route 66.

In 1926 construction began on an American institution—Route 66. Upon completion, the highway "reached across more than 2,400 miles, three time zones, and eight states"[1] from Chicago to Santa Monica, California. In time, Route 66 became a symbol of America's heritage of travel and of our desire to make a better life for ourselves by moving west. The road was especially important to rural areas. Many small, sleepy towns came to life as the road snaked its way through them. Restaurants, gas stations, truck stops, and other businesses sprang up along the road to accommodate Dust Bowl refugees, business travelers, and vacationers who traveled Route 66. As America grew, with the resulting demand for faster and safer roads, the original two-lane road was replaced by a four-lane highway that closely paralleled the first, but skirted the towns. Some businesses moved closer to the road; others counted on the "Business Route 66" signs to funnel traffic off the new four-lane and into their places of business. During World War II, the road served as a major military corridor, which, ironically, may have been the origin of its decline in importance. General Dwight Eisenhower (soon to be president of the United States) is said to have been so impressed with the speed and efficiency of traffic on the German autobahn that he determined to replace American highways with superhighways, to be called interstates; and so, in time, the four-lane highway that had relegated Route 66 to a "Business Route" was replaced by an even more efficient, and impersonal, pavement: the interstate.[2]

By mid-1984, when the last section of Route 66 was bypassed near Williams, Arizona, a grass-roots resurgence of interest began to grow, until by the early 1990s, all eight states through which the road passed had organized associations to promote and preserve the road and accompanying businesses. Many people now travel the road as a destination in and of itself. For instance, on the second weekend in June, the Route 66 Association of Illinois takes a two-day motor tour between Chicago and St. Louis, involving several hundred people, stopping along the way to visit historic sites and some of the people who have given the road its unique character. The association also maintains a Hall of Fame at the Dixie Trucker's Home in McLean, into which it annually inducts those people and places in Illinois which best exemplify the Route 66 spirit. The Hall of Fame has been featured in several documentaries, including a PBS feature called "Great Roads," narrated by Robert Townsend and starring many Hall of Fame members.

In the fall of 1991, I taught an interdisciplinary colloquium at Illinois State University, Normal, Illinois, in which twenty-five honors students enrolled. Most of the students were between eighteen and twenty-one years old; there were three nontraditional (twenty-five years or older) students in the course. Their majors ranged from English to history to accounting and communication. Titled "Route 66: 1926 to the Present," the course provided the history of the road as well as materials and popular culture associated with the route. Students also conducted oral histories with people who lived or worked along the road and compiled the interviews into a book. (Students signed a copyright release form, which meant that any proceeds from the sale would be designated for honors scholarships.) Although taught at the college level, this course on the social history and popular culture of an American highway could also be adapted easily for a high school U.S. history course or any interdisciplinary course in American culture, since it strongly relies on activity-based learning.

I began the course by talking about my interest in Route 66. Personal anecdotes seemed especially effective at conveying the mystique of Route 66 and prepared the students for the interviews they would conduct with people who had traveled the road.

During the early class sessions, students were taught about the history of roads in America, beginning with the Native American and buffalo trails that preceded European settlement. They learned about the muddy, often impassable, National Road that began in Maryland in 1803 and reached Vandalia, Illinois, in 1840. I covered the Federal Aid Acts and Laws and spent time discussing the "Father of Route 66," Cyrus Avery, of Oklahoma. Avery was appointed the state highway commissioner of Oklahoma in 1923 and was the first chairman of the State Highway Commission, which laid out the state highway system. He was also the leader of the American Association of State Highway officials. At their 1924 meeting, they proposed that the secretary of agriculture select and designate a comprehensive system of interstate routes. As a result, Avery was chosen to lay out and create what would be known as the United States Highway System. On November 11, 1926, a committee of federal and state highway officials met in Pinehurst, North Carolina, and signed documents that made Route 66 official.[3]

I frequently began or ended the class period by asking students to write essays on topics designed to stimulate their thinking about the road and/or personal experiences related to the road. These essays also gave me useful insight into their thoughts. For instance, the initial assignment was to write about "my first car ride." Another essay required them to write about the day they got their driver's licenses, which proved for many to have been a nerve-wracking experience.

We were fortunate to have Tom Teague, author of *Searching for 66*,[4] as a guest speaker. The book was required reading for the students because it dealt with two important topics: Tom's own journey along the road in 1985 and the interviews he conducted. It was very helpful for the students to be able to ask him questions about the situations and people he encountered along the road and his experiences in collecting oral history. Hearing Tom's story gave them confidence in their ability to conduct their own interviews.

One class period was devoted to showing the movie, *The Grapes of Wrath*, based on the John Steinbeck novel. John Ford directed the movie, which effectively captured the desperation of the 1930s Dust Bowl refugees as it focused on the Joad family and their flight from poverty and near starvation in Oklahoma. The movie followed them along Route 66, contrasting their hopes of employment and a better life in California with a realistic portrayal of the experiences of many nameless, faceless others who traveled the road in search of salvation. The black-and-white photography by Gregg Toland created "sweeping panoramas of the dustbowl road-scape [that] have a kind of bleak grandeur."[5]

I wanted my students to experience a ride along the entire highway in Illinois. Students had been prepared through lectures and guest speakers for the sights they would see. They were not quite as well prepared for the physical hardships encountered on such a long trip. Early one morning, we left in a van for Chicago, returned to Normal for lunch, and then left immediately for St. Louis. We stopped at various historic places along the way, including the Welco Truck Stop in Joliet, Funk's Grove, and the Cozy Dog Restaurant in Springfield. The Welco Truck Stop impressed the students but not necessarily in a positive way. One student wrote:

> most of the group went to encounter the slovenly waitress. I went into the gas station office instead, past smoking truckers sitting around a grimy table watching TV. The restrooms were down a long, dark hallway that wound deep into the building. Foul propositions on the wall above the urinals invited me to knock on the third stall door and ask for Bubba. I didn't.

Fortunately, our stop at the Cozy Dog Restaurant turned out to be a very pleasant experience as students met the famed Ed "Cozy Dog" Waldmire:

> Arms flailing wildly, he flagged us to a stop in front of the restaurant. Warily, I stepped down from the van with the fear that this energetic little man would pick me up and swing me around in his excitement. Inside the Cozy Dog, he showered us with little presents—notebooks, maps, pencils—all bearing the Cozy Dog logo, of course. I can definitely say that Ed Waldmire was one of Route 66's true characters.

We also saw the Chain of Rocks Bridge crossing the Mississippi River into Missouri before heading back. After a brief stop at the Illinois Route 66 Hall of Fame at the Dixie Trucker's Home in McLean, we returned to Normal just after midnight. Perhaps because of the length of time they spent on this trip and the level of discomfort produced by bouncing around in the van, students who went along on the field trip "bonded" with each other and with the images of earlier Route 66 travelers. Students wrote an essay about their bone-rattling experience and the images it provoked. One said:

> As we were taking our trip, I tried to imagine what it would have been like to travel on 66 in the 1940s and '50s, and I tried to piece the road back together with what I knew about it, in order to make the picture complete. I couldn't help but feel anger for people who don't let anything stand in the way of "progress." They tear down old houses to make way for gas stations and parking lots. They tear down interesting old buildings to make way for corporations enclosed in glass and steel. And they push aside old highways like 66 in exchange for a way we can get somewhere faster. In doing so, highways have lost the human aspect that used to be so important to people. No one is anyone's neighbor anymore because they don't have time to stop and talk. No one notices the scenery anymore because they're driving by too fast. That's why most of the new interstates just cut through the land instead of following the hills and dips and plains that make it interesting and beautiful. I can understand the need to get somewhere quickly sometimes, but why are we always hurrying today? I think that now I understand why people are still so fascinated by Route 66. People miss going a little slower and being able to stop and talk to people along the road. They miss *real* people; not the robots in McDonald's uniforms, programmed to say certain things. And they miss the feeling of adventure that the land has always brought with it.

Another major activity for the class involved oral history, a historical research method that records the spoken memories of eyewitnesses to events. These memories are important to the understanding of events and their effect upon the people who experienced them.

I trained the students in oral history collection, beginning with such basics as tape recorder operation and selection of cassette tapes, as well as how to set up the interview, establish rapport, ask open-ended questions, and so on. Students were referred to the *Oral History Guide* by Elizabeth Bryant Merrill[6] for further guidance. Some students had family members or friends whom they would be able to interview; those students who did not were assigned a person. Because of time and geographic restrictions, our interviews were limited to people who had lived or worked along the route in Illinois, although some interviews were conducted with those fortunate individuals who had used the road for vacation purposes.

After learning about the history and popular culture of the road, students compiled a list of questions to use as an outline for the interviews. These questions included:

- What memories do you have of your first trip on Route 66?
- Why did you travel on Route 66 and how did the new interstate affect this?
- When was the last time you were on Route 66? For what reason?
- In what ways has Route 66 changed or influenced your life?
- Why do you think Route 66 is so important to many people?
- Was there any one experience that happened on 66 that stands out in your mind?

Students were told not to read the list to the interviewee but to use it as an outline to guide the interview.

A total of forty-one interviews were conducted by the twenty-five students. Students found that they formed friendships with those people whom they interviewed; one student in particular made many trips to a nursing home to visit her new friend. Another student interviewed her father, an Illinois state policeman who spent his entire twenty-seven-year career on Route 66. She gained an insight into his life and her own as well:

> I learned about Route 66, but I discovered something about myself as well. . . . I know how much his life was affected by his experiences on Route 66. As a child, I remember my father being gone on Sundays, holidays, at night, and in bad weather. I know about the nights he didn't sleep because he had witnessed a bad accident. And now, I understand.

Students were warned that transcribing would be the hardest part of the process, requiring many hours of uninterrupted tedium and concentration. Even with repeated warnings, many of them put off the transcribing until the last minute, which was reflected in the quality of their transcription. Once the interview was transcribed, students then had to edit it into a coherent and useful document. How-to sheets were provided to help in this process.

Students participated in other classroom activities as well. They were given a form with the outline of a T-shirt and asked to create a design that incorporated images of Route 66, Illinois State University, and the honors colloquium. This proved to be a very popular exercise and even those who claimed no artistic ability turned in crudely drawn but well-thought-out designs.

Another project involved Burma Shave jingles. Burma Shave, a brushless shaving cream, was advertised by the unique marketing technique of placing a set of six rhyming one-foot-by-three-foot signs at one-hundred-foot intervals along Route 66 and other highways. The literary quality of the signs varied, but they were generally corny, utilizing folk humor and wit. Contests were held beginning in the early 1930s, with a prize of $100 for a rhyme selected for use by Burma Shave.[7] Students were given examples of the 1927 through 1963 signs and a form with spaces for them to write two of their own sets. For instance, two original Burma Shave signs read:

> Riot at / drug store / calling all cars / 100 customers /
> 99 jars / Burma Shave (1936)[8]

and

> When you lay / those few cents down / you've bought /
> the smoothest / shave in town / Burma Shave(1953)[9]

The students thought up their own signs, including:

> The lights may be dim / the mood / just right /
> but a stubbly face / brings an early "good night!" / Burma Shave

And as a reflection of the changing status of women:

> Women have always / been deprived / now we can gloat /
> we've finally arrived / Burma Shave / for women

Burma Shave finally was sold to Philip Morris in 1963, and in 1964 a set of signs was given to the Smithsonian, which declared "Shaving Brushes / You'll Soon See 'Em / On the Shelf / In Some Museum," a fitting epitaph for an art form that provided pleasure for motorists for so many years.[10]

In another activity students role-played the part of a business owner along the recently bypassed old Route 66. They were divided into small groups and asked to devise ways to lure business off the road and into their town. Students were especially intrigued by this exercise as they took on the roles of gas station, motel, and restaurant owners who must find ways to revitalize the town and their own businesses. Students gained valuable insight into the dilemma faced by those in this position and they offered creative ideas for this revitalization. They understood why towns might want to "cash in" on the current Route 66 nostalgia boom, which includes motor tours, festivals, and so on.

When the course was over, I extended an invitation to the students to continue working with me to edit the interviews into the book; four students volunteered and named the manuscript *Route 66: Illinois Remembers*. These students have been especially faithful to the project, helping to edit the interviews as well as collect additional information as necessary. One student described the process:

> Over several semesters we tunneled through a mountain of transcripts and other assorted resources, hoping to divine some understanding from and impose some order on the mass of materials we had collected. The effort to do so is staggering: with nearly 1000 single-spaced pages of transcripts to study, we spent over a month just cataloguing and summarizing the interviews. . . . None of the chapters evolved as we had anticipated. Writing around other people's words required a delicate touch. Too much narration on our part stifled their voices, while too little narration left them floating in space and time.

The book is in the final editing stages; maps and photographs are being selected, and a query letter found three publishers willing to read the manuscript.

On the first day of class, when faced with traditional-aged students, I had some doubts about the success of the course. How could I communicate something to them that they had not experienced? But, of course, that is what all historians must do. It did, indeed, prove to be challenging; it was also extremely rewarding. Besides providing students with historical information and with the practical and very useful skill of conducting interviews, I tried to be creative in my approach, incorporating activities such as creating the T-shirts and Burma Shave jingles. In addition, I was able to watch the students "bond" with each other and with their interviewees. A side effect, which I had not anticipated, was intergenerational: the opening up of dialogue between the students and their parents and grandparents, who remembered Route 66 or a road for which they felt similar affection. Students reported that their parents and grandparents called to ask what they had learned in class that week and to share stories of their own about cruising, drag racing, and road trips. Students discovered a common bond with their elders, which, in some cases, surprised both.

Students became introspective and contemplative as they considered their current "in a hurry" lifestyles. Commenting on the mystique of Route 66, one said:

> Route 66 is much more than just pavement. More than just a go-between, Route 66 is a place to go. For years, I have traveled [Interstate] 55 and other highways and turnpikes, feeling extreme satisfaction with the speed and convenience of my trips. However, looking back at the history of Route 66, I now wonder what it is we are missing by opting for the non-stop method. The answer to that question appears in the faces and words of the people whose lives were touched by the route. After reading about and talking to these people, I find myself, an outsider, removed by both time and locale, caught up in Route 66.

Another student commented on the legacy of the road:

> For some, it was a road of dreams. For others, it was more than that. It was a road that had many meanings. . . . [B]ecause of the aura that 66 has projected over the years, it is a road that will *never* die. The mystique and vision of old 66 will linger in the minds of current generations, and generations to come, and because of this, stories of escape, salvation, vacation, exploration, and trips from here to there will live on as well.

I am encouraged about the future of the road. The torch has been passed as the next generation "hits the road."

Three years after I taught the Route 66 course, I became intrigued with the question of why foreign visitors travel Route 66. In the fall of 1994, I visited my friends, Glaida and Steve Funk, who operate a maple sirup[11] camp at Funk's Grove in Illinois. I was amazed to find that Glaida's guest book contained signatures from hundreds of visitors from such faraway places as Austria, Belgium, England, France, Germany, the Netherlands, Japan, Luxembourg, Switzerland, and Thailand. American Route 66 travelers profess to deep feelings of affection for the road, combined with nostalgia and longing for a simpler time. It seems that the road serves as a time machine, transporting travelers, however temporarily, back to prosperous and happy days. I wanted to know what the attraction was for international visitors and what they found on their journey.

I sent a survey to those whose signatures and addresses were legible. In all, I was able to distinguish 114 names and addresses from ten countries. Eight of my surveys were returned with insufficient addresses, and of the 106 presumed delivered, I received 45 replies, representing eighty-eight people from eight countries, a return rate of 42 percent. By far, the greatest number of replies, 22, were from Germany, which constituted 58 of the 114 surveys sent, a response rate of 38 percent. A follow-up letter, sent to all forty-five people, received 12 replies from five countries, a 27 percent return rate.

The average age for female travelers was just under thirty-three, and just under thirty-eight for males. Nearly without exception, the international visitors traveled from Chicago to Los Angeles for a period of three to four weeks, in rented vehicles. Few undertook the trip alone and most traveled with other couples, with one friend, or in small family groups.

Responses to the question "How did you learn about Route 66?" elicited literary answers. Some had read John Steinbeck's *The Grapes of Wrath* and had become intrigued with the struggles of the fictional Joad family. Most had access to recent books about the road, including those by Tom Snyder, Susan Kelly and Quinta Scott, Michael Wallis, Tom Teague, and the Jack Rittenhouse reprint.

Many had read articles in travel magazines, newspapers, and publications by their motor club equivalent of our AAA. Some belong to Route 66 associations in their own countries, which provided additional information, including maps and travel guides written in their own language.

Television documentaries abound, and it was interesting to hear that in some areas of the world people are watching the original *Route 66* television series with Tod and Buz zipping around in their Corvette, seemingly ageless, in a 1960s America.[12]

Other sources of inspiration included a poster in a Munich library which showed the 1950s route and a *Life* magazine article from the 1950s with a photograph of the road in New Mexico, a hauntingly beautiful image, which had stuck in someone's mind.

Of course, many mentioned that music had lured them here. "Get Your Kicks on Route 66," that lyrical travelogue written by Bobby Troup and first recorded by Nat King Cole in 1947, served as the Pied Piper for some of the travelers. The song has, of course, since been covered by dozens of artists. Most of the visitors who mentioned the song, however, had heard the rollicking Rolling Stones version.

The overall impression that international visitors have of the road is that it is the "real America." Most of the visitors are quite sophisticated in their travels, having made multiple trips to the United States prior to their Route 66 experience. Several people had traveled to the United States two to three times, one person had traveled to the United States four times, and one person listed this as his ninth excursion. They reported that their Route 66 journey was not the usual face of the United States, such as the more tourist-oriented cities of New York or Los Angeles. They found the people friendly, and for one the trip was the realization of a dream: "my youth fulfilled." They found the road to be "a good overview of the U.S. You can see big cities and very small towns, rich people's houses and poor villages. You can see lots of things that are common all over the country and you can see the regional specials." One couple called it "A very special trip. Wonderful architecture. Wide landscape. We saw another America: not the wealthy of NY or LA, but hard working people, sometimes desperately trying to make a living." One family, in particular, reported "feeling the past, seeing the past, smelling the past." At least one person described feeling "totally free!" Another questioned why they couldn't "put the interstate a few miles further [away]? For the first time of my life I felt like a traveler!"

Route 66 was an unforgettable adventure for some, not a "usual road, but a state of mind." Most travelers discovered that Route 66 was not the United States of the movies, but the real America. They seemed particularly fascinated with the great distances, vast horizons, open spaces, and changing scenery from big cities to rural areas, farms to deserts, mountains to plains, Lake Michigan to the Pacific Ocean.

The surveys eloquently expressed the travelers' delight with the road:

> It was a great pleasure to drive along the Mother of Roads and revive most stories of the legendary Route 66. We will be fans of Route 66 for a long time. Traveling is about seeing new places, but Route 66 was never ordinary. We must have driven on the most magical road in the whole world. After swinging from the Pacific, across rivers, plains, mountains, deserts, and canyons of 8 states and several Native American Reservations, we ended two thousand miles later in [a] "mega" city like Chicago on our fourth trip to America. We

are able to say that we saw the true America. We recognized the deeper value of a Route 66 Revival!

They agreed on certain key memorable people, mostly those who were featured in Route 66 books. Many, however, named everyday people—truckers, waitresses, farmers, and taxi drivers—as the most memorable they had encountered along the way. Whether well known or anonymous, each of these people had had something to say to the European visitors about the road and the American way of life. And travelers expressed pleasure and surprise that people had taken so much time to speak with them and to share stories of the road.

Some travelers reported that they did not buy typical road souvenirs, choosing instead some other reminders of America and American culture. But most seemed delighted with their Route 66 treasures, including maple sirup from Funk's Grove, T-shirts, books, records, postcards, and even boxer shorts featuring Route 66 images! It's fun to think that these Route 66 objects now decorate homes and bodies in at least eight countries. At least two respondents sent along photographs of their souvenirs on display at home. One German couple holds a party on the last day of each month, inviting friends to their home as they turn their Route 66 calendar to the next month, revealing the next colorful image of the road.

The question was asked if they would repeat the trip and, if so, what they might do differently. Only one person responded negatively, saying that she and her friend had enjoyed the trip but that they enjoy traveling in America and there was still much to see besides the road.

Most people said they would definitely travel it again but more slowly. They would see more places, make more stops, meet more people, and regardless of the amount of time they had on the road, they wanted more time to explore. Those who traveled only part of the road expressed a desire to come back to travel the whole road, and those who had chosen favorite sections wanted to visit again and spend more time. They also wanted enough time for just "drifting around." Some, however, would change their mode of transportation. Many expressed the desire to travel the road on motorbikes or motorcycles (particularly Harley-Davidsons), and one said that he would buy a classic car in which to travel. One respondent felt the need to make the trip in a convertible, and one thought the trip might best be repeated on a bicycle. However they traveled, they found the road memorable. Said one person, "Some days I can visualize whole stretches of old Route 66. I found out that I am a real roadie." When asked for general comments, most pleaded with anyone responsible to "keep that American dream!"

Preservation of the road was a primary concern. One respondent seemed bemused by the fact that a sixty-year-old road would be called "historic." Others seemed worried about the condition of the road and the lack of historical awareness of Americans. They expressed their sorrow that the road is not renovated and that the signs which should direct travelers to the road are missing or slow to be erected. They noticed neglect and complained about the commercialization of some parts of the road. They are sad that "the real Route 66 generation is becoming less and less. . . . Some parts of Route 66 [are] neglected." Many sounded a preservation "wake-up" call: "Let the Americans get aware that they have to preserve the historical things they have. It's so important for their future, so [worthwhile] to keep all these things unique for the world alive."

Another respondent said, "you Americans should in my opinion realize that the Route 66 is a known historical feature, also in Europe. Not only for touristical reasons but also for historical reasons you Americans should be more careful about it." Another commented, astutely, "It's still a very lively road, but many of the old buildings and sites disappear little by little. Of course you can't keep everything, but it is necessary to take care of certain key buildings, if you still want Route 66 to be an attraction to overseas visitors." One person gave advice to those who wish to travel the road: "Don't wait too long to do this trip. What will happen in the near future is (1) a lot of things will disappear (demolished), and (2) more diners, motels, etc. will be modernized too much."

Do the reasons international visitors give for traveling the road differ from those of Americans? There does not appear to be much difference. An element of nostalgia, a longing for an earlier America, is evident in the returned surveys of the European travelers. Many mentioned that the road evoked the 1950s and 1960s era for them. How can a European be nostalgic for something not previously experienced and so intrinsically American? Perhaps it is similar to the experience of those who were far too young to remember when the road was in its prime but who can, nevertheless, experience it through learning about it. The international visitors are quite sophisticated and know a lot about America and American culture. For many years they have vicariously experienced our popular culture through books, film, music, and television. It seems that most respondents found the earlier America they sought—with real Route 66 "characters" along the ribbon of concrete giving the constantly changing scenery a unique personality.

My friend Glaida calls me from Funk's Grove whenever a foreign visitor has time to spend. If I can, I dash down the ten miles or so to serve as a goodwill ambassador for my beloved Illinois road. I suppose that, in the process, I also become one of the anonymous "characters" along the "Mother Road."

NOTES

1. Michael Wallis, *Route 66: The Mother Road* (New York: St. Martin's Press, 1990), p. 1.
2. Wallis, p. 25.
3. Susan Croce Kelly and Quinta Scott, *Route 66: The Highway and Its People* (Norman: University of Oklahoma Press, 1990), pp. 12–13.
4. Tom Teague, *Searching for 66* (Springfield, IL: Samizdat House, 1991).
5. Mark Williams, *Road Movies: The Complete Guide to Cinema on Wheels* (New York: Proteus Publishing Company, 1982), p. 66.
6. Elizabeth Bryant Merrill, *Oral History Guide* (Salem, WI: Sheffield Publishing Company, 1985).
7. Frank Rowsome, Jr., *The Verse by the Side of the Road: The Story of the Burma Shave Signs and Jingles* (New York: Viking Penguin, 1990), p. 24.
8. Rowsome, p. 82.
9. Rowsome, p. 113.

10. Rowsome, p. 67

11. Hazel Funk Holmes, a Funk descendant, was a stickler for this spelling, insisting that it was the preferred spelling, according to the Webster dictionary. The United States Department of Agriculture also uses this spelling.

12. This television program aired from 1960 to 1964, and although very few of the episodes were really shot along Route 66, it quickly became a symbol of the road.

SELECTED BIBLIOGRAPHY

Kelly, Susan Croce, and Quinta Scott. *Route 66: The Highway and Its People.* Norman: University of Oklahoma Press, 1990.

Kerouac, Jack. *On the Road.* New York: Viking Penguin, 1976.

Rittenhouse, Jack D. *A Guide Book to Highway 66.* Albuquerque: University of New Mexico Press, 1989.

Rowsome, Frank, Jr. *The Verse by the Side of the Road: The Story of the Burma Shave Signs and Jingles.* New York: Viking Penguin, 1990.

Snyder, Tom. *The Route 66 Traveler's Guide and Roadside Companion.* New York: St. Martin's Press, 1990.

Steinbeck, John. *The Grapes of Wrath.* 1939. New York: Bantam Books, 1970.

Teague, Tom. *Searching for 66.* Springfield, IL: Samizdat House, 1991.

Wallis, Michael. *Route 66: The Mother Road.* New York: St. Martin's Press, 1990.

Williams, Mark. *Road Movies: The Complete Guide to Cinema on Wheels.* New York: Proteus Publishing Company, 1982.

PART III

PIONEER "STARGAZERS": TWENTIETH-CENTURY TRAVEL PERSONIFIED

Touring America in a Model T

DAVID TOMLINSON

WHEN THEY MARRIED in April 1912, Olive and Ben King had a dream: a year's tour of the United States. They could not take such a honeymoon just after the marriage, yet they dreamed. "Always this year of stargazing danced ahead, an utterly delightful vision which we doubted not could some day be realized. Our wait was only nine years."[1]

Although the couple lived in Washington, D.C., in the early 1920s, their car tour began from Kirkwood, Missouri, the home of kin. Olive explained, "We'd have started from Washington, D.C. in the Ford, but that several very proper visits demanded we do credit to our relatives—a credit hardly possible out of suitcases" (1). They made those visits, and then they bought a car for the trip.

The car, which they christened "Stargazer," since it was to be the vehicle of their dreams, was not the ideal chariot. At the beginning of the travel diary she kept of the journey, a journal she called "Log of the Stargazer," Olive first denounced the purchase. "Great was my disgust," she complained, "over the purchase of a *second hand* Ford" (1). However, a secondhand car was the best they could do. They would have had to wait six weeks or more for delivery of a new vehicle, and mechanics advised the couple that no car should begin a cross-country jaunt without having been broken in, a matter of a thousand miles' driving.

"Shortly Stargazer was ours," Olive lamented, coming a step closer to accepting the machine, "Ours to be trundled home and put thro preliminary paces. Most lame those paces! Our solicitous family waxed lugubrious as one and all saw how long it took to start her, how she refused the hills, how she stopped betimes for no apparent cause. One confided to another that there was no doubt about it, the car was quite impossible—we'd never get out of the state of Missouri in her" (1). With some pride, Olive boasted, "We did, tho—and back into Missouri, eleven months after" (1).

What we will do is to trace the trials and tribulations of half that journey, the trip from Missouri to the West Coast. It all began on July 1, 1921. "Many expectations to the contrary, Stargazer's engine *did* actually go, and we rolled out of the front yard of the old home shortly after 10 A.M., amid a shower of rice and old shoes" (1). Obviously, the whole family accepted the trip as a honeymoon nine years delayed and treated it so. At the end of the day, Olive could note, "Ben is still chuckling over the rice, which is everywhere among our duffel bags. It's really much nicer than a first honeymoon. After getting acquainted in matrimony for more than nine years, we have so much more to start on than we did the first time" (2).

They did not travel far that first day, only seventy-five miles; but the trip which would take slightly more than an hour today took much longer over poorly maintained roads. Olive, still suffering from a sore jaw after having had oral surgery three days before (an impacted wisdom tooth had had to come out), was happy to find a nice wooded campsite and get rest.

The couple did not look for hotels along the way. They camped. They did not have to pitch a tent in the evenings, however: they merely shifted the equipment in the truck-like rear of Stargazer to make room for sleeping. Then they spread out their bedding, put down the curtains of the car/truck, and enjoyed relative comfort and privacy wherever they happened to be. This nifty arrangement saved them both time and difficulty in a number of situations; and it, in part, accounted for their sticking with Stargazer in spite of frequent mechanical difficulties.

By July 3, the car had begun to produce what was to become an unending litany of mechanical troubles. This first set made Olive meditate about the name and the sex of the machine: "I've been hesitating over whether to refer to Stargazer as he, she or it. Somehow one always thinks of a Ford and a donkey as feminine, and after last night's display of perversity, 'she' she shall be henceforth" (2).

At Moberly, Missouri, what they thought was engine trouble delayed them. Otherwise, they had been satisfied with the performance of the car. Earlier in the day, Olive had crowed, "Stargazer gave us 20 miles an hour thro very pretty country, growing flatter all the time" (3). The landscape was not always trouble-free, however. When there was talk at a filling station of a "terrible hill," the couple listened intently. They heard that people had been killed on the hill the day before. The Kings soon learned that one person's nemesis is often no difficulty at all to others. "The hill was so mild we never recognized it," Olive reported in a relieved tone (3).

The next morning, Ben spent an hour or two trying to track down the engine difficulty, but his work was to no avail. From the nearest farmhouse, they had to call a garage. The difficulty was not so serious as they had feared: the car battery needed replacing.

Ten hours later, Olive could report, "We are 80 miles—or rather hills—further on" (6). After getting the new battery, the Model T had shown great energy, taking "hill after hill like a bird. They were rough hills, too" (6).

This early enthusiasm soon gave way to a more sober assessment: "On the last few hills Stargazer stopped halfway, and I got out and pushed. The getting out helped, thus removing 125 pounds, and I insist the pushing helped too, but Ben just grins" (6). This first attempt at coaxing the perverse vehicle was not the last. Later, Olive could easily have claimed that she had pushed Stargazer most of the way across America.

July 4 may have been Independence Day, but for Ben and Olive it was a day which emphasized their dependence upon the kindness of others. Gas stations were sparse, and Stargazer ran out of the necessary liquid on a hill. The couple were reduced to visiting nearby farmhouses to beg for enough gas to get them to a station. Far from embarrassing them, the visits confirmed their feelings of faith in their fellows. Olive could brag, "Country-people hereabout are certainly kindly. I've been to 2 farm houses after gasoline, and always the people smile so cordially, and do what they can to help. Just the smile is a lot, whether they have anything you want or not. So far it has indeed been a 'friendly road.' "

Perhaps part of the friendliness came from the Kings themselves. They rarely seem to have found indifferent or hostile people along the way. At Bloomfield they joined people out to see an Independence Day parade and to await fireworks. In spite of the holiday, however, Olive was able to find a dentist to help her with her sore jaw; and they located a mechanic who looked at Stargazer, pronouncing her fit.

But the Kings' fears about Stargazer were justified by subsequent events. On the road toward Ottumwa, Iowa, with the skies darkening, Stargazer got stuck again on a hill. By the time Ben was able to phone garages, they were all closed. The help of two boys who joined Olive's efforts meant that the car made it up that hill. The boys gave the Kings the name of a good mechanic at Ottumwa, a town ten miles away. In spite of the odds against them, the couple decided to urge Stargazer on. After Ben poured carbon remover in the engine, they set out with high hopes, only to get stuck on another hill.

"Along came a jovial tramp. 'Let me push,' said he, 'I hate to see a partner in distress, and this is the worst grade between here and Ottumwa.' It seemed hopeless, but Ben started up again, and with the tramp and I both pushing our hardest we got her over the brow, foot by foot" (9).

Once they were over the crest of the hill, Olive and the tramp jumped in for a ride down the other side. After a few miles, the tramp left them and headed into the woods. Olive soon got out herself because she feared that with her aboard the car would be unable to negotiate the hills ahead. "I walked nearly all the way to Ottumwa. . . . It was a wonderful feeling to tramp along the soft woodsy road, and see Stargazer ahead, caterpillaring up an incline, with a creep feeble but sure" (9). Finally, they reached the town and found the mechanic. After extracting a promise from him to look at the car the first thing the next morning, they camped, enjoying "hours of oblivion, and a wood thrush singing close by" (9).

Camping in Stargazer had certain drawbacks over staying in hotels. One, of course, was that the car had no running water. The Kings were always looking for some place where they might have a good bath, feeling that relaxing was easier when they were clean. In Ottumwa, the couple sought out the local Y.M.C.A. and Y.W.C.A. "and soaked, first in hot and then in cold water" (10).

Stargazer had her mechanical ills cured, and Olive found a dentist to change the dressing in her jaw. "He took a look at my mouth, said he hadn't the proper things in his office, went on 2 trips to a drug store after them, treated the deep hole most gently and carefully, and then fixed me 2 bottles of disinfectant and a box of iodoform gauze and a dropper, so that I could treat the place myself everyday, it being well on the road to healing. For all of this, he charged me $.50. We are still marveling" (10). If they marveled in 1921, the service to strangers seems even more a wonder in the 1990s.

Once again, after being given mechanical attention, Stargazer had more energy than the two remembered her showing. The grades were steep, but "Stargazer bounded up them, and could hardly be restrained coming down. She did so want to run" (11). To the Kings and even to the reader of the log, Stargazer takes on a personality. On this day, the car with personality took the couple 150 miles.

Not all troubles of the trip were related to Stargazer either. On July 6, Olive reported burning a child's foot. "I was making coffee for the thermos bottle," she said, "and 4 little youngsters were hopping around, asking every manner of question—why didn't we have a house? Was Ben my papa? How did I make my pants stay up?—and I hated to send them away, as they showed much interest in the thermos bottle. I filled it, and a little boy knocked it over, sending a splash on his sister's foot. Of course she shrieked with all the force of 2 healthy lungs, and said she hated me and wished she hadn't come—for which I didn't blame her. We found her mother and explained things and tried to help, but instead of using linseed oil and lime water, they used grandmother's pain killing salve" (12).

As they traveled west, the couple noticed changes in landscape and an inevitable enterprise among the country's people. One day, Olive noted, "We passed a sign 'O. C. Snow—Furniture and Undertaking'—nothing like a diversity of occupation" (12). The same day, July 7, she could also say, "The hayfields have changed from clover to alfalfa, and the country is flattening to rolling plains" (12). That evening they reached Fremont, Nebraska, and treated themselves to a steak dinner. The meat was priced at $.25 a pound; and since they cooked it themselves, they were able to enjoy nature with the meal. They watched a rose-breasted grosbeak, "so rare a sight in Washington, D.C. that I can never look my fill at them," Olive opined (12).

The next day brought flat tires which could not easily be fixed. "It began to cool as evening came on," Olive wrote, "and when we were 11 miles from Grand Island [Nebraska], a terrific 'popp fizz' rang out from a back tire. A blowout, our second tire trouble since starting. . . . We had several new tubes, but on pumping them up, found they leaked air badly thro the valves. New valves helped not at all, and there was no garage near. Just then a heavy car came by, fellow tourists of the camp of the night before. The driver, a young man, drew up and helped till there was no hope for any one of our tubes, and then, offered to drive Ben to the city, 22 miles round trip, to get a new tube. We demurred but he insisted, and it ended by his mother and little girl and I sitting on a bank, while he and Ben went for a tube. There are few friends who would do as much, let alone a chance acquaintance of the night before. It was cool now, and the 3 of us ate fruit and cheese sandwiches and listened to the corn rustle, and watched the sky turn salmon, and the moon and stars come out" (14).

After dark, Ben and the good Samaritan returned, "and we almost ruined our precious tube before we realized it was our pump which was wrong and had spoiled the other tubes. We got the tire on, and landed at the camping place at 10:30, so weary we could hardly walk" (15).

The next day, they discovered that the inner tubes were not the only problem. The tire itself on that wheel was badly rimcut. It could not be repaired. The log keeper lamented, "It had gone less than 1000 miles, and should have served for 5 or 6,000" (15). (Automobiles have changed drastically in the more than seventy years since the Kings took their trip; one measure of the change is the life expectancy of tires.)

On July 10, the travelers ran into an unusual roadblock: a drove of steers. A cowboy finally cleared a path so that the car could pass. Once they wended their way past the animals, they had to contend with a weak bridge. Before they got to it, they met a sign reading "Go slow! Dangerous Bridge! This means you!" (17) and at the foot of the bridge itself another that read, "Hit me easy! I'm old and feeble" (17). They survived the crossing of the Platte River and arrived at a tourist camp which had hot and cold shower baths. "My second honest-to-goodness bath in 10 days!" Olive exclaimed (17).

Tire trouble continued. As they stopped, they discovered that a nail had caused the third flat of the trip, which Ben fixed before he washed up. The acquaintances who had helped them over the previous flat were in the same camp. Ice cream was available, so the Kings threw a party for the kind folks to thank them for the care they had given.

The next day, Stargazer performed beautifully, giving the couple the easiest day of travel they had had. "We went 180 miles in all, and hardly realized it, the roads were so good, except for half a mile into Cheyenne, when we nearly turned over" (19). Mail from family and friends awaited them at Cheyenne, and they carried it with them to a campground by a lake, where they had "thick lamb chops, new potatoes, green beans and little nut cakes" (19) for supper.

It had taken eleven days to get to Cheyenne; and once there, the couple knew they wanted to be present for the Frontier Days celebration at the end of the month. They decided to take a side trip until the celebration began, a trip to Rocky Mountain National Park where they could enjoy the beauties of nature.

The initial evening of the side trip, they had their first campfire where they "got all the aluminum so beautifully blackened that we feel the pickings of true campers' spurs" (20). They did not rough it completely, using paper and matches to start the fire. Olive thought it better to use the modern materials "than rub [sticks together] for the rest of our lives" (20).

They were in the mountains luxuriating in the cooler weather; but the rough territory which suited them did not suit Stargazer so well. After camping overnight in Thompson Canyon, they went through Estes Park, a village in a crescent of the mountains which Olive described as "blue and snowy and fir covered" (20). After the village there was "a long, winding climb, which poor Stargazer crept up with groanings of spirit. She doesn't appreciate the mountains, and she doesn't like the altitude. After perhaps 5 miles she gave up, and went stone dead on us. Due investigation showed that she'd take us back down, but if we wanted to go any upper, we'd have to navigate ourselves. She'd been thoughtful enough to stop in a lovely spot for camping, with swift running water and a great pine tree" (20). They did not sleep in the car but pitched a tent. They gave that enterprise up after one evening, however, because sleeping outside was too cold. They returned the cots to Stargazer the next morning and opined, "We like our house on wheels better every time we see other people's, and realize our advantages over theirs" (21).

Necessity kept the Kings exploring on foot. There were not many others walking. "We almost never pass anyone afoot, just a steady stream of autos and horses" (25), Olive noted. With such traffic, there were definite disadvantages to walking along the roadside. For example, once an "inconsiderate machine plunged into a mud puddle" (25) and splattered Olive from head to toe. "Everyone thought it very funny, as it was—only I had a clean pongee waist on, and it should have done for a week" (26).

After the Cheyenne festival, the twosome and their cantankerous car were back on the road by July 29. Olive's diary entry is so completely concerned with the car and the virtues it could engender in people that I will give it to you in its entirety:

> We are in adversity. One of the great things about such a trip as this, is the serene patience which one gradually acquires. For me it is hard come-by, I note[,] being by nature very patient. One simply has to take everything as it comes, and cultivate a tra-la-la feeling, thankful when the car does well, and grateful it's no worse when the car does very badly. At present it's badly.
>
> We were a few miles out of Cheyenne, when Stargazer died on us going up a hill. I removed my pounds, as usual, and Ben backed down and tried her again, only to stop a few feet higher up. A very heavy road machine came chugging along, and without a word its mechanic saw our plight, hitched Stargazer behind his powerful engine, and towed her up the hill. He refused all pay but thanks, and we ran along a mile or so, till another hill stumped us. In half an hour the road machine got there, and once more towed us over the top. We couldn't get back, and tho we knew something bad was the matter, there was nothing to do but some how [*sic*] reach the next garage—some 40 miles ahead. Being right high up by now, there was comparatively level going for a while, and then another Waterloo loomed before us. A Ford came down it as we went up, and just as a matter of course the man and woman in it got out, and added their pushes to mine. That is the way of the road, out west.
>
> The next hill was a corker, and we went to the side of it, wondering what we'd do. No garage for many miles, no houses. A Dodge came by, its driver took out a cable, pulled us up, and kept near us the rest of the way to the next town, towing us 8 or 10 times. What a lot of human kindness is still in this world!
>
> When we finally pulled into the funny little town—bare, flat, sandy, a few houses, 2 banks, 6 garages and a huge grain elevator, also a railroad track—we found a place to get some dinner and give some to our friend in need and his wife. Afterwards we spent the afternoon in a garage getting new transmission bands, and had an hour's beautiful ride that evening to the next town, a cool breeze in our faces, the distant hills a heavenly blue.
>
> Early next morning we started gaily, with a contented all-fixed-up feeling. For 10 miles we stayed fixed, and then our same trouble began,—and the

> nearest town 30 miles away. For the next 6 hours the program was repeated—go as far as we could, get a passerby with more power than he needed to haul us over a grade, and then do it all over. It was funny as well as tragic.
>
> All afternoon we spent in a garage having done over again the same work done 24 hours before. I shall never understand how those bands burned out in 40 miles. They should have lasted for 5,000. Next thing was a blowout. We got into camp about 7:00, calming our weary souls by eating dinner on the river bank, hills before us, and the last faint glow of a perfect sunset. (31–32)

And the trouble did not stop on July 29. By August 1, the Kings were again seeking the help of a garage. The repairs took several days. Olive tried to be philosophical, saying, "After the fine work Stargazer gave us, against tremendous obstacles, we can't complain if her 'innards' are pretty much out of kilter now" (33). While the car was being repaired in Thermopolis, Wyoming, the couple ventured to sights close by, including a sulphur spring; but they were cautious. When the mechanic said Stargazer was ready to go, they tried her out, only to have her refuse the first hill. She went back to the shop to have her valves ground, a mountain gear and some bearings added, and two new tires put on. By the time they headed out toward Yellowstone, fifty-five miles away, almost a week had passed. By noon they were at Pahaska, Buffalo Bill's ranch. There gasoline sold for the outrageous sum of $.50 a gallon, "probably because you simply *have* to have it, and it's the only place you can get it" (35). The car held $2.50 worth of gas, and once they got to the entrance of Yellowstone, a green buffalo sticker pasted onto their windshield giving them access to the park cost them $7.50.

They started toward Sylvan Pass. Other travelers told the Kings they faced "a perfect 'luau' of a hill" (35). "It was all of that," Olive reported, "8 or 9 miles long, four hairpin curves, low gear all the way, a 3000 ft. climb in altitude—and oh how a car hates altitude—a very high, narrow drive. It was perfectly beautiful, tho, close to the edge, a forest of fir and cedars, far, far below us. An unruly car, or a little carelessness meant certain death—but a beautiful death, so clean and quick. Not that I'm wishful for one, but there's far less tragedy in that than in a long slow illness, and great suffering" (35). Ironically, before she died in 1981, Olive was to suffer that long, slow illness she detested in 1921.

In the park, gasoline was $.40 a gallon, but the couple found prices at the stores there quite reasonable. They did not need much from the stores, however. "All one needs in Yellowstone to have a wonderful time," Olive mused, "is a capacity for enjoyment. Some tourists lack it, and wish they hadn't come, and don't see anything so grand about the park" (36).

The transmission bands failed again. After coming down from Dunraven Pass, the Kings recognized the signs. They learned the nearest garage was twenty-three miles away and the cost of having the car towed there would be $75, unthinkably high in those days, when a car was priced at only a few hundred new. Even without the requisite tools, Ben bought bands at a park store and determined to try to install them himself.

The installation proved an adventure. Olive "put down clean papers, and wrapped up the different bunches of screws in separate little bundles. Ben rolled around under the car or poked into it, black grease to his elbows. He hadn't the proper wrenches and could neither borrow nor buy any. About noon a Ford drove in, with a Canadian and his English wife. He had the wrenches, and lent them to Ben while they walked to the Falls. When they returned, he got interested in Ben's plight, and he actually put on overalls and worked with Ben the whole afternoon, with me as a weak third hand, tool passer, and screw finder. I didn't do anything, but I got greasy to my wrists and felt very knowing" (37–38). Before sundown, the car was repaired. That repair job proved the best they had found. The bands did not have to be replaced again.

With only a little trouble of other sorts, the travelers got past Mammoth Hot Springs and Old Faithful, past Golden Gates and the Hoodoos, past Yellowstone Lake, and, even with the delicate Stargazer, past Teton Pass. The Teton Pass was not an easy achievement, though. After a first attempt, they had to turn back to find a garage. A wire had come loose, they found out. Even repaired, the car had to stop often for water and to let her engine cool while climbing the steep grade. Olive walked the distance to keep from being a burden to Stargazer. The car beat her to the summit by only five minutes.

In Idaho, they began to see Mormon settlements. The Kings had a great curiosity about the beliefs and lifestyles of the Mormons, a curiosity which they partially satisfied by a two-week sojourn in Salt Lake City. Then the journey began again on September 14:

> The desert once more, and a lumpy, scalloped roadbed, with long exquisite climbs, and miles of rocks, and then miles of 18 inch dust, sifting over everything like fine flour, choking our throats and parching our skins, with ruts a foot deep and thousands of chuck holes! We forged ahead like a boiler explosion, bang! crash! smash! expecting any minute to see Stargazer's front run merrily off leaving her back behind. Wonderful how an engine of cold metal can keep on sending up and down its valves and pistons, headless of the cars [*sic*] gymnastics! As Ben said, a car needs double joints. Often I could have wept and wrung my hands over the feats we demanded of our [car]. She has never yet failed us in a bad place. Her lapses have always occurred when help was reasonably near. (59)

The roads, as you will have surmised, were not in those days the same smooth ribbons of asphalt we know so well today. In relatively dry areas, many were, at best, hardened earth surfaces; yet even in the desert, those surfaces did not remain smooth. On September 18, road conditions caused the Kings a problem.

> We started at 7, bumping gaily over holes and ruts, till something happened—we were going very queerly.
>
> "What on earth!" said Ben—and with that came an awful crash in the rear, and I leaped out to find a back wheel 30 ft. behind us in the road.
>
> "Whew! broken axle," said Ben with a whistle. "aren't we lucky to be just 3 miles from town!" (62)

Six hours later, after the Kings had phoned for help, Stargazer was whole again; and the travelers were on their way, passing through Reno on September 21 and into California by September 24.

They easily passed inspection at the border of California and headed toward Yosemite. "Stargazer was most amiable for a season, running up the long grades in a manner quite too good for any Ford. We knew it couldn't last, and soon she wearied in well-doing. Followed a spell of hill-pushing, and then the spark control came unattached and she began to leak oil, and a steady trickle of gasoline fell from the carburetor—$.50 gasoline too" (71).

When they crawled into Yosemite late in the afternoon, they found that the nearest help for the car was sixteen miles ahead. They took these difficulties on October 6 in stride and had Stargazer repaired. Their touring resumed. All the while they wended their way slowly toward Laguna Beach, where they planned to spend the winter.

On November 5, when they were still sixty miles from their goal, car trouble struck again. Stargazer "blew up on us. Not actually, but it sounded like it—8 miles from a garage, too. So Ben made her go anyway, and her lamentations and raspings were almost unendurable to us. She must have suffered horribly. The first garage was in a pretty Quaker city called Whittier, and when a mechanic had listened to her, he said it would be several days before we could drive her" (80–81).

Several days afterward, the two completed their trip. At first they camped at Laguna. Then for two weeks, they house-sat for a woman they met there, and finally they rented a house for the winter. When they reached this last level of comfort, they stored Stargazer for the season. They relegated themselves to walking. Olive observantly wrote, "For a sight of true contentment, one should see Stargazer. Back wheels jacked up, she hibernates in the pretty brown garage beside our cottage, so comfortable, she doesn't care if she *never* goes again" (96).

She did go again, however. At the beginning of April, the Kings left the interesting people of Laguna behind and started home via the southern route. That way agreed more naturally with Stargazer's disposition; and the pushing was less frequent, as were garage visits. By May, they returned to Missouri, and the train took them home to Washington, D.C. soon after.

The Kings lived long lives together after this early trip, but Olive never wrote anything of consequence after the log of Stargazer, though her sister Frances Warfield contributed regularly to the *New Yorker* and other magazines. That she kept track of the trek across America lets us know a great deal about the culture of the country in the 1920s, gossip which F. Scott Fitzgerald and other authors of note missed.

After her return to Washington, Olive remained active at the National Cathedral, eventually donating two large windows and, at her death, leaving the cathedral property valued at over $5 million. She and Ben helped renovate Georgetown as well, and in the mid-1920s they moved to Maryland to an area now known as Crofton, where they lived on 1,500 acres of land. There they adopted four children and lived until Ben died in 1961 and Olive followed him twenty years later. Both are buried in the graveyard at St. Stephen's Episcopal Church, three or four miles from their home. The house, now known as Linthicum Walks, is on the national register of historic places, for it had a long history even before the Kings occupied it. The earliest parts of it were built before the Revolutionary War and the newer part was added in the mid-nineteenth century. The couple never demanded luxury for themselves either on the trip across America or at home, but they did enjoy helping to build America's future and to preserve its past. No wonder they wanted to see the great country they loved so much by taking one trip across it—no common achievement in the 1920s.

NOTE

1. All quotations in this essay come from the unpublished typescript "The Log of the Stargazer." The pages of the typescript which are the sources for quotations follow each quotation in parentheses. The quotations appear here with the permission of the script's owner, Margaret Argent, daughter of Olive King. The typescript, which none of the surviving relatives had ever seen previously, was found among Mrs. King's things at the Farmers National Bank in Annapolis, Maryland, after her death in 1981.

~

Learning Our Way Around the World: The Overseas Teaching Subculture

RUTH CARRINGTON

WHEN THE SMALL navy plane settled down on a hot, dusty, almost deserted airfield near the U.S. Navy base at Tsoying, Taiwan, in August 1956, any illusions I might have had about the exotic Orient vanished. This place held no more excitement than the farm country in Montana where I had grown up. No wonder they called the Taiwan assignment a "hardship area" and added extra pay for teachers who were willing to be sent to this drab, lonely location. We were each to be paid $4,500 for the school year, somewhat more than most elementary and high school teachers earned in Montana.

Riding from there to Kaohsiung, however, in the navy jeep that met us, my husband, Clyde, and I encountered a landscape entirely unfamiliar to me. We traveled on narrow dirt roads that crossed flooded rice paddies, the water held inside neat squares by earthen dikes. This was far different from the vast dry fields of wheat in Montana! Farther on, we passed even more lush fields of garden crops being watered and fertilized by coolie women in woven hats with peaked brims, their faces, arms, and legs covered with multicolored scraps of cloth to protect their skin from the sun. They carried water in buckets slung on bamboo poles across their shoulders. And some were dipping buckets into wooden tank wagons pulled by horned, black water buffalo. The tanks, we later learned, were filled with natural liquid fertilizer; this nightsoil was dipped by hand from sewers in the city and sold to the farms by the drivers of the vehicles that Americans called "honey wagons."

The jeep driver honked the horn many times as other water buffalo, ducks, chickens, and pigs wandered across the road in front of us and children stood dangerously close to watch us go by. More coolies walked along the same road, barefoot, bearing baskets filled with fish or vegetables balanced on bamboo poles. For the first time, I saw "pedicabs," large rickshaws each powered by a wiry man on a bicycle, often loaded with whole families and bundles of cabbages, or chickens in cages, being brought to market.

As we approached the city of Kaohsiung, we saw brick houses and bamboo huts, all built closely together, and crowds of men, women, and children on the narrow streets as we drove through the city itself. Pedicabs wove in and out among the crowds, as did the hundreds of bicycles and the very few taxis and other automobiles. Coming from Montana—as sparsely populated as most of Australia, where much of the state has fewer than five people per square mile—to the teeming throngs on the island of Taiwan was the first culture shock. But after two years of living there, then two years in the Philippine Islands, and three in Morocco, with trips to Hong Kong, Japan, Vietnam, Thailand, Cambodia, Singapore, Malaysia, Burma, India, Europe, and the Middle East, I discovered knowledge of the world that one cannot gain merely from seeing these places in movies, on television, and in books and magazines.

Clyde and I had been hired to teach in the Navy Dependent Schools, later known as DOD schools, under the Department of Defense. We made up part of a diverse but unique group that became a formal entity known as the Overseas Education Association, with seven thousand members at one time (now about six thousand), which sends delegates to the National Education Association annual meeting, just as the teachers' associations in the fifty states of the United States do. We taught in these schools for seven years, two at Tsoying in Taiwan, two at Subic Bay in the Philippine Islands, and three on the navy base at Port Lyautey in Morocco.

These public school teachers from all parts of the United States became world travelers after World War II, when thousands of American families were installed on military bases on five continents. Planners who set up bases for army, air force, navy, and marine occupation and surveillance had determined that having wives and children accompany military personnel added to the effectiveness of these forces. In 1950, about a hundred thousand dependents of servicemen were on overseas bases; by 1960 it was five hundred thousand. And as tours of duty lasted at least two or three years—sometimes much longer—it was necessary to provide schools for the children in these families. The American servicemen and their families, we teachers, and other civilians who worked on the bases experienced world travel as no other large group of Americans had ever done before. Although missionaries have often brought their children with them when they worked in foreign lands, their circumstances limited them in ways that did not limit us.

On this first assignment, to Taiwan, we made up part of a six-member faculty, four men and two women, who taught about 150 students, from grades one through twelve. Another young couple, the Byars, came from Colorado; the principal from Tennessee; and a single man from New York. My experience and Clyde's had been mainly in junior high and high school, but the principal asked me to teach the second grade and the other female, Eleanor Byars, the first grade. The principal took the third grade and assigned my husband a double load, forty-eight pupils in grades four and five because Clyde had insisted that the forty first and second graders should not be combined into one classroom. Clyde's large group met in an open Quonset hut that accumulated pools of water during the frequent tropical rains. Since my second graders were dismissed at 2:30 each day, I assisted Clyde by teaching music class two days and remedial reading two days. On Fridays we taught them square dancing and other folk dances. Then a parent asked me to teach social dancing to her daughter and another student. So I held a class in the base recreation hall on Saturdays for eight weeks, teaching twenty-four eager-to-learn fourth and fifth graders to waltz, foxtrot, and jitterbug. The parents organized a party for the final session on March 8, where fathers and mothers danced with the children, and they presented me with an orchid corsage, gold earrings, and a silver tray for my efforts.

On Saturdays Eleanor and I rode in our pedicab to downtown Kaohsiung, where we had our hair shampooed and set for twenty-five cents and had stylish dresses made for about two dollars each. The post exchange imported fine British cotton cloth and raw silk material, and we acquired chic wardrobes. The Taiwanese seamstresses did not need patterns. We simply brought them a picture of what we wanted, and they copied it exactly.

On one of the first trips downtown, Eleanor said, "Just think, in a year we'll be able to read all those signs." Our Chinese lessons, however, did not continue long. There were too many different dialects, too many ways of pronouncing each of the symbols. Clyde spent many hours with the young Chinese students who came to our home to practice speaking and reading English. I taught American dances to the little daughters of our neighbors, helped our housegirl, Meyo, learn to read English, and talked with the high school girls who came to see us after school. So instead of learning their language, we found ourselves bringing American culture to receptive Chinese and Taiwanese friends.

We had a lot to learn about life outside the United States. Some of the men had traveled during World War II, but for Eleanor and me, it was our first experience overseas. Fortunately, Clyde had served four years in the navy in the South Pacific and had returned to Guam with a construction crew for five years after the war. He understood both the intricacies of navy regulations and the procedures we needed to follow to live in an Asian country—to peel all fruit from the market, for example, and to soak vegetables in a chlorine solution to avoid illness.

One reason we loved Taiwan so much was that we lived among the Chinese and Taiwanese people, rather than in a compound on a military base. The island had just begun the tremendous industrial expansion of the postwar years. We lived simply in a small house made of concrete bricks, with an address that translated as "Rice Paddy Alley." We had a terrazzo floor in the living-dining room, a raised bedroom with a polished wood floor, and another small room with tatami mats on the floor and sliding doors. The square shower-tub was concrete, as were the kitchen floor and the small courtyard in the back, where the toilet was located.

Across the bamboo fence lived the Chens, a friendly, cultured family with five young daughters and one son, who had come to the island with Chiang Kai-shek's government, only seven years before we arrived in Taiwan. We learned that Mr. Chen, Chen Chong Kow, owned a fishing vessel which made trips to the Pescadores Islands. He had been an officer in the Chinese navy, then—when the navy was destroyed by the Japanese—a colonel in Chiang Kai-shek's army. A Cantonese, he had worked on the Burma Road with General "Vinegar Joe" Stilwell and spoke excellent English. His wife, Chen Wei, was from Fuchien Province and was well educated, but her English was like my classroom French; she said very little. The

Chens often brought us Chinese food, and Mrs. Chen let me watch her and take notes as she made (no recipe, of course) the chicken with cashews, ginger-flavored clams, beef with peppers, and sweet-and-sour pork. The dishes I learned to make in her kitchen have been served to appreciative guests for many years and have helped me understand the economical Chinese lifestyle, which includes, for example, cutting a small amount of chicken or pork into many pieces to serve a large family, with rice as the basic part of the meal.

We became good friends with the Chens, and we four went to the movies together, usually in their pedicab as it was larger than ours. The movies, usually American, including *To Catch a Thief, The Eddie Duchin Story, South Pacific, Moby Dick, Designing Woman,* and *Anastasia,* began with the playing of the Nationalist Chinese anthem and pictures of the Nationalist troops marching, preparing for the mythical day when they would take back their homeland from the Communists. From the Chens and other friends there we learned of the conflicts between the Chinese who had come with Chiang Kai-shek in 1949 and the Taiwanese, who had lived on the island some three hundred years, including the recent fifty years (1895–1945) when it was controlled by Japanese. Our hard-working pedicab boy, Agana, and delightful housegirl, Meyo, were Taiwanese. (One easily adopts the proprietary "our" and "my," along with servants!) The Taiwanese and Chinese had to be civil to each other, but they usually avoided social contact. The Chinese from the mainland remembered the Japanese occupation of their country and preferred not to associate with Taiwanese, who spoke Japanese as well as their own Taiwanese dialect and, if well-educated, Mandarin. One of the conclusions I was to draw from living overseas is that in every country, tensions exist between groups that the traveler does not experience until they are brought to her attention, often by some painful encounter. In Taiwan we made friends among both groups, and the younger generations became friends with each other at school. The Chens' daughters were often in our house, and the mayor's daughter (Taiwanese) became a good friend also.

During the summer session in 1957, we took our American students to the presidential troop review, where we took pictures of Chiang Kai-shek addressing the Chinese soldiers. We also saw the shah of Iran, in a black limousine, as his entourage drove through the narrow streets of Kaohsiung that summer. That part of his state visit apparently caused little commotion as the industrious Taiwanese continued about their work as usual. Our social life included official dinner parties with both American and Chinese officers in uniform, sitting with their wives at round tables in either the American or Chinese officers' club. We smiled at each other, made introductions, and talked about where we came from in the States, small talk—with the men mostly, their wives being pleasant but saying very little. Leaders of each group proposed toasts to the other. Sometimes a small orchestra played American music, and we exchanged dances with the Chinese and American couples at our table.

Occasionally, some incident caused tension between U.S. troops and the Taiwanese. Martial law was invoked in Taipei in the spring of 1957 when a serviceman named Reynolds was declared innocent of some offense. Crowds rioted and stormed the U.S. Embassy. Even in Kaohsiung, some two hundred miles south,

Americans were ordered to stay in their homes, out of the streets. From these contacts began my introduction to the realities of international politics, a view of the world that had never before concerned me outside certain of my college courses. Like most public school teachers, I was absorbed with the narrow world of my job, family, and social life. I seldom read newspapers or paid attention to radio news. Clyde and I didn't discuss politics; perhaps he did with other people. But after our two years in Taiwan, then two years teaching high school in the Philippine Islands, and three years in Morocco, I understood more about the divisions and social structures that separate people in every country. Being a part of a military operation, with its hierarchical structure, made me more aware of the privileges accorded to rank. The public schools, however, operated as a great equalizer, and students we knew formed friendships and selected leaders without regard to their fathers' positions on the base. Occasionally an officer would try to secure privileges for a student because of his position, but most teachers and administrators where we worked insisted on fairness. Discipline problems in DOD schools were rare; students knew that getting "out of line" would have repercussions at home and could even threaten a parent's military career.

Our traveling differed from tourism in that we adjusted to conditions that tourists do not experience when visiting countries on short vacations. For example, we chose not to spend a great deal for first-class American standards. When we traveled, we seldom made a reservation for lodging in advance. But we always found adequate accommodations, often very modest, with shared baths and ceiling fans, but no air conditioning, hot water, radio, television, or room service. In our travels we saw firsthand the ordinary lifestyles of each country and talked with people who were not accustomed to seeing Americans driving through the barrios and villages or across the desert country unaccompanied by a guide. On our six-week drive through Europe in 1962, we made use of the campgrounds provided and set up our green tents, cots with sleeping bags, and butane cooking tanks. Camping out was much more common throughout Europe than in the United States then, and campsites often provided laundry facilities and grocery shops as well as showers and rest rooms. Several families would be camped near us, and we would exchange information when using the common water tap. Every second or third night, we would find a country inn that would take us without a reservation or a "youth" hostel that accepted travelers of any age.

Most of our fellow teachers also ventured out, taking every opportunity to see some of the world on weekends, summer breaks, and during Thanksgiving, Christmas, and Easter holidays. Like us, they wanted to see and experience as much as they could on modest budgets. While teaching in Taiwan we visited the Philippine Islands, made several trips to Hong Kong, and in the summer of 1957 toured Southeast Asia for three weeks, spending a few days each in Singapore, Bangkok, Saigon, Angkor Wat and Pnom Penh in Cambodia, and in Kuala Lumpur, making a brief visit to a rubber plantation. The young Scottish manager, Mr. Edington, welcomed us graciously and invited us for tea in his large bungalow. Later he had one of the workers tap a rubber tree to show us the process. He showed how they poured the white liquid into large vats and solidified it into sheets to be shipped elsewhere for manufacturing. It was early evening when we went out and we saw only a few of the Malayan workers, but they had an easy, relaxed relationship with the manager and seemed happy to show us how the work was done. Mr. Edington told us, though, of the crisis a few years before, when many of the English managers were murdered by terrorists. We were to hear similar stories of anticolonial rebellion from missionaries in Morocco a few years later, as they related narrow escapes when hundreds of French farmers were massacred there during the terror of 1956. Our summer visit to Malaysia in 1957 coincided with the country's independence from the British, and the Malayans were preparing to celebrate the event on August 31. Back in Kuala Lumpur, at a newly built railroad station, we talked with Malayan university students who were eager to tell us about the struggles with both the British colonial government and the Communist guerrillas in gaining their independence. They admitted there would be problems in the new government, but in their talk and expressions they showed pride and optimism.

The second two years, in the Philippine Islands, we taught in a brand new American high school on the navy base at Subic Bay, appreciating the privileges of dining and dancing in officers' clubs, shopping at the large post exchange on the navy base, and enjoying the year-round warm weather, the tennis courts, and the Olympic-sized swimming pool. Our modern two-bedroom, American-style house on the base had tropical wood furniture and was surrounded by a lawn and blooming gardenia bushes. We spent several weekends in the cool luxury of the navy's "r and r" resort in the mountains at Baguio. During our first Christmas vacation there, we explored the various islands of the Philippines by plane, making overnight stops, for example, on Negros; Cebu, where Magellan is buried; and Zamboanga, where we saw the sights in a "calesa," a light, horse-drawn carriage. We sailed in a "venta," a tiny native boat with colored sails that looks like a child's toy, to little Santa Cruz Island, then flew in a small plane to Jolo, where rebel Moros, the Muslims of the southern islands, were still fighting Filipino troops. The mayor of Jolo treated us like honored guests and gave Clyde a Sulu hat, once worn by a native of that southern archipelago, as a unique souvenir of our visit. Shaped like a pillbox of tightly woven straw, it was decorated with boars' teeth and a strip of red cloth with white shirt buttons sewn onto it.

During the summer of 1959 we went to Japan for two weeks, visiting Tokyo again, where we attended a kabuki theater and a glittering Japanese musical show with dancers like the Rockettes. In Nikko the colorful shrines to the shoguns are large and impressive, but the natural beauty of the waterfalls and lakes in the national park impressed us more. In Hakone we took a cable car up the side of a mountain at night, from where we could see spectacular fireworks and look down at the colorful costumes and huge flaming torches of a folk dance called the "bon odoro." At Nara we fed tame deer. We stayed in country inns, where we wore the customary cotton kimonos, called "yukatas," took hot baths in wooden tubs, and tried the flat, green, rather bitter seaweed that was served for breakfast on low tables placed on tatami mats. We made the tour of Pearl Island, the Mikimoto pearl farm where we were shown the process of making cultured pearls. We bought pearl jewelry in the Yokohama post exchange for all our women relatives.

With a dozen Japanese travelers, we toured the Peace Museum in Hiroshima, where photographs show the destruction left by the bomb. The shell of one building near the blast remains as a reminder. Otherwise, even then, the city had been rebuilt, with wider streets. I thought we would see many people who had been scarred by burns, but I saw only one or two. The skeleton of that one structure, the peace monument, and the museum were the only evidences we saw of the destruction of the city.

In the years we traveled in the Orient, North Africa, Europe, and the Middle East, we never encountered any animosity toward us as Americans, nor any outright resentment of us personally for the obvious differences between our comparative wealth and the widespread poverty in the places we were. In Calcutta, on our Christmas visit in 1959, we saw coolies wearing only breechcloths and pouring hot tar in blistering heat. That night we attended a performance of part of India's great epic, the Ramayana, where we saw more affluent Indians, the men in dark business suits and the women wearing jewels and gorgeous saris of every color.

The World Agriculture Fair was being held in Old Delhi, where we stayed in a hotel that housed American agricultural advisers and some 4-H young people. We became acquainted with an American Indian couple (Hopis) who were demonstrating their Native American crafts at the fair. We spent an entire day at the fair and went back a second time before we left Delhi. We watched a two-hour program of classical dance performed by a single Indian woman, accompanied by a small group of musicians. One exhibit, a display of incubators and brooders in which little chicks were being raised on wire, especially attracted the attention of families there. For some reason we, too, attracted as much attention as any of the exhibits. We were constantly surrounded by a throng of people who regarded us with great interest. Two students attached themselves to us, and one of them invited us to his home. He was sixteen years old and was to study in England the next year. I do not remember why we did not go, but we wished afterward that we had.

We hired a man with a 1940s Bentley for a drive to see the Taj Mahal at Agra. On the way we saw peacocks running wild and a jackal. The driver pointed out remains of ancient fortresses scattered throughout the countryside, reminders of violent tribal warfare in India's past. We had toured the Red Fort in Delhi, a medieval fortress with walls of red stone. In the pink city of Jaipur, named for the same stone, we explored a palace built during the Mogul period, which had ramps for the elephants that brought people into the palace. In Benares we rode on a kind of houseboat along the Ganges, with a philosopher-guide who explained to us the importance of the Ganges to Hindus, the custom of bathing in the waters to heal disease, and the "burning ghats," where family members cremated their dead along the riverbanks and put their ashes into the sacred river. We marveled at the lengths of multicolored saris displayed in the silk markets and bought them as gifts for the families at home, where some of them were made into dresses. Until it is draped by the skillful hands of an Indian woman, a sari is merely five meters of cloth. Again, we saw the contrast between those who, like us average Americans, could afford to travel and buy luxuries, and the thousands of others who lacked bare necessities.

We made friends in every country and for some time exchanged letters and holiday greetings with the Chens. In the Philippine Islands we met Filipino teachers and a couple we liked very much, who took us with them to the annual ball, sponsored by a society organized just for that purpose. The men wore black trousers and beautiful embroidered dress shirts called "barong tagalogs," but the women wore costly formal gowns of varied style and fabric. Filipinos love all kinds of dancing, and the ballroom or the town plaza looks like a kaleidoscope as they waltz, tango, and perform the modern ballroom dances. One evening as we walked through the lobby of the Manila Hotel, we saw the "upper level" of Filipino society arriving for a ball. We asked a guest what the occasion was, and he, a Dr. Bautista, graciously invited us to sit with the group at his table. It was the grandest social affair I had ever witnessed. Such a display of magnificent gowns as they performed the opening "rigodon," like an intricate grand march!

We wore the native costumes and enjoyed the dancing. I even tried doing the tinikling and other folk dances of the country. My American students invited young people from local Filipino high schools to parties on the base and to exchange musical programs.

One of the new experiences for postwar overseas teachers was the availability of servants. Like the navy families, we were expected to hire cooks, gardeners, housekeepers, and chauffeurs, or some combination of those. Their wages were set by local custom, and we were warned not to raise those amounts as doing so would upset the balance that had been established. Our perfect housekeeper in the Philippines, Rosa Fuentes, who took over all the cleaning, laundry, and cooking (she made delicious chicken adobo), for example, received only forty dollars a month, the maximum because she was considered by Americans on the base to be the best housekeeper one could find in Subic Bay. Agana, our pedicab boy in Taiwan, received fifteen dollars a month for being at our disposal all day Saturday and Sunday as well as evenings during the week. The rest of the time he was at his regular stand. Although I realized the necessity of adhering to local hiring policies, I caught a glimmer of understanding of the world's economic realities.

One of the benefits of overseas teaching was that some of the people who worked for us became like younger sisters and brothers. We taught them to read English; they taught us words of their language and invited us to their homes. From them we learned more about the family life and the economics of their countries. In Taiwan I had marveled at the efficiency of Mrs. Chen's housekeeping and the compactness of their family home, where two adults and six children lived congenially in two small rooms. In Morocco, we sat on small cushions around a low table in the home of our maid, drinking sweet mint tea and eating rich sweet cakes. The table covered most of the room.

As we traveled, Clyde mentioned certain important people and events: in Saigon, for instance, in 1957, he commented on seeing a large picture of Bao Dai, a name that meant something to him, but nothing to me. My memory of Saigon then is of French-looking shops, almost empty, since the French owners had fled in 1954 after the defeat at Dien Bien Phu. We saw short, dark men in uniforms and green berets, and we rode in a "motorcyclo," a mechanized pedicab whose driver spoke French.

He asked us in French which way we wanted to go, and when he understood my French reply, I was thrilled. It was the first time I had spoken French outside the college classroom. Later, in Morocco and other places, knowing some French helped me communicate with native people who explained to me the injustices they felt under the colonial system.

We happened to be in Manila on Rizal Day, the last day of 1957, when President Carlos Garcia was inaugurated. We saw the parade in honor of Jose Rizal y Mercado, born in 1861, who showed in his novels the evils of Spanish rule, inspired Philippine nationalism, and worked for political and social reforms. In 1896, the year of the Philippine insurrection, an unjust military court ordered that Rizal be shot. In the parade were Vice President Macapagal and the old hero of Philippine independence, Emilio Aguinaldo, then age eighty-eight, who had fought first against Spain and later against the United States. Such events gave me a heightened sense of history.

I said earlier that I was a typical "apolitical American" when I went overseas. That is, although I had heard lectures comparing different political philosophies, had participated in college debates about the role of government, and had listened to a few discussions about inequalities in society and abuses of human freedom, I had never thought deeply about wrongs in society or taken actions to promote justice. When we traveled in the mid-1950s, television had not yet brought images of political campaigns and the Third World into our homes. By the time we returned to the United States, to attend graduate school, the ferment of the sixties had begun. Having been in Saigon, I attended meetings where faculty and students discussed the political situation in Vietnam. I began thinking seriously about our country's role in world affairs. We teachers were not treated as ugly Americans. Wherever we went, people liked us. Barefoot children in the Philippines gave us a thumbs-up sign as they said, "Americano, O.K.!" But I had also heard Filipino teachers there talk about land reform and about the campaign of the Huks. I had seen bar girls in Taiwan and in Olongapo, and I knew that the American presence in these places was not universally welcomed. Though the French and Arabic teachers in Morocco were charming and seemed to like us, I sensed their reservations about Americans in general. They advised us not to discuss politics as we drove across Algeria, Tunisia, and Libya. We were at the beach in Morocco the night King Mohammed V died, and we were warned to stay on the base to avoid political unrest during a change in power. Foreign residents told us about the "terror" that had occurred before Morocco received its independence, just four years before we arrived. And I had conversations with our teacher of Arabic, a Palestinian refugee, who lived more as an internationalist than a partisan, the type who, Cervantes says, "saw life and saw it whole." As we went through each country on our drive around the Mediterranean, I studied guidebooks to find historical sites on our way. Firsthand observation piques one's curiosity about a country's history and politics.

We may not have been the typical visiting Americans in the three countries where we lived. I probably read more books than most, Clyde talked more with workers and students in every country, and we both belonged to a tiny group who discussed Plato and Aristotle, Lucretius, and Descartes in the Great Books discussion groups on the base in Port Lyautey. During the winter a troupe from the Comedie Francaise, sponsored by Les Amis du Theatre Francais, presented plays in Kenitra; we saw *La Vie Est un Songe*, *Amphitryon*, *Hernani*, *Les Caprices de Marianne*, and *Le Cid* during the 1963 season. I was able to buy copies of the plays at the French bookstore so I could read them through first; but the dialogue was much too fast for my untrained ear. It was the same at the Cine Club that met in Kenitra. We saw classic films, such as *Les Remorques*, starring Jean Gabin and Michele Morgan; *Le Mort de Siegfried* (1923, German); and Bergman's *Une Lecon d'Amour* (in Swedish, with French subtitles), and we listened to the discussion of the movies afterward. Though I understood very little, I was impressed—amazed—at the seriousness and intensity with which the audiences analyzed the films; I had never encountered Americans who talked about the movies they saw! We also played bridge, and we were, I believe, representative of the thousands of DOD teachers who have transplanted to foreign soil classrooms like those in the suburbs of America. A few were less adaptable; they missed the amenities and familiar scenes of home and often stayed only two years, or even managed to leave at the end of the first. But we have known teachers who took families with three or four children on their teaching assignments to not one but several bases in Europe, the Middle East, Asia, Africa, or the Pacific islands. My friend Eleanor Byars, who taught with us in Taiwan, continued teaching for thirty years in the Philippine Islands, Morocco, Spain, Italy, Germany, Turkey, and Spain again, retiring in 1986. She has settled down in Colorado and says she never wants to get on a plane again. As I said, we were unique—but diverse. *My* story is different!

After those seven years as a DOD teacher, the circumstances of my life changed dramatically. I began to read the diaries I had kept, sift through those experiences, and then to write about them. During those years we traveled I had also set educational goals for myself: to become fluent in French; to learn some Arabic (which we did, in Morocco); to read as many significant books as I could. For example, I read the Bible from cover to cover in 1959 and 1960, and another year I searched out and read biographies and autobiographies, those by Benjamin Franklin, Lincoln Steffens, Pearl Buck, and Clarence Darrow. I read the plays and novels that I knew should have been part of my background as an English teacher. And I read some travel books: *Kim* and *Home to India* when we were going to India; *Tales of the Alhambra* (twice, when we made two trips to Granada); Agnes Keith's *Bare Feet in the Palace* (about the Philippine Islands) and *Three Came Home* (about her life in a Japanese prison camp); Edith Wharton's *Morocco*; *Highlights of Spanish History*; and Mark Twain's *Innocents Abroad*. I kept lists of the books I had read, even tallied the number each year. I also learned to account for my expenditures as Clyde was extremely conscious of not wasting money; he asked me to write down the cost of each item I bought. That habit has helped me to live and travel more economically than I could have otherwise.

In 1965 I was in New York City, writing about my experiences overseas, when the Tonkin Gulf incident occurred. The protest meetings that followed it, hearing Senators Morse and Gruening at the teach-ins at Columbia University, a debate at the Overseas Press Club, and speakers such as Paul Krassner (editor of *The Realist*) at street rallies—all these catapulted me into the peace movement. Out of that, I became involved in political life and have since become a quiet activist. As an internationalist, I relate to others who are concerned about world affairs and who are involved in efforts to promote world understanding. The contrast between our privileged lives and those in places we visited sharpened my awareness of the inequities in the world, the contrast between our affluent American society and the way of life of most other people of the world. The differences between rich and poor in the countries we visited often presented themselves so starkly that I could not ignore them. For example, we took our pupils to Rabat on a Friday to watch the weekly ceremony when the king went to prayer in an ornate gold carriage that we were told had been given to his great-grandfather by Queen Victoria. We saw several of his other palaces and watched his plane land after a visit to the United States—loaded, we were told, with furnishings for his twelve homes, gifts, they said, from President Kennedy. And in our drives through the deserts and mountains of Morocco, we had seen barefooted children and workers who appeared to own nothing, to have only the one garment they wore. We had been guests in their tiny, crowded homes.

As to the effect this subculture has had on others, I can only speculate. Perhaps it gave someone the germ of an idea which became the Peace Corps. I have always believed that a chief benefit of that agency has been to give Americans the opportunity to experience the real world outside their own country. As travelers write letters and show slides of their travels, they open up possibilities and arouse in others a desire to see foreign places. The travels of those thousands of Americans overseas, service personnel and their dependents, undoubtedly broadened their outlook. In 1985 I attended a reunion of the students who attended George Dewey High School at Subic Bay in the Philippine Islands during the 1960s. Their happy expressions and conversation, as they met again after many years of separation, showed that their school years overseas gave them strong bonds. And the teachers who loved to travel made up an important part of the children's responses to being overseas.

Though I never again traveled as intensely, I have returned to Europe four times, have spent eighteen months in Asia, and have visited in Australia, New Zealand, and Latin America. I have continued to make friends in new places around the world, and I carry on a fairly extensive correspondence with them. Many of us now look at the world as our community and feel a responsibility for its welfare. Those years of teaching overseas led me into more remarkable adventures, including the peace movement, then politics, more travel, and further teaching, writing, and learning as a part of the Fulbright program. For me, being a part of the DOD overseas teaching experience has made a considerable difference in the way I react to events in my own country and in the world. Devoted as ever to my own biological family, I have come to feel that people in the countries I visited belong to my extended family, and I am concerned about them. Writing afterward about those years of travel, I called that section of the book "My Other Family." For just as my essential character was largely formed by the close-knit associations with parents and siblings on the isolated farm in Montana, so the person I have become has been enlarged by the new experiences, the friendships, and the knowledge of the world I gained in those seven years of travel, discovery, and discipline as an overseas teacher.

~

Annotated Bibliography

IF THE TRAVEL CULTURE is as broad a field as we say it is, then of course its bibliography is bound to leave things out. First, I am leaving out the practical travel guide books, though many of them go beyond the practical, and some are downright poetic. Limiting the bibliography to books about travel, I omit almost all the failures. "Failure," of course, is subjective: too much interior journeying—too much "looking for oneself"—does me in, but my threshold may come sooner (or later) than yours. Obviously, I will have missed some books; also, every good novel, memoir, autobiography, or biography, and other "true" stories, give a sense of place and sometimes of journey too. In early 1997, for example, Walter Cronkite's *A Reporter's Life* gives a sweet sense of growing up in Kansas in the early years of the twentieth century and an unwitting, "shadow"-picture of the travel in this century that was most significant to many men and women: the "travail" through war. Many superlative writers saw a place askew (my call) because their eye was on their subject or themselves—for example, Norman Mailer, on the 1968 Democratic and Republican Party conventions, and on Norman Mailer (of course), in *Miami and the Siege of Chicago.* Nonetheless, Mailer's peripheral (sometimes downright blind) view is intriguing because his mind's eye is so superb. This bibliography, then, can only *introduce* the novel, autobiography, and so on, as travel writing; it is arbitrary, is it not, to limit the fiction writers to those who wrote at least one travel book per se? Who caught Paris (or New York) better than F. Scott Fitzgerald, especially in his short stories? Perhaps John Cheever did New York better, in his short stories. Or perhaps Thomas Wolfe did . . . I will add to the genres introduced some that may be new to you, such as cookbooks; but I will also put off—sadly—filmography (for example, that haunting picture of the dark island off the state of Washington in *Five Easy Pieces*). This is, however, a start.

~

Adams, Percy. *Travel Literature and the Evolution of the Novel.* Lexington: University of Kentucky Press, 1982. Valuably, it places travel literature in the (roiling) mainstream.

Adler, Judith. "Travel as Performed Art," *American Journal of Sociology* 94:6 (May 1989): 1366–91.

——. "Youth On The Road: Reflections on the History of Tramping," *Annals of Tourism Research*, 12 (1985), 335–54.

Alexander, Caroline. *The Way to Xanadu*. New York: Knopf, 1994. Alexander visits places she thinks moved Samuel Taylor Coleridge to write "Kubla Khan" (1797): Shangdu (Chinese Mongolia); Florida's swamps; Srinagar, in Kashmir; and "Mt. Abora," in Ethiopia.

Alexander, Lamar. *Six Months Off: An American Family's Australian Adventure*. New York: Morrow Quill, 1988. The 1996 Republican Presidential candidate and Tennessee politician's story on the family more than the place, thus strong(er) on traveling than the places traveled to.

Algren, Nelson. *Chicago: City on the Make*. Chicago: University of Chicago Press, 1987. A tough guy's romantic view of the city on the lake, on the make.

Appiah, Kwame Anthony, and Henry Louis Gates, Jr., eds., *The Dictionary of Global Culture*, New York: Knopf, 1997. "Madres de la Plaza de Mayo, Maeterlinck, Magna Carta, Mahabharata": this is a new world encyclopedia, indeed; and it is the opening shot in the battle between the global and the multinational cultures. See introduction to this text, and Shapiro entry, below.

Ascanio, Pam. *White Men Don't Have Juju: An American Couple's Adventure Through Africa*. Chicago: Noble, 1992. A Florida couple burned out in social service and academia spend a year in Africa. Practical information too, is given in the notes.

Batten, Charles L. *Pleasurable Instruction: Form and Convention in Eighteenth Century Travel Literature*. Berkeley: University of California Press, 1978.

Bedford, Simi. *Yoruba Girl Dancing*. New York: Penguin, 1994; London: Heinemann, 1991. In the genre of women's coming of age and clash of cultures.

Bell, Gertrude. *Syria: The Desert and the Sown*. London: Heinemann, 1907 (out of print). A classic for Arabists (see Robert Kaplan, *The Arabists*).

Bernstein, Jeremy. *In the Himalayas: Journeys Through Nepal, Tibet, and Bhutan*. Rev. ed. New York: Lyons & Burford, 1996. Photographs. A pioneer in the U.S. "mountain aesthetic" (a view he sold to William Shawn, the legendary editor of *The New Yorker*, for which he then wrote), the 1996 book is a revision of Bernstein's account of his treks through Nepal, first written in 1967. He added Bhutan and Tibet (newly reopened by the Chinese) for a 1989 revision and rewrote the whole book after a 1994 trip. The history and peoples of the region—the Sherpas, the Chinese Communists, and so on—as well as the unbelievable mountains are here in a definitive book of the area by a definitive figure in the craft and art of joining science, travel, and teaching.

The Best of Granta Travel. London: Granta Books, 1991. Includes the men in the spring 1989 issue of *Granta* and also Gabriel García Márquez, "Watching the Rain in Galicia"; Martha Gellhorn, "Cuba Revisited"; Salman Rushdie; and others.

Blackburn, Julia. *Daisy Bates in the Desert*. New York: Pantheon, 1994. A postmodern, personally infused re-creation/biography of Daisy Bates in the Australian desert in 1913, at age fifty-four.

Blaise, Clark, and Bharati Mukhergee. *Days and Nights in Calcutta*. 1977. St. Paul, MN: Hungry Mind Press, 1995. Michael Gorra in *The New York Times Book Review* calls it "one of the best travel books about India," especially in the "vivid" outsider's view Blaise has of the country of his then new wife, the fiction writer.

Blocksma, Mary. *The Fourth Coast: Exploring the Great Lakes Coastline from the St. Lawrence Seaway to the Boundary Waters of Minnesota*. New York: Penguin, 1995. A fresh region—in people as well as place—from which Blocksma draws uncommon history and encounters.

Blythe, Ronald. *Akenfield: Portrait of an English Village.* 1969. New York: Pantheon, 1980. A model social study of a place.

Boorstin, Daniel. *The Image,* 1987. The 25th anniversary edition of the classic cultural study originally published in 1961as *The Image or What Happened to the American Dream.* See introduction to this text. The chapter, "From Traveler to Tourist: The Lost Art of Travel," is particularly historic to travel culture.

Boswell, James. *Boswell on the Grand Tour: Germany and Switzerland, 1764–1765.* The Yale Edition of the Private Papers of James Boswell. New York: McGraw, 1953.

——. *Boswell on the Grand Tour: Italy, Corsica, France, 1765–1766.* The Yale Edition of the Private Papers of James Boswell. New York: McGraw, 1955.

——. *Boswell's Journal of a Tour to the Hebrides with Samuel Johnson, LL.D, 1773.* 1785. The Yale Edition of the Private Papers of James Boswell. New York: McGraw, 1962.

——. *James Boswell's London Journal, 1762–1763,* edited by Frederick A. Pottle. New Haven: Yale University Press, 1992.

Bourdieu, Pierre. *Distinction.* London: Routledge & Kegan Paul, 1984. See introduction to this book.

Brown, Dona. *Inventing New England: Regional Tourism in the Nineteenth Century.* Washington, DC: Smithsonian Institution Press, 1995. Illustrations. Scholarly but readable, and ironic, history of how "New England" was invented in the nineteenth century as a middle-class American tourist venue and how the tourist business was created after New Englanders wiped out their first occupations: whaling, herring fishing, lumbering, and farming (plowing "rocks," as New Englanders say). Brown focuses on the Maine coast, the Massachusetts islands of Martha's Vineyard and Nantucket, the White Mountains, Vermont, and twentieth-century Cape Cod.

Brown, J. D. *Digging to China: Down and Out in the Middle Kingdom.* New York: Soho, 1991. Brown, a writer living in Xi'an, makes Xi'an so dreary and *not* adventurous that, after reading him, my son, working in Asia, chose against traveling in China.

Browne, Ray B. "A Lion's Share of Tourism in the 21st Century." In *Preview 2001+: Popular Culture Studies in the Future,* edited by Ray B. Browne and Marshall Fishwick. Bowling Green, OH: Bowling Green State University Popular Press, 1995. See introduction to this book.

Bryson, Bill. *The Lost Continent: Travel in Small-Town America.* New York: Harper, 1989.

——. *Neither Here Nor There: Travels in Europe.* New York: Morrow, 1992. Bryson is laugh-out-loud funny, but he also unearths the telling truths (in the details).

——. *Notes from a Small Island.* New York: Morrow, 1995. Bryson on Britain.

Burnaby, Frederick. *On Horseback Through Asia Minor.* 1877. New York: Oxford, 1996. In 1876 newspapers reported Turkish atrocities against Belgian Christians. Burnaby sought the truth, balancing cases made by Muslims, Christians, and "others" (Kurds, Armenians, Turks). Timely.

Buzzi, Aldo. *Journey to the Land of the Flies and Other Travels.* Trans. Ann Goldstein. New York: Random House, 1996. Essays revised for the English translation on Italy and Sicily (less known places, such as Gorgonzola) and Russia, particularly its writers and architecture (Buzzi, appropriately in love with the nutty paradoxes that are [in part] Russia, is an architect in Milan).

Cahill, Tim. *Jacquars Ripped My Flesh.* New York: Bantam, 1987. The first collection of the journalist (*Rolling Stone, Outside,* etc.). Under the humor and machismo beats a (funny) ecologist.

——. *Pass the Butterworms.* New York: Vintage, 1997. Honduran rivers, the Mongolian grassland, the Peruvian jungle, and more. The Savvy Traveler *Newsletter* (Spring 1997) says of *Butterworms* that Cahill writes "with the crazed humor his fans relish."

——. *Pecked to Death by Ducks.* New York: Vintage, 1993. Reprinted essays of adventures from Baja to the Marquesas and to Kuwait's oil fires; paeans to the llama, the moose, and others.

——. *Road Fever: A High-Speed Travelogue.* 1991. New York: Vintage Departures, 1992. From Tierra del Fuego to Prudhoe Bay in twenty-three and a half days (a record)—cheaply, "by the seat" (bike).

——. *A Wolverine Is Eating My Leg.* New York: Vintage, 1989. "Vertical Caving," "Drunken Diving for Poison Sea Snakes"; the bad guys ("An On-the-Scene Report from Guyana"); good animals ("Love and Death in Gorilla Country"); and other adventures and eccentrics, all without a false note.

Capote, Truman. *The Muses Are Heard.* New York: Random House Modern Library Paperbacks, 1956. The novelist's account of a visit to the Soviet Union, rare in 1955, and like everything by Capote, rare in its writing. The wounded war veteran who pours his vodka into his empty eye socket: now there's an unforgettable image.

Caro, Ina. *The Road from the Past: Traveling Through History in France.* New York: Harcourt Brace Harvest, 1994. Provence, Languedoc, the Dordogne, Loire Valley, and the Ile-de-France. Thick, complex history for Francophiles.

Chase, Sarah Leah, and Jonathan Chase. *Saltwater Seasonings: Good Food from Coastal Maine.* Boston: Little, Brown, 1992. Photographs by Cary Hazlegrove. An A+ example of the popular "multi-genre," the cook- and place-book.

Chatwin, Bruce. *Anatomy of Restlessness: Selected Writings, 1969–1989.* New York: Viking Penguin, 1996. Collection of unpublished or generally unknown essays, stories, and reviews.

——. *In Patagonia.* 1979. New York: Penguin, 1988. See also Chatwin and Paul Theroux, *Nowhere Is a Place: Travels in Patagonia.* San Francisco: Sierra, 1992.

——. *The Songlines.* New York: Penguin, 1988. The masterwork of the "travel writer's travel writer": Australia (the Aborigines) and Chatwin's metaphysic that travel—"walking"—is the human being's natural life.

——. *The Viceroy of Ouidah.* 1980. New York: Penguin, 1988. A novel about a Brazilian "nobody" who went to Dahomey for the slave trade and became the viceroy. It is the basis for Werner Herzog's film *Cobra Verde.*

Clark, Miles. *High Endeavours: The Extraordinary Life and Adventures of Miles and Beryl Smeeton.* New York: HarperCollins, 1991. Tracking the adventures of a dauntless twentieth-century pair: sailing, trekking, and climbing all over the world, and pioneering in the western Canadian wilderness.

Clarke, Thurston. *California Fault: Search for the Spirit of a State Along the San Andreas.* New York: Ballantine, 1996. Regional history and the gimmick of seismology.

——. *Equator: A Journey.* New York: Morrow, 1988. From 1984 to 1987, Clarke traveled the line of the Equator, through strange, intriguing places and people in South America, Africa, and the South Pacific.

Clavell, James. "The Asian Saga": *Shogun:* 1600; *Tai-Pan:* 1841; *Gai-Jin:* 1862; *King Rat:* 1945; *Noble House:* 1963; *Whirlwind:* 1979. New York: Delacorte, 1993; Dell, 1994. Japan, Hong Kong, a Japanese World War II prison camp, Iran—all novels of the Caucasian meeting the East. *Shogun, King Rat,* and *Noble House* were also filmed. If the twenty-first is the "Pacific Century," these topical books and films will be seen as wavelets in the sea-change.

Cliff, Michelle. *No Telephone to Heaven.* 1987. New York: Vintage, 1989. Autobiographical novel by a Jamaican creole (and poetic writer) divided between her homeland and the sophistications of the United States and London.

Cocker, Mark. *Loneliness and Time: The Story of British Travel Writing.* New York: Pantheon, 1992. A (still) rare, and excellent, scholarly overview of travel literature.

Cody, Robin. *Voyage of a Summer Sun: Canoeing the Columbia River.* New York: Knopf, 1995. Cody, a novelist who grew up on the rivers of Oregon, brings knowledge of what makes the river give, and take, and he brings love, but not an intrusive self.

Condon, Sean. *Sean and David's Long Drive.* Melbourne: Lonely Planet, 1996. Two guys, four thousand miles around Australia in a '66 Falcon. Quirky insights and subtle, sharp writing.

Cooper, Rand Richards. "Travel." *New York Times Book Review,* June 5, 1994, 54–55, 61. Besides the annual summer review of books, a typography of travel literature.

Coster, Graham. *A Thousand Miles from Nowhere: Trucking Two Continents.* New York: North Point and Farrar, Straus & Giroux, 1995. A Brit rides with truckers, first to Russia, then west across America. A different, engrossing viewpoint on traveling.

Cox, Christopher R. *Chasing the Dragon: Into the Heart of the Golden Triangle.* New York: Henry Holt, 1996. Cox, a Boston *Herald* reporter, and Jay F. Sullivan, a Vietnam veteran on his ninth trip looking for U.S. POWs in Southeast Asia, travel in Thailand and Myanmar (formerly Burma), turning up the issues that are dilemmas: heroin grown and smuggled by poor farmers, the spread of AIDS, Thailand's sex industry, the Shan people's revolt against "their" aggressive Myanmar government (the Shan leaders promising to stamp out opium). Timely politics and precise writing to boot.

Coyne, John, ed. *Going Up Country: Essays by Peace Corps Writers.* New York: Scribners, 1994. A collection of Peace Corps members who turned out to be leading today's brigade of travel writers.

Crossette, Barbara. *So Close to Heaven: The Vanishing Buddhist Kingdom of the Himalayas.* New York: Vintage Departure, 1996. Bhutan in particular.

Dalrymple, William. *City of Djinns.* 1993. London: HarperCollins Flamingo, 1994. The British author of *In Xanadu* lived in Delhi, and his artist-wife Olivia Fraser illustrates this memoir, novel-like in its vivid detail and characterization. *Djinns* is the best kind of history as it takes off from the present to the past in reverse chronology: to the Sikh massacres after the assassination of Indira Gandhi, the partition of India, the British empire, the ancient Mughal empire, and so to prehistory through archaeology.

Danziger, Nick. *Danziger's Adventures: From Miami to Kabul.* 1992. New York: HarperCollins Flamingo, 1993. The sequel to *Danziger's Travels* from an epitomical contemporary writer-photographer "daredevil."

David-Neel, Alexandra. *My Journey to Lhasa.* 1927. Boston: Beacon, 1993. A classic in a new edition, with a foreword by the Dalai Lama. At age fifty-five, disguised as a pilgrim and trekking through amazing terrain, David-Neel became the first European woman (she was French) to enter Lhasa, the forbidden city of Tibet—where her *Journey* shows her to be awesomely intrepid and innovative. (An unforgettable excerpt is in Mary Morris, ed., *Maiden Voyages*; see also Bernstein, who writes about her.)

Davidson, Cathy N. *36 Views of Mount Fuji: On Finding Myself in Japan.* New York: Dutton, 1993. Based on her teaching at Kansai Women's University in 1990, coming home (?) to the United States, and three further visits to Japan.

Davidson, Robyn. *Desert Places.* New York: Viking Penguin, 1996. Trekking with the Rabari, pastoral nomads of Rajasthan in northwest India. Like *Tracks,* adventure and the poignancy of threatened cultures (but see Kobak entry for a negative review).

——. *Tracks.* 1980. New York: Vintage, 1995. Alone—but with dog, four camels, snakes, including human ones (Australian men).

Didion, Joan. *Salvador.* 1983. New York: Vintage International, 1994. Didion is a journalist-novelist whose field is politics and whose scene is usually a humid "backwater." Reportage like *Salvador* and *Miami* is the straightforward "nonfiction" form of novels such as *Democracy,* one of the best books on southeast Asia (1984; Vintage International, 1995), *A Book of Common Prayer,* on Central America (1977; Vintage International, 1995), and *The Last Thing He Wanted,* on the Caribbean—and (not uncommonly for Didion) Hollywood (New York: Knopf, 1996).

Dinesen, Isak. *Out of Africa and Shadows on the Grass.* 1937. New York: Vintage, 1989. The Danish Baroness Karen Blixen's lyrical memoirs of her years as a plantation owner in the veldt. The basis of the Meryl Streep–Robert Redford movie.

Doughty, Charles M. *Travels in Arabia Deserta.* 2 vols. 1888. New York: Dover, 1980. A classic influence on U.S. missionaries and diplomats to the Middle East. See Gertrude Bell.

Douglas, Norman. *Old Calabria.* 1915. Introduction by Jon Manchip White, 1993. Evanston, IL: Marlboro Northwestern University Press, 1996. Another classic work of travel literature, reissued.

Duncan, David Douglas. *Yankee Nomad: A Photographic Odyssey.* New York: Holt, Rinehart & Winston, 1966. The autobiography of one of the modern world's best photographers, and a writer not to be sneezed at either.

Dunlop, M. H. *Traveling the Nineteenth-Century American Interior.* New York: Basic, 1995. Scholarly but lively summary of how foreign travelers, such as Charles Dickens, the wonderfully gimlet-eyed Frances Trollope, and her son Anthony, the novelist, compared the United States to Europe: we're gauche, yes, but—whether they like it or not—democratic too.

Durrell, Lawrence. *Prospero's Cell: A Guide to the Landscape and Manners of the Island of Corfu* (1945); *Reflections on a Marine Venus* (1953); and *Sicilian Carousel* (1976). New York: Marlowe, 1996. Lyrical, lucid re-releases (*Reflections* is on the island of Rhodes). Durrell's novels—indeed, his whole corpus—could be in this bibliography.

Enzensberger, Hans Magnus. *Europe, Europe: Forays Into a Continent.* New York: Pantheon, 1989. Political science focusing on change and Sweden, Italy, Spain, Portugal, Poland, and Hungary—not the main players; in this, the West German Enzensberger was prescient on European politics before the big change at the turn of the decade of the 1990s.

Esquivel, Laura. *Like Water for Chocolate.* 1992. Garden City, NY: Doubleday Anchor, 1993. Not travel literature (any more than Enzensberger is just a travel writer), Esquivel's novel is as rich a picture of Mexican culture as the recipes that thread the magical, funny story.

Farber, Thomas. *On Water.* Hopewell, NJ: Ecco Travels, 1994. Literary and mythic wellsprings.

Fenton, James. *All the Wrong Places: Adrift in the Politics of the Pacific Rim.* New York: Grove-Atlantic, 1987. The fall of Saigon, wartime Cambodia, the Corazon Aquino revolution in the Philippines, and more from what is now history.

Fermor, Patrick Leigh. *Between the Woods and the Water: On Foot to Constantinople from the Hook of Holland: The Middle Danube to the Iron Gates.* 1986. New York: Penguin, 1987.

——. *A Time of Gifts: On Foot to Constantinople: From the Hook of Holland to the Middle Danube.* 1977. New York: Penguin, 1979. The British adventurer recorded his walk across *Mittel Europa* in the mid-1930s when Hitler was a shadow on the "blue" (really brown) Danube and golden Transylvania. This old-fashioned stylist could teach us all how to write.

Fletcher, Colin. *The Thousand-Mile Summer.* 1964. New York: Vintage, 1989. Fletcher wrote this one about a 1958 walk, and also wrote *The Man Who Walked Through Time* (1968) and other "felt," sensual books about walking through California: the Mojave Desert, Death Valley, the High Sierras.

Fonesca, Isabel. *Bury Me Standing: The Gypsies and Their Journey.* New York: Vintage Departures, 1996. Fonesca, a journalist, traces the route and thousand-year history of the Gypsies, wanderers originally from India or perhaps Egypt. About travel, but even more, about persecution—and the persecution of a brilliantly faceted culture.

Fowler, Brenda. "Where Did He Go?" Review of *The Neanderthal Enigma,* by James Shreeve. *New York Times Book Review,* December 17, 1995, 21.

Fowler-Billings, Katharine. *Stepping-Stones: The Reminiscences of a Woman Geologist in the Twentieth Century.* New Haven, CT: Connecticut Academy of Arts and Sciences, 1996. The autobiography of a seven-decade-plus geologist, conservationist, and adventurer in the American West, Africa, Australia, Peru, and Alaska.

Frantz, R. W. *The English Traveller and the Movement of Ideas, 1660–1732.* Lincoln: University of Nebraska Press, 1967.

Fraser, Keath, ed. *Bad Trips.* New York: Vintage Departures, 1991. Collection from Paul Theroux, Jan Morris, Martha Gellhorn, Colin Thubron, Mary Morris, and some you might not expect to be travel writers, such as William Trevor and John Updike.

Frater, Alexander. *Chasing the Monsoon.* 1990. New York: Henry Holt Owl, 1992. Set in India, and in the popular contemporary travel subgenre of the "gimmick" (and yet another good writer).

Fussell, Paul. *Abroad: British Literary Travel Between the Wars.* New York: Oxford, 1980; paper, 1982. A breakthrough in seeing travel as literature, history, and social study.

Fussell, Paul, ed. *The Norton Book of Travel.* New York: Norton, 1987. More than eight hundred pages of excerpts from Herodotus through the eighteenth century era of the Grand Tour, to a "Heyday" in the nineteenth and twentieth centuries (Byron to Kerouac), and on to "posttourism" (Naipaul, Theroux, et al.). Almost wholly limited to British and U.S. travelers (after "The Beginnings").

Gellhorn, Martha. *Liana.* 1944. New York: Penguin, 1987. In addition to vivid, wise travel essays, the journalist wrote *Liana,* which is set in "St. Boniface," a French-Caribbean island a lot like Saba, and which is a novel with an ahead-of-its-time plot of interracial marriage.

Geyer, Georgie Anne. *Waiting for Winter to End: An Extraordinary Journey Through Soviet Central Asia.* New York: Macmillan Brassey, 1994. In her account of a journey in 1992, the veteran "foreign" correspondent illuminates new/old states, such as Kazakhstan, Uzbekistan, and Russia, and the dangers to them from old Soviet pollutions and new zealous missionaries, entrepreneurs, dictators, and other pols.

Ghosh, Amitar. *In an Antique Land: History in the Guise of a Traveler's Tale.* 1992. New York: Vintage, 1994. Egypt past and present through the perspective of an Indian following up on a reference to a twelfth-century Indian slave.

Gissing, George. *By the Ionian Sea: Notes of a Ramble in Southern Italy.* 1901. Evanston, IL: Marlboro Northwestern University Press, 1996. Another classic reprinted; a bitter-sweet view.

Glass, Charles. *Tribes with Flags: A Dangerous Passage Through the Chaos of the Middle East.* New York: Atlantic Monthly Press, 1990. The journalist (print and ABC network) planned to decode the political history of the fragmented peoples of the Middle East with a trip from Turkey through Israel, but was taken hostage in Beirut in 1987. He escaped after sixty-two days; his account of his captivity is a short crucible at the end of a long, rich history book.

Gorra, Michael. "Travel." *New York Times Book Review*, December 3, 1995, 7, 49–50. Typical of the twice-a-year *New York Times* reviews of travel literature.

Gould, Jean, ed. *Season of Adventure: Traveling Tales and Outdoor Journeys of Women over 50.* Seattle, WA: Seal Adventura, 1996. Adventures in Guatemala and up the Amazon; historical "women homesteaders," but also city gardeners and women who run, who climb, who swim at age seventy-plus, and so on.

Govier, Katherine, ed. *Without a Guide: Contemporary Women's Travel Adventures.* St. Paul, MN: Hungry Mind Press, 1994. A collection generally of newer, less known women often from the less traveled countries; for example, "Cairo Is a Grey Jungle" by Hanan al-Shaykh; Wendy Law-Yone, from Burma (Myanmar); Ysenda Maxtone Graham, an English woman, in the Grand Canyon; Robyn Davidson, "Alone Across the Outback"; Kirsti Simonsuuri on "Kaamos, the Darkest Time of the Year," from her 1981 travel book *Northern Notebook*, on Finland; and Alice Walker on China.

Granta 26, spring 1989. The British journal—part of Penguin, which publishes travel writing heavily—lit fires under the travel boom in the 1980s. This volume on travel collects some Chatwin (and is dedicated to him; he died January 18, 1989), Amitar Ghosh on the "four corners" in the U.S. Southwest, Colin Thubron on China, Ian Buruma on Taiwan, Bill Bryson on "More Fat Girls in Des Moines," and lots more.

Greene, Graham. *Journey Without Maps.* 1936. New York: Viking Penguin, 1980. Across Liberia in 1935, when it was *really* untouched by the Western world. Greene is masterful in his description and his psychological and political insights (e.g., on why the Liberian people prefer to be governed by whites).

——. *The Quiet American.* 1955. New York: Viking Penguin, 1977. "Right-minded" Washington economic advisers move in on Saigon while the colonist-French are being beaten by the Vietminh in *their* war, in 1955. The narrator, Fowler, speaks his author's understanding of the Vietnamese as *people,* a viewpoint not that common then. In *our* war in Vietnam, Greene's clear look at America's huge power, and huge righteousness, became a foreshadowing classic. (Hollywood's 1958 movie turned the terrorist bomber from an American zealot to—what else in the Cold War?—a Communist.)

——. *Stamboul Train.* 1932. New York: Viking Penguin, 1975. Greene classified his spy tales as "entertainments"; today we see them as classics of popular culture *noir. Stamboul* is the essential Orient Express thriller—from Ostend to Constantinople—with dissolutes and the hard-boiled, with realists and romantics, and, at the center (of *all* of Greene's stories), romantics who make themselves romantics because they are realists in this world.

Grimes, William. "Travel." *New York Times Book Review*, June 16, 1996, 13, 44.

Hakluyt, Richard. *Hakluyt's Voyages.* 1589. *Voyages and Discoveries*, ed. Jack Beeching. New York: Penguin, 1972; also other editions. Explorations, mainly British, from circa 517 (King Arthur's) through late sixteenth-century voyages to America and sailings (Spanish) across the Pacific to Japan. Surprisingly, many of the British voyages before 1066 (the Norman conquest) are to Russia, via the Arctic Ocean and far northern Scandinavia.

Halliburton, Richard. *The Royal Road to Romance.* 1925. Westport CT: Greenwood, 1969. A classic.

Harrison, Barbara Grizzuti. *Italian Days.* New York: Weidenfeld & Nicholson, 1989. Such a long, lyrical paean to Italy that even the most passionate Italiaphile might overdoes, as on Asti Spumante. Harrison has also written *Islands of Italy* (New York: Ticknor & Fields, 1991), with meltingly sensuous photographs by Sheila Nardulli of the warm Italian islands, the Aeolians, Sicily, and Sardinia. Art, architecture, food, people, land, and always the sea.

Heat-Moon, William Least. *Blue Highways: A Journey into America.* New York: Fawcett, 1986. Started the popular contemporary "rambles" through rural and small-town America.

Heinlein, Robert A. *Tramp Royale.* New York: Ace, 1992; paper, 1996. Written in 1953–54 and still not only vivid but up-to-date even when he discusses the effect in Peru of the 1950s hunter of Communist "witches," U.S. Senator Joe McCarthy—timely *especially* when he discusses the "past." San Francisco, New Orleans, South America, South Africa, Indonesia, Australia, and New Zealand are covered.

Hemingway, Ernest. *Green Hills of Africa.* New York: Scribner's, 1935. Equally gorgeous (compared to Hemingway on Africa) is his writing of place and of journey in the short stories about the Upper Michigan peninsula; Spain in the 1920s (*The Sun Also Rises* [1926]) and in its Civil War (*For Whom The Bell Tolls* [1940]); the French Riviera, in *The Torrents of Spring* (1972); Paris after World War I, in the memoir *A Moveable Feast* (1964); and so on.

Heyerdahl, Thor. *Kon-Tiki: Across the Pacific by Raft.* Trans. F. H. Lyon. Chicago: Rand McNally, 1950. A classic inspiration to the generation of post–World War II children.

Hiassen, Carl. *Native Tongue.* 1991. New York: Fawcett Crest, 1992. Also *Lucky You* (New York: Knopf, 1997), *Strip Tease* (1993; New York: Time-Warner, 1994), and *Skin Tight, Double Whammy, Tourist Season.* Southern Florida is the place of this imaginative mystery/thriller writer.

Hiestand, Emily. *The Very Rich Hours: Travels in Orkney, Belize, the Everglades, and Greece.* Boston: Beacon, 1992. Birds and her mother, in Scotland; her lover and the ancient Calusa people, in the Everglades; Belize, haunted by the Mayans; Greece: all these past/presents are held together by the author's sensibility.

Hillaby, John. A classic travel writer whose works include *Hillaby's World: Adventures Across the Three Continents* (North Pomfret, VT: Trafalgar, 1993); *John Hillaby's London* (New Brunswick, NJ: Transaction Publishers, 1988); *Journey Through Britain,* (Brunswick, NJ: Transaction, 1986); and *Journey Through Europe* (Chicago: Academy, 1982).

Hillerman, Tony. *The Great Taos Bank Robbery, and Other Indian Country Affairs.* 1973. Albuquerque: University of New Mexico Press, 1993. Essays on New Mexico.

——. *A Journey Through the Southwest with Tony Hillerman.* 1991. New York: HarperCollins, 1993.

——. *New Mexico, Rio Grande, and Other Essays.* New York: HarperCollins, 1993.

——. *A Thief of Time.* New York: HarperCollins, 1990. This book is one of his many other mysteries set in the U.S. Southwest.

Hitt, Jack. *Off the Road: A Modern-Day Walk down the Pilgrim's Route into Spain.* New York: Simon & Schuster, 1994. Five hundred miles from France to the shrine of St. James's bones, along with the wayside scene, pilgrims, unholy dogs, and other humor.

Hodgson, Michael, ed. *No Shit! There I Was . . . : A Collection of Wild Stories from Wild People.* Foreword by Todd Skinner. Merrillville, IN: ICS, 1994. Bears, bikes, falling planes, a "yak attack," and so on.

Hoffman, Eva. *Exit into History: A Journey Through the New Eastern Europe.* New York: Viking, 1993; paper, 1994. Post-Communist travel through Poland (her homeland), the two Czechoslovakias (Slovakia and the Czech Republic), Hungary, Romania, Bulgaria. Just right for its time.

Hofmann, Paul. *The Seasons of Rome: A Journal.* New York: Henry Holt, 1997. Illustrations by Joanne Morgante. One year (of more than thirty) of Hofmann's daily life in the city of "the arrangement"—a place as sinuous, but lucid, as Hofmann's words.

——. *The Spell of the Vienna Woods: Inspiration and Influence from Beethoven to Kafka.* New York: Henry Holt Owl, 1994.

——. *The Sunny Side of the Alps: Year Round Delights in South Tyrol and the Dolomites.* New York: Henry Holt Owl, 1995.

Homer. *The Iliad.* Trans. Robert Fagles. Introduction and notes by Bernard Knox. New York: Viking Penguin, 1990. The "prequel" to *the* classic travel story, Homer's *Odyssey, The Iliad* tells of the Trojan War—especially well in Fagles' acclaimed new translation.

——. *The Odyssey.* Trans. Robert Fagles. Introduction and notes by Bernard Knox. New York: Viking Penguin, 1996. "Sing to me of the man, Muse, the man of twists and turns / driven time and again off course, once he had plundered / the hallowed heights of Troy." So opens the premier travel adventure of Western civilization, Odysseus' winding way home to Ithaca and Penelope, after the Trojan War. The new translation is tough and sinewy, and it sings. No wonder the Norwegian Cruise Line, in 1997, echoes the poem (12,109 lines long) some 2,700 years old: "Sing, Muse, of the travels of Ted and Kate / upon the winedark sea. Of wily Ted, broker of stocks, who renounced wingtips."

Hongo, Garrett. *Volcano: A Memoir of Hawaii.* 1995. New York: Vintage Departures, 1996. Poetic history, natural and personal, as well as general history (densely specific) of the prototypical South Sea island.

Horowitz, Paula. *Finding Our Way: A Mother's Journey with Her Son.* Birmingham, AL: Menasha Ridge Press, 1994. A memoir of thirteen years, from when Jason was six, backpacking and otherwise traveling through New England, Europe, Nepal, India, and South America.

Horwitz, Tony. *Baghdad Without a Map and Other Misadventures in Arabia.* 1991. New epilogue by the author. New York: Plume, 1992. The title catches the style, but the details of this important, isolated contemporary city are illuminating.

——. *One for the Road: Hitchhiking Through the Australian Outback.* New York: Vintage Departures, 1988.

Hudson, Peregrine. *Under a Sickle Moon: A Journey Through Afghanistan.* 1986. New York: Atlantic Monthly Press, 1987. An in-the-midst war adventure, this one with more Sarajevo, 1994–type realism than Rudyard Kipling–style romance.

Hunt, Christopher. *Sparring with Charlie: Motorbiking down the Ho Chi Minh Trail.* Garden City, NY: Doubleday Anchor, 1996. A sensitive young man and keen writer (son of Richard Hunt, a TV reporter in Vietnam during the war) limns Vietnam, and a bit of Laos and Cambodia, as they fold themselves back into America's ken.

Iyer, Pico. *Falling off the Map: Some Lonely Places of the World.* New York: Knopf, 1993; Vintage Departures, 1994. Of places like Cuba, Paraguay, and North Korea and (typical Iyer) the weird, usually corrupt things that happen to the clear-eyed visitor because of their isolation. Iyer has mastered the poignant detail; for example, the Bhutan telephone directory.

——. *The Lady and the Monk: Four Seasons in Kyoto.* New York: Knopf, 1991; Vintage, 1992. The most serious Iyer meets Sachiko, a Japanese wife.

——. *Tropical Classical: Essays from Several Directions.* New York: Knopf, 1997. Mainly the "direction" is East, and includes essays (on Ethiopia, Nepal, Bombay, New York, and California); British Raj history; and reviews and biography of other travel writers, such as Norman Lewis.

——. *Video Night in Kathmandu, and Other Reports from the Not-So-Far East.* New York: Random House, 1988; Vintage Departures, 1989. Life and politics in all the Asian countries, except Bhutan, which he saved for *Falling off the Map.*

Jakle, John A. *The Tourist: Travel in Twentieth-Century North America.* Lincoln: University of Nebraska Press, 1967. An early scholarly study.

James, Henry. *Italian Hours.* 1909. Hopewell NJ: Ecco Travels, 1987. Ecco has also reprinted Edith Wharton's *Italian Backgrounds,* Charles Dickens's *Pictures from Italy,* Ford Madox Ford's *Provence,* and other classics from the "eliter" era of traveling (and writing).

Jerome, Christine. *Adirondack Passage: The Cruise of the Canoe Sairy Gamp.* New York: HarperCollins, 1994. Jerome, in a similar light canoe, retraced the 266-mile paddle and portage made in 1883 by naturalist George Washington Sears through the Adirondack Mountains in northern New York. She incorporates historical tales and reports from local newspapers of Sears's time.

Jerome, John. *Blue Rooms.* New York: Henry Holt, 1997. The physics and psychology of swimming—which we love because of the primacy of the sense of touch, he says, and which he studies in many beautiful swimming "holes."

Johnson, Diane. *Natural Opium: Some Traveler's Tales.* New York: Knopf, 1993. Good title to describe travel. Essays by the novelist (*Health and Happiness, Le Divorce,* etc.), who traveled, often with her doctor-husband, to, among other places, the Great Barrier Reef, "The heart of Pakistan," Egypt, Hong Kong, Switzerland (wjere she experienced a terrifying night sled ride that may haunt you). So will the monied travelers (such as the author), among the many importuning others.

Johnson, Samuel. *Journey to the Western Islands of Scotland.* 1775. Ed. Mary Lascelles. Vol. 9, *The Works of Samuel Johnson.* New Haven, CT: Yale University Press, 1971.

Jones, Lloyd. *Biografi: A Traveler's Tale.* New York: Harcourt Brace Harvest, 1994. A New Zealand fiction writer universalizes a trip to Albania, where the dictator (Hoxha) had a double and the citizens made up their official lives (*biografi*). Travel as metaphor for postmodern metaphysics.

Kane, Joe. *Savages.* 1995. New York: Vintage Departures, 1996. Photographs. On the spot, Kane reports the aftermath of the discovery of oil in a remote Amazon region of Ecuador, home to the Huaorani Indians. Dark comedy, turning "civilization" on its head.

Kaplan, Robert D. *Balkan Ghosts: A Journey Through History.* New York: St. Martin's, 1993. History and current politics, embedded in a focus on place, as is this writer's gift. Kaplan is also the author of *The Arabists: The Romance of an American Elite* (New York: Free Press, 1993), an unusually informative history of the roots of the U.S. Arabphiles in missionaries, educators, and a certain U.S. East Coast elite.

——. *The Ends of the Earth: A Journey to the Frontiers of Anarchy.* New York: Vintage Departures, 1996. "From Togo to Turkmenistan, From Iran to Cambodia": Kaplan, as he says in his preface, "folds international studies into a travelogue." As usual, he "give[s] personal meaning to the kinds of issues raised in Paul Kennedy's *Preparing for the Twenty-first Century.*" And "personal meaning" comes via the rich details.

Kern, Stephen. *The Culture of Time and Space, 1889–1918.* Cambridge, MA: Harvard University Press, 1983. Complex study of a big era in technology: for example, the effects of speed ("the bicycle was about four times faster than walking"), artificial illumination, new perspectives such as Cubism, and much more. This encompassing, synthesizing work emphasizes our notions and assumptions as much as the technology.

Kobak, Annette. "Chasing After Nomads." *New York Times Book Review*, February 16, 1997, 26. Kobak (herself the author of a travel book, *Isabelle*, a biography of the nineteenth-century traveler, Isabelle Eberhardt) reviews Robyn Davidson's *Desert Places,* the latest trek-in-the-wild-with-an-endangered-tribe, and raises the ethical question of exploitation: Davidson, not unusually, was subsidized.

Kowaleski, Michael, ed. *Temperamental Journeys: Essays on the Modern Literature of Travel.* Athens: University of Georgia Press, 1992. One of the first American collections, with a "Selective Chronology" and bibliography since 1900.

Krich, John. *Music in Every Room: Around the World in a Bad Mood.* New York: Atlantic Monthly Grove, 1988. Krich (who also loves and writes about baseball) is today's light-hearted (clear-eyed) traveler—as, for example, in his irreverent gloom.

——. *Why Is This Country Dancing: A No-Hope Samba Through Brazil.* New York: Simon & Schuster, 1993.

Krotz, Larry. *Tourists: How Our Fastest Growing Industry is Changing the World.* London: Faber, 1966. Travel packages versus adventure.

Langewiesche, William. *Sahara Unveiled: A Journey Across the Desert.* New York: Pantheon, 1996. Colonial history, nomads, Islam, and desert tales, as well as strong description.

Lattimore, Eleanor Holgate. *Turkestan Reunion.* 1934. New York: Kodansha, 1994. Introduction by Evelyn Stefansson Nef; introduction from the 1975 editon by Owen Lattimore; and "Decorations by Eleanor Frances Lattimore" (only a few, but lovely line drawings). See Owen Lattimore entry.

Lattimore, Owen. *The Desert Road to Turkestan.* 1929. New York: Kodansha, 1994. With previously unpublished photographs (by Owen Lattimore) and a new introduction by David Lattimore (and Owen's introduction to the 1975 edition). See next entry.

——. *High Tartary.* 1930. New York: Kodansha, 1994. The most famous "old China hand" (blamed by postwar U.S. reactionaries for "selling out" China to the Communists and hounded out of the State Department by Senator Joseph McCarthy), Owen Lattimore traveled across Inner Mongolia in 1927 in one of the last camel caravans in the rail era (which was brand new there). Rebel Mongolian troops, fellow travelers not to be trusted, a blizzard, drought in the desert, and more, marked the journey, which he wrote of in *The Desert Road.* He journeyed to meet his bride, Eleanor, who wrote of her "easier" (he had thought) journey to him across Siberia (more than four hundred miles by sled after the railroad ended); "she was . . . the better road-finder" (of the two of them), he writes in his introduction to the 1975 edition of her book, *Turkestan Reunion.* They met in Urumchi, capital of what is now Xinjiang, and made their way together through the high mountain pastures and passes of Chinese Turkestan and over the Himalayas to India. His book of this part of the "adventure" is *High Tartary.* Their books—and lives—are uncommonly amazing and admirable. (As a writer, she is less learned about the languages and geography of the regions they travel, but at least equally observant and even more engaging, perhaps because her book was first written as letters to her family in Evanston, Illinois.)

Lawrence, D. H. *Sketches of Etruscan Places.* Ed. Simonetta de Filippis. Cambridge edition of the Works of D. H. Lawrence. Cambridge: Cambridge University Press, 1992.

——. *Twilight in Italy.* 1916. New York: Clarkson Potter, 1990. Lawrence wrote much now-classic travel writing (e.g., *Sea and Sardinia*); these are the two works in print in 1997.

Leavitt, David, and Mark Mitchell. *Italian Pleasures.* San Francisco: Chronicle, 1996. Illustrations. Alternating original essays by Leavitt and Mitchell on Florence and Tuscany, Rome, Naples, and lots of food, and other lyricisms.

Le Carre, John. "Quel Panama!" *New York Times Magazine,* October 13, 1996, 52–55. On how a small "paradise"—Panama—may be being ruined by "sloth, corruption and stupidity"—and how a larger one, England, irretrievably is. Le Carre's whole corpus of spy novels could be in this travel bibliography.

Leed, Eric. *The Mind of the Traveler: From Gilgamesh to Global Tourism.* New York: HarperCollins Basic Books, 1991. Stimulating, synthetic analogy of travel and psychology, specifically, the human lifetime "passages." See introduction to this book.

——. *Shores of Discovery: How Expeditions Have Constructed the World.* New York: HarperCollins Basic Books, 1995. "We *are* our paths, not our places," Leed says in the preface, and he traces the paths of "ancestors" such as Moses, Agamemnon, the Caesars, the Crusaders, and Cortez and what they meant to our world.

Lelyveld, Joseph. *Move Your Shadow: South Africa, Black and White.* New York: Random House, 1985; paper, Penguin, 1986). A Pulitzer Prize winner and my nomination for best title: *susa lo-mtunzi gawena* tells the caddies at the country club to move even their shadow out of the white man's way.

Lévi-Strauss, Claude. *Tristes Tropiques.* 1955. Trans. John and Doreen Weightman. New York: Atheneum, 1975. The anthropologist would not let his title be translated; it would be something like *The Sadness of the Tropics* or, says Paul Fussell, editor of *The Norton Book of Travel,* perhaps *The Melancholy of the Foreign* (761). In his travel writing, Lévi-Strauss, one of the premier structural analysts of twentieth-century popular culture, represents the postmodern, anti-industrial, anti-Western ennui of the traveler. And he writes with epitomical French intelligence and *les mots juste.*

Lewis, R. W. B. *The City of Florence: Historical Vistas and Personal Sightings.* New York: Farrar, Straus, Giroux, 1995; paper, Henry Holt Owl, 1996. Lewis's Florence, lived in (part-time) some fifty years, is full of history, which means art history as well as a lot of political history, often murderous.

Lindqvist, Sven. *"Exterminate All the Brutes."* Trans. Joan Tate. New York: New Press, 1996. Incorporates adventure travel (across the Algerian Sahara to Chad) in a political history that sees the roots of Nazi genocide in European imperialism, particularly British colonialism in Africa.

Lukacs, John. *Destinations Past.* Columbia, MO: University of Missouri Press, 1994. The Hungarian historian's travel essays from the late 1950s to the 1990s, covering Finland to Philadelphia, but mainly European history. Learned, lucid melding of a personal and national past; for example, on the passing of Winston Churchill.

Lundberg, Donald E. *International Travel and Tourism.* 2nd ed. New York: Wiley, 1993.

——. *The Tourist Business.* 6th ed. New York: Van Nostrand Reinhold, 1990.

Lyon, Nancy. *Scatter the Mud: A Traveller's Medley.* Montreal: Nuage, 1995. Essays from a lifelong traveler and travel writer (for *New York Times, Ms., Travel and Leisure,* the

Chicago *Tribune*, etc.). On New York City, Mexico, Ireland, Europe, Montreal, and other spots.

Maalouf, Amin. *Leo Africanus*. 1986. Trans. Peter Sluglett. New York: New Amsterdam Books, 1992. Of the travels of the trader five hundred years ago, in Granada, North Africa, Cairo, and Turkey, among Muslims, Christians, and Jews who, perhaps most interesting, seem both modern and "ordinary."

MacCannell, Dean. *The Tourist: A New Theory of the Leisure Class*. New York: Macmillan, 1976. 2nd ed., 1989. See introduction to this book.

Maclean, Norman. *A River Runs Through It and Other Stories*. 1976. New York: Pocket, 1992. Montana, earlier in the twentieth century, when it was even cleaner. Stories in the Hemingway vein, of sport and lifestyle quiet enough to hear the "code." The surprising success of these personal stories by the University of Chicago English professor—and of the movie made by Robert Redford—opened doors for this subgenre (and gates to "big sky country").

Madsen, Axel. *Silk Roads: The Asian Adventures of Clara and André Malraux*. New York: Pharos, 1989. Real and exotic derring-do of the French novelist and his wife when they were young and poor and bent on "liberating" relics from Khmer temples in "Indochine." Discovering Asian culture and colonial rule, however, they became *provocateurs* instead, first by starting a newspaper in Saigon. A rich, *foreign* yarn, of a different time as much as a different place.

Mahfouz, Naguib. *Palace Walk*. Vol. 1 of *The Cairo Trilogy*. Trans. William Maynard Hutchins and Olive E. Kenny. New York: Doubleday Anchor, 1991 (*Bayn al-Qasrayn*, 1956). A Muslim family saga, starting during British occupation in the early twentieth century. Volume 2, *Palace of Desire*, takes place in the 1920s as more freedom roiled Egyptian society, seen through this "ordinary" family (Doubleday 1991, Anchor 1992; *Qasr al-Shawq*, 1957). In volume 3, *Sugar Street* (Doubleday 1992, Anchor 1993; *Al-Sokkariyya*, 1957), independence grows and, with it, Marxism and also Muslim activism. Egypt is a key to our world's fate, and this soap opera story clarifies why, perhaps more than the political tomes can.

Malcomson, Scott L. *Empire's Edge: Travels in South-Eastern Europe, Turkey and Central Asia*. London and New York: Verso, 1994. A historically and politically informed journal, a form which personalizes and makes immediate and dramatic the news of what's happening today in the "Ottoman Empire."

Maspero, François. *Roissy Express: A Journey Through the Paris Suburbs*. Trans. Paul Jones. New York: Verso, 1994. In 1994, Mort Rosenblum gave us the Seine he lived on, from its springs to the emptying in the English Channel. Maspero gave us a more real and more political panorama (with photographs by Anaik Frantz) of the Paris RER B-line from Roissy-Charles de Gaulle Airport through thirty-eight stops and thirty-seven miles across the city to St.-Rémy-lès-Chevreuse. It is a dark urban world of today's poor African immigrants, but also Drancy, where the Nazis stored French Jews (ten thousand) before sending them to the death camps.

Masterson, Graham. *Maiden Voyage*. New York: St. Martin's, 1984. Amazingly, (excepting the *Titanic* "industry") there are relatively few novels or movies set in the golden age of trans-Atlantic travel by dirigible, "Pan Am. Clipper," but mostly, steamship. This novel set in the 1920s drops the names of movie stars Rudolph Valentino, Mary Pickford, Douglas Fairbanks, and others and captures this buoyant era, now bittersweet because we know how it all ended.

Matthiessen, Peter. *African Silences*. New York: Random House, 1991; paper, 1992. Following *A Tree Where Man Was Born* and *Sand Rivers*, about eastern and southern Africa,

African Silences covers a 1978 expedition to the west, to Senegal, Gambia, the Ivory Coast, and eastward to Zaire and a 1986 expedition in central Africa, in the Congo Basin. Both expeditions looked for rare, endangered animals and birds—and also saw ruinous political and economic greed and corruption.

——. *The Cloud Forest.* 1961. New York: Viking Penguin, 1989. Like all of Matthiessen's travel writings (which are also nature and also political writings), *Cloud Forest* is a personal chronicle, this one of the South American wilderness.

——. *The Snow Leopard.* 1978. New York: Viking Penguin, 1987. Nepal, and Matthiessen's Zen Buddhism.

——. *Under the Mountain Wall.* 1962. New York: Viking Penguin, 1987. A New Guinea tribe. Still other works from this modern giant in personal, ethical naturalism and travel include *Indian Country* (New York: Viking Penguin, 1992) and *Blue Meridian* (New York: Viking Penguin, 1997) about searching the white shark off Australia.

Mayle, Peter. *Anything Considered.* New York: Knopf, 1996. A typical "production" from the ex-advertising man and British expatriate to the south of France, who is making a career we all envy, of writing best-sellers about his new home area. This one is a novel about a British expatriate, with a plot of the type best called a "caper" (as the book jacket calls it).

——. *A Dog's Life.* New York: Knopf, 1995; Vintage, 1996. Drawings by Ed Koren. Boy (a dog and a native) tells his side of life in Provencal with Peter Mayle, nominally his master.

——. *Hotel Pastis.* New York: Knopf, 1993; Vintage Departures, 1994. After his two hit memoirs of Provence, Mayle wrote a novel, which became another best-seller, about the same sensuous area in the south of France.

——. *Toujours Provence.* New York: Knopf, 1991; Vintage Departures, 1992.

——. *A Year in Provence.* 1989. New York: Knopf, 1990; Vintage Departures, 1991. This best-seller begat *Toujours* and a hit PBS TV series about the Great Escape.

McCarthy, Mary. *The Stones of Florence.* New York: Harcourt Brace Jovanovich, 1963; paper, 1976. Photographs by (mainly) Evelyn Hofer. History and art history by one of the century's best writers, and large photographs (this is a coffee-table book), mostly black and white, that communicate Florence as few others do.

——. *Venice Observed.* 1956. New York: Harbrace Harvest, 1963. They are opposites: Venice is light-struck and Florence is umber and dense. McCarthy catches each of them extraordinarily, through erudition, but also through the offbeat detail so many have emulated.

McPhee, John. *Coming into the Country.* 1977. New York: Farrar, Straus, Giroux Noonday, 1979. Alaska; and one of the best Alaska books, by a research writer of the old *New Yorker* school.

Mehta, Gita. *Raj.* 1989. New York: Fawcett Columbine, 1991. A novel of the Raj, that is, of princely India, from the British Queen Victoria's Diamond Jubilee (1887) to the civil wars of independence in the late 1940s, focusing on one woman's journey out of the traditional purdah into independence and power. A contemporary old-fashioned "good read."

——. *A River Sutra.* New York: Random House, 1993; Vintage International, 1994. Another fictional but realistic story of India today.

Michener, James. *Mexico.* 1992. New York: Fawcett Crest, 1994. Also *Hawaii, Alaska, Poland, Texas, Caribbean, Chesapeake, Tales of the South Pacific* (Oscar Hammerstein II and Richard Rodgers' book for *South Pacific*)—and even *Space.* Michener was not the snappiest writer, but he was a solid researcher and a best-seller, and thus an important educator of Americans.

Middleton, Nick. *The Last Disco in Outer Mongolia.* London: Phoenix, 1992. One of the first Westerners to visit, in 1987 and 1990, before and after some liberalization.

Miller, John, and Kirsten Miller, eds. *Istanbul.* San Francisco: Chronicle, 1995. A pretty, small book collecting essays by Mary Lee Settle, Michael Palin, Simone de Beauvoir, Lady Mary Wortley Montagu, Herman Melville, and others.

Miller, Tom. *Trading with the Enemy: A Yankee Travels Through Castro's Cuba.* 1992. New York: Basic Books, 1996. Eight months of access and travel through the cities and rural areas of Cuba by the author of *The Panama Hat Trail* (1986); with a 1996 introduction.

Minta, Stephen. *Aguirre: The Re-Creation of a Sixteenth-Century Journey Across South America.* New York: Henry Holt, 1994. Retracing the steps of a 1560 Spanish trek through South America looking for El Dorado; Minta emphasizes how hard it is to trace ancient "facts."

Mistry, Rohinton. *A Fine Balance.* New York: Knopf, 1996. A "fat" novel of ordinary people—Parsi's—living modern Indian history.

Mojtabai, A. G. "An Accidental Family." *New York Times Book Review*, June 23, 1996, 29. Review of *A Fine Balance* by Rohinton Mistry.

Morris, Jan. *Among the Cities.* New York: Oxford University Press, 1985.

——. *Destinations: Essays from "Rolling Stone."* New York: Oxford University Press, 1980.

——. *Fifty Years of Europe: An Album.* New York: Villard (Random), 1997. Snapshots of political and cultural history.

——. *Journeys.* New York: Oxford University Press, 1984.

——. *O Canada: Travels in an Unknown Country.* New York: Harper, 1992. Morris, one of today's top travel writers, has written of many *Locations* (1992), mainly cities, like *Hongkong* (1988), *Sydney* (1992), and *Manhattan, 'Forty-Five* (1987), but also her homeland, in *The Matter of Wales: Epic Views of a Small Country* (1986).

Morris, Mary. *Nothing to Declare: Memoirs of a Woman Traveling Alone.* New York: Penguin, 1988. Living in Mexico (a small, northern town) and (briefly) traveling in Central America. One of the leaders in the current recording of physical *and* psychological journeying.

——. *Wall to Wall: From Beijing to Berlin by Rail.* New York: Penguin, 1991. Another personal travel writing, trundling from Asia to Russia and Berlin, involving the nuclear meltdown at Chernobyl and her new, problematic pregnancy.

Morris, Mary, ed. *Maiden Voyages: Writings of Women Travelers.* New York: Vintage, 1993. A particularly strong collection, from Lady Mary Wortley Montagu discovering the *freedom* of eighteenth-century Turkish women behind their veils, and pioneers in America and (my favorite) Lady Mary Anne Barker, who matter-of-factly trudged the nearly impenetrable hills and gorges of nineteenth century New Zealand, and so on through modern pioneers such as Alexandra David-Neel in Tibet, Box-Car Bertha, and Joan Didion.

Morrison, Toni. *Tar Baby.* New York: Knopf, 1981; Signet, 1983. A vivid novel of the Caribbean, with Morrison's special descriptive power and re-creation of the tragic "multiculture."

Mowat, Farley. *Aftermath: Travels in a Post-War World.* Boulder, CO: Roberts Rinehart, 1996. The nature writer (*Never Cry Wolf*, etc.) journeyed through England, France, and Italy in 1953, seeking peace by visiting sites where his Canadian comrades had fallen during World War II. Moving and, in the late 1990s, poignant.

Myrdal, Jan. *Report from a Chinese Village.* New York: Pantheon, 1981. And *Return to a Chinese Village* (Pantheon, 1984). Social anthropology in the tradition of his Swedish sociologist parents, who pioneered in exposing *An American Dilemma* (1944), by Gunnar Myrdal, about the moral and psychological dilemma of the United States, committed to racial equality, but committing inequality.

Naipaul, V. S. *Among the Believers: An Islamic Journey*. New York: Knopf, 1981; Vintage, 1982. One of the first and still best books clarifying contemporary Islam. Naipaul journeys through Iran, Pakistan, Malaysia, and Indonesia.

——. *India: A Million Mutinies Now*. London: Penguin, 1990; New York: Viking Penguin, 1991; paper, Penguin, 1992). Again, an epitomical multicultural man explores his roots today. Naipaul's whole body of work is a journey.

——. *A Way in the World*. New York: Knopf, 1994. Fiction (?), memoir, history, with Columbus, Raleigh, and Francisco Miranda (1750–1816), a failed Venezualan revolutionary; and, finally, philosophy of the human traveler.

Narayan, R. F. *My Dateless Diary: An American Journey*. New York: Penguin, 1988; Indian Thought Publications, 1964. A middle-aged Indian gentleman-Odysseus comes to New York, Chicago, and Los Angeles and encounters celebrities (the great Garbo!), muggers, commuters. A clear view from askance of the United States from this prolific writer.

Newman, Steven M. *Worldwalk*. New York: Morrow, 1989. A young Ohio journalist who was the first person to walk the world. Four years through the United States, Ireland and Britain, France, Spain, Italy, Greece, North Africa, Yugoslavia, Turkey, India, Thailand, Malaysia, Australia: meeting up with bandits, flash floods, jail, but mainly good people of all sorts. When, in his last months, he reached the third grade at Emerald Elementary School in Bozeman, Montana, which had followed his trip, he found Ms. Robin Morris's students knew more about the world's geography than most "high-schoolers I had spoken to" (503).

Newsham, Brad. *All the Right Places: Traveling Light Through China, Japan, and Russia*. New York: Villard, 1989; Vintage Departures, 1990. Well-written odyssey from one life to another and one of the best written of today's characteristically confessional travel writings. For example, Newsham is too young for World War II, but when Japanese schoolchildren at the War Museum in Hiroshia run into the large (to them), young American, they are both terrified and enthralled, and Newsham, and we, are completely moved, angry, and guilty.

O'Faolain, Sean. *An Autumn in Italy*. New York: Devin-Adair, 1953. "[A]nd below us the Mediterranean goes flashing and flashing between the flitting houses" (15): train travel, of course. Typical of the "golden oldie" travel books to be found in old bookstores and yard sales.

O'Hanlon, Redmond. *Into the Heart of Borneo*. New York: Vintage, 1987; Edinburgh: Salamander, 1984; New York: Random House, 1985. The naturalist O'Hanlon and James Fenton, also a travel writer (see entry), went by river into the jungle in 1983. This is the kind of "clash of cultures" that erupts into laughter—and then understanding.

——. *In Trouble Again: A Journey Between the Orinoco and the Amazon*. New York: Vintage Departures, 1988.

——. *No Mercy: A Journey to the Heart of the Congo*. New York: Knopf, 1997. A typical "journey" of today: through change, irony, and pain, to no clear end.

Packer, George. *The Village of Waiting*. New York: Vintage Departures, 1988. A Peace Corps teacher in Togo writes a parable of the cruel catch 22 of illusive "development" that forms an addition to the novels of Chinua Achebe of Nigeria: *Things Fall Apart*, a classic modern fable of the tragic clash of the tribal old and "progressive" new; its sequels, *No Longer at Ease* and *Anthills on the Savannah*; and the extraordinary short stories *Girls at War and Other Stories.*

Palin, Michael. *Around the World in Eighty Days.* 1989. Foreword by Jan Morris. San Francisco: KQED Books, 1995. Photographs. Companion to the PBS series. One foot at a time, you can't stop reading on, the specifics are that distinctive.

——. *Pole to Pole: North to South by Camel, River Raft, and Balloon.* 1992. San Francisco: KQED Books, 1995. Photographs by Basil Pao.

Paretsky, Sara. *Guardian Angel.* 1992. New York: Dell, 1993. And a half dozen or so other detective novels and short story collections starring Chicago detective V(ictoria) I. Warshawsky, the model for today's feisty women private investigators, in adventures in (mainly) blue-collar Chicagoland; for example, the Calumet ship canal or (one of my favorites) the locks on Lake Superior (*Deadlock*).

Parks, Tim. *An Italian Education: The Further Adventures of an Expatriate in Verona.* 1995. New York: Avon, 1996.

——. *Italian Neighbors, Or a Lapsed Anglo-Saxon in Verona.* 1992. New York: Ballantine Fawcett Columbine, 1993. The titles tell you the story and preview the light, intelligent style of these true tales.

Paton, Alan. *Cry the Beloved Country.* 1948. New York: Collier, 1987. A classic, the poetic telling of South Africa's tragedy, and the story for the musical play *Lost in the Stars.*

Pindell, Terry. *A Good Place to Live: America's Last Migration.* 1995. New York: Henry Holt Owl, 1996. Pindell looks across America and Canada for places to live that have a "sense of community." He charts what this means and, in particular, what it means in about fifteen communities, from Portsmouth, New Hampshire, to San Luis Obispo, California (and Asheville and Wilmingon, North Carolina; Ithaca, New York; Minneapolis-St. Paul, Minnesota, etc.), plus Vancouver and Kelouna, British Columbia. Then he goes home to Keene, New Hampshire. A sound book about, indeed, our foundations.

Pindell, Terry, with Lourdes Ramirez Mallis. *Yesterday's Train: A Rail Odyssey Through Mexican History.* New York: Henry Holt, 1997. Following "rail odyssey[s]" across America (*Making Tracks*, Henry Holt Owl, 1991), and Canada (*Train to Toronto*, Henry Holt, 1992). Current sociopolitical issues and history are linked illuminatingly.

Pirsig, Robert. *Zen and the Art of Motorcycle Maintenance: An Inquiry into Values.* New York: Morrow, 1974. Perhaps on the road to being a classic? The motorcycle and its philosopher travel America, loosely (picaresquely) and musing—but really thoughtfully: this is *serious* philosophy.

Polo, Marco. *The Travels.* Trans. R. E. Latham. New York: Penguin Classics, 1958. Polo (1254–1324) traveled westward for some twenty years from Italy across Asia. While he was a prisoner in Genoa, a romance writer, Rustichello of Pisa, collaborated in composing his now classic history and generic "travel adventure."

Pratt, Mary Louise. *Imperial Eyes: Travel Writing and Transculturation.* London and New York: Routledge, 1992. A singularly important reading of travel as a key source of "transnationalism." See the introduction to this text.

Pyle, Ernie. *Ernie's America: The Best of Ernie Pyle's 1930s Travel Dispatches.* Ed. David Nichols. Foreword by Charles Kuralt. New York: Random House, 1989. Nichols picks from columns that the beloved World War II correspondent (creator of "G.I. Joe") wrote while traveling around the United States. The columns, from 1935 to December 15, 1941, for the Scripps-Howard newspapers, communicate with a simple clarity that seems to tell the whole story of the 1930s Dust Bowl and Great Depression and places, especially small ones, and American people startlingly like those Charles Kuralt found a long time later.

Quammen, David. "National Parks: Nature's Dead End." *New York Times*, July 28, 1996, 4:13. In this essay, Quammen applies to the parks the important idea of his book *The Song of the Dodo*: that islands (or national parks), by their isolation, help create extinctions.

——. *The Song of the Dodo: Island Biogeography in an Age of Extinctions.* New York: Scribner's, 1996. See Bryson essay in this text.

Raban, Jonathan. *Bad Land: An American Romance.* New York: Pantheon, 1996. The British traveler and writer has written picaresquely of America before in *Arabia: A Journey Through the Looking Glass* (1979), and *Old Glory: An American Voyage* (1981). *Bad Land* grows from a series of drives by Raban from his (new) home in Seattle to eastern Montana and the western Dakotas; it celebrates the pioneers who tried to live in this harshest place and (uncritically) those who now live off "welfare ranching." Controversially, Raban links the land and its current libertarians, such as the Aryan Nations, Mark Fuhrman, and Ted Kaczynski. See Page Stegner.

Rambali, Paul. *In the Cities and Jungles of Brazil.* New York: Henry Holt, 1994. Rambali, after several visits, aimed (well) for the contradictions and dilemmas of a nation of wide and deep poverty, pristine—and vulnerable—resources, and equally extreme dynamism. From rain forest to shantytown megalopolis to soap opera literacy, a rich stew.

Robinson, Jane, ed. *Unsuitable for Ladies: An Anthology of Women Travellers.* New York: Oxford University Press, 1994. Another cornucopia, this one of almost five hundred pages, starting in Victorian England and ending in "North America," after being all over the world, especially where wild things are (and the undaunted women).

Rogers, Jim. *Investment Biker: On the Road with Jim Rogers.* New York: Random House, 1994. The first travel/finance book merger.

Romer, Elizabeth. *The Tuscan Year: Life and Food in an Italian Valley.* 1985. New York: Farrar, Straus, Giroux North Point Press, 1989. The valley joins Tuscany and Umbria; the food is the "everyday": *bella!*

Rosenblum, Mort. *The Life of the Seine.* New York: Addison-Wesley, 1994. To see the houseboats moored along the Paris quais is to envy those who get to live on them. Now Rosenblum, an ex-*International Herald-Tribune* newspaper editor and one of the lucky ones, tells the story of the river from start to end—of both its length and history—and nails our envy. "The Seine was calm but by 8 A.M. *La Vieille* [his boat: "the old one"] was rocking gently. . . . The air bore a pleasant nip" (10); "A glance at the river in Paris tells you what is going on in France. If it is not slopping over its stone quais at the new year, farmers had a bad time with drought" (3): this is the insider's knowledge the lover of Paris longs for. And did you know that the word *paris*—as in Parisii, the first tribal settlers of Paris—is Celtic for "boat"?

Runciman, Steven. *A Traveller's Alphabet: Partial Memoirs.* New York: Thames and Hudson, 1991. A gimmick that works to give the historian Runciman "pictures" of his many travels, from Athos to Zion (and "Ampersand" and "Others"). Witty, wry, wise "takes" on the old, elegant days by an elegant who was there—mainly in the elegant places; but Runciman can make even Los Angeles elegant or at least gossipy.

Rushdie, Salman. *The Jaguar Smile: A Nicaraguan Journey.* New York: Viking Penguin, 1987; New York: Henry Holt, 1997. Interpreting a 1986 visit to the contradictory, complex country (like all countries are), then socialist under Daniel Ortega and threatened by the United States and its Contras and "la CIA."

Sacks, Oliver. *The Island of the Colorblind and Cycad Island.* New York: Knopf, 1997. The neurologist and writer (*Awakenings, An Anthropologist on Mars*) is also a scholar of islands—particularly a botanist—though there is no compartmentalizing this "traveler" among academic fields.

Salzman, Mark. *Iron and Silk.* New York: Random House, 1986; Vintage, 1990. China tales from an English teacher and martial arts student, evoking the culture like a tai chi gesture.

——. *The Laughing Sutra.* New York: Random House, 1991; Vintage, 1992. Salzman's novel set in China.

Savage, Barbara. *Miles from Nowhere.* Seattle: The Mountaineers, 1983; paper, 1984. Barbara and Larry Savage biked 23,000 miles in twenty-five countries for two years, and Barbara wrote a vivid report. As her book was about to be published, she was killed in a biking accident in Santa Barbara, California, near home.

Schivelbusch, Wolfgang. *The Railway Journey: The Industrialization of Time and Space in the Nineteenth Century.* Berkeley: University of California Press, 1986. An important study focusing on a particular technology as galvanizer of sea change. See also Stephen Kerr entry. See Tom Gunning's essay in this text; Gunning cites Schivelbusch in connecting the panoramic view from a train with the film perspective, born with the train.

Scot, Barbara J. *The Violet Shyness of Their Eyes: Notes from Nepal.* Corvallis, OR: Calyx, 1993. Recognizes almost too sensitively the pain, and the *right*, of the Nepali to become "modern."

Seal, Jeremy. *A Fez of the Heart: Travels Around Turkey in Search of a Hat.* New York: Harcourt Brace Harvest, 1985. Improbably, this feels like a full and vital picture of Turkey, even with that title and even strung cutely on the history of the fez, the national headgear until 1925, when Turkey's modern leader Kemal Ataturk outlawed it as a symbol of backwardness.

Sears, John. *Sacred Places: American Tourist Attractions in the Nineteenth Century.* New York: Oxford University Press, 1989. A good example (like Dona Brown's *Inventing New England)* of travel history focused on a specific place but also thematic.

Seth, Vikram. *From Heaven Lake: Travels Through Sinkiang and Tibet.* New York: Vintage, 1987. A Chinese-speaking Indian goes home via Tibet and mainly in an old truck. Memorable places and people.

Settle, Mary L. *Turkish Reflections: A Biography of a Place.* New York: Simon and Schuster Touchstone, 1992. Illustrations. The first in the current spate of visits to Turkey, and because Settle's observations and writing were so winning, "the word" went out and a trend was born.

Shapiro, James. "From Achebe to Zydeco." Review of *The Dictionary of Global Culture. New York Times Book Review*, February 2, 1997, 7. See introduction to this text and Appiah entry, above.

Shenon, Philip. "The End of the World on 10 Tugriks a Day." *New York Times Magazine,* June 30, 1996, 34–37.

Shreeve, James. *The Neanderthal Enigma: Solving the Mystery of Human Origins.* New York: Morrow, 1995. A *Discover* magazine editor argues—controversially among anthropologists—that the Cro-Magnons beat out the Neanderthals as ancestors of the modern human being because the Cro-Magnons traveled out of their intimate group for mates and (it followed) for bright new ideas.

Siddons, Anne Rivers. *Colony.* New York: HarperCollins, 1992; paper, 1993. The Maine coast, plus a knotty story centered by a heroine who grows old richly.

——. *Hill Towns.* New York: HarperCollins, 1993; paper, 1994. About Tuscany. Before *Colony*, her breakthrough, Siddons had written about her native Southeast: *King's Oak, Peachtree Road, Fox's Earth, The House Next Door,* and *Heartbreak Hotel.* In 1995, HarperCollins published *Fault Lines*, about California (paper, 1996). Siddons walks the tightrope, but does seem to weight her stories toward plot and character, rather than description of place.

Siebert, Charles. "The Cuts That Go Deeper." *New York Times Magazine*, July 7, 1996, 20–25; 34; 40; 43–45. "Traveling in place" as a metaphor for cosmetic surgery.

Simeti, Mary Taylor. *On Persephone's Island: A Sicilian Journey.* 1986. New York: Vintage Departures, 1995. Illustrations by Maria Vica Costarelli. An American woman married and stayed in sunny, ancient Sicily, and she writes from this complex insider/outsider perspective.

Simony, Maggy, ed. *The Traveler's Reading Guide.* Rev. ed. New York: Facts on File, 1993. Annotated guidebooks, background reading, history, and novels, by regions.

Smith, Valene L., ed. *Hosts and Guests: The Anthropology of Travel.* Philadelphia: University of Pennsylvania Press, 1977; 2nd ed., 1988.

Smith, Valene L., and William E. Eadington, eds. *Tourism Alternatives: Potential Problems in the Development of Tourism.* Philadelphia: University of Pennsylvania Press, 1992; forthcoming in paper from Wiley.

Stark, Freya. *Baghdad Sketches.* 1938. Evanston, IL: Marlboro Press/Northwestern University, 1992. With an introduction by Barbara Krieger. Stark was a British "spinster" of thirty-five when, after her father died, she completed her dream of traveling to fabled Baghdad. Her *Sketches* were the start of a life—as a travel writer. Among a number of works, those in print in 1997 are *Alexander's Path: From Caria to Cilicia* (1958; New York: Overlook Press, 1990); *A Winter in Arabia* (1940; New York: Overlook Press, 1987); and *The Journey's Echo.* (Hopewell, NJ: Norton Ecco, 1988).

Stark, Peter. *Driving to Greenland.* New York: Lyons & Burford, 1994. Essays on snow and ice, sports such as luge, the Arctic, and driving to Stark's fantasyland—Greenland— in a 1974 minibus.

Stegner, Page. "The Plains That Broke the Plow." Review of *Bad Land*, by Jonathan Raban. *New York Review of Books* 44, no. 2 (Feb. 6, 1997): 32–34. In a generally complimentary review of Raban's tour of the Badlands, Stegner questions "one of [Raban's] few dubious conclusions": a causal connection between the region and the "survivalists" and other antiestablishment types abounding there these days (Randy Weaver, Timothy McVeigh, Mark Fuhrman, etc.) Stegner also betrays the old notion of travel writing as lesser: "*Bad Land* is regrettably the kind of book often disparagingly categorized as 'travel literature'—a misnomer here because travel is merely the thread" (32). Reading that putdown surprises; one rarely hears the old elitism in these days, when just about everyone "goes." See Raban entry.

Steinbeck, John. *Travels with Charley in Search of America.* New York: Viking, 1962. A pioneer modern political travel writer, Steinbeck foreshadowed his travel writing (*A Russian Journal* was written in 1948) in the masterwork, *The Grapes of Wrath* (1939), where the pictures of the 1930s Dust Bowl in the American West and the Promised Land of southern California, were indelible (*Wrath* is often cited by contemporary travel writers as a youthful seed).

Stevens, Stuart. *Night Train to Turkistan: Modern Adventures along China's Ancient Silk Road.* New York: Atlantic Monthly Press Traveler, 1988. One of the "retracing the steps" genre; here, in 1986, the five-thousand-mile "road" across China to Kashgar that the

British traveler Peter Fleming traced in 1936—with detours and the plus of Stevens's wit.

Stevenson, Robert Louis. *An Inland Voyage.* Irvine, CA: Reprint Service, 1992. About a trip in Europe in 1878. The author of *Kidnapped* and *Treasure Island*—stories at the heart of the traveler's fantasy—has a number of travel books, but few are in print in 1997.

——. *South Sea Tales.* Ed. Roslyn Jolly. New York: Oxford University Press, 1996. Stevenson's South Sea travel books are not in print, but his tales are realistic (even having "explanatory notes") and are based on his own expatriation to Samoa in 1890—where his writings, including these short stories, were critical of imperialism and colonialism and sympathetic to cross-culturism.

——. *Travels with a Donkey in the Cevennes.* 1879. Evanston IL: Marlboro Press/Northwestern University, 1996. Stevenson's record of his twelve-day, 120-mile walking tour in an isolated area of France in 1878.

Storace, Patricia. *Dinner with Persephone.* New York: Pantheon, 1996. One of the best new writers. Storace lived in Greece for a year, and she weaves the personal and place, present and past. The *New York Times* reviewer of *Persephone* (Barry Unsworth) rightly noted Storace's "effective indirect comment," as when she sketches a Greek icon painter huckstering, while a butterfly lights on a garish towel, opening and closing its wings because it believes it is resting on a flower (9).

Stowe, William W. *Going Abroad: European Travel in 19th Century American Culture.* Princeton, NJ: Princeton University Press, 1994. Contemporary (i.e., politically conscious) scholarly work presenting Margaret Fuller, Ralph Waldo Emerson, Mark Twain, Henry James, and others as languid social climbers traveling two easy roads to "productivity": travel and writing about it.

Strassberg, Richard E. *Inscribed Landscapes: Travel Writing from Imperial China.* Berkeley: University of California Press, 1994. The UCLA professor of Chinese translates and introduces fifty accounts which show that guilt over traveling, and the quest for justification for it, are ancient—including the seemingly "new age" justification that our unconscious knows each of us better than restrictive human reason does.

Terkel, Studs. *Division Street: America.* New York: New Press, 1993. Division Street, Chicago, is the microcosm. Terkel's Americans—the oral histories he, more than anyone, popularized—bring his places to life, wherever they are; another example is *Hard Times: An Oral History of the Great Depression* (New York: Pantheon, 1986).

Theroux, Paul. *The Great Railway Bazaar.* Boston: Houghton Mifflin, 1975. The first, and maybe still the best, work from the man who started the current boom in journey journals. This one took us through Asia, most memorably on the Siberian Express, and was exotica—at least in 1975.

——. *The Happy Isles of Oceania: Paddling the Pacific.* New York: G. P. Putnam's, 1992; paper, Ballantine Fawcett Columbine, 1993. New Zealand and Australia, Melanesia (the Solomons, etc.), Polynesia (Western Samoa, Tahiti, the Marquesas, Cook Islands, and Easter Island), and, at last, Hawaii. He entitles this section "Paradise," although other sections are titled "Melanesia" and so on; Hawaii is, one sees in his almost last words, the world Theroux loves best: "It was a world of intimidating magic in which anything could happen" (527, Columbine ed.).

——. *The Kingdom by the Sea: A Journey Around Great Britain.* New York: Houghton Mifflin, 1983; paper, Washington Square Press, 1984. Theroux travels by foot through Britain, and may be too self-indulgent. Theroux needs an editor who will tell him, "*Enough* kvetching!" His bad moods seem to dog him, and the places and people he met in Britain were too similar to one another. Can it be that Great Britain in the early 1980s had become too homogeneous?

——. *My Other Life: A Novel.* Boston: Houghton Mifflin, 1996. Like a number of his "fictions" (particularly *My Secret History*), this novel turns on travel and seems autobiographical.

——. *The Old Patagonian Express: By Train Through the Americas.* Boston: Houghton Mifflin, 1979. From the Boston subway (the "T") to the end of Argentina, mainly by train. Theroux's second book, and the making of the guru: his winning technique is making us want to know what and who are in that town down the line.

——. *The Pillars of Hercules: A Grand Tour of the Mediterranean.* New York: G. P. Putnam, 1995; paper, Ballantine Fawcett Columbine, 1996. The gimmick here is touring a rough oval all around the Mediterranean, from Spain, France, and Italy to Albania, Bosnia (at war), Greece, the Levant, Morocco, and so on. (My favorites are Mallorca and Corsica and other "small" places.) Theroux's persona sounds less whiney here, perhaps because he turns self-reflexive about that curmudgeonly persona. If we can put up with him, no one paints more vital pictures of what (and whom) he sees: we are there, and we remember.

——. *Riding the Iron Rooster: By Train Through China.* New York: Ivy, 1989. This one really needs editing—how many gripes about "hawking and spitting" are too many, even for Theroux's curmudgeonly persona? But the end of the book—over mountain-top plain by taxi to Tibet—is wondrous and worth all.

——. *Sailing Through China.* Boston: Houghton Mifflin, 1984. Mainly a picture (coffee-table) book, as China, it seemed then, opened up to the world.

——. *Sunrise with Seamonsters: Travels and Discoveries, 1964–1984.* Boston: Houghton Mifflin, 1985; paper, 1986. Short essays, from his 1960s years in the Peace Corps in Africa, onto the best, a 1984 piece on rowing off Cape Cod, which demonstrates that the greatest adventures and the toughest tests of body and spirit take place a few, unbridgeable yards from home.

——. *To the Ends of the Earth: The Selected Travels of Paul Theroux.* New York: Random House, 1991; Ivy, 1994. Excerpts from all his travel books.

Thesiger, Wilfred. *Arabian Sands.* 1945. New York: Viking Penguin, 1985. A classic about this region.

Thorn, John, and David Reuther, eds. *The Armchair Traveler.* New York: Prentice Hall, 1986. A strong collection including Peter Benchley, "Fair Skies for the Caymen Islands" (1985), on the good news/bad news of growing tourism in these islands; a typical "wise guy" Tim Cahill piece ("World Class Attractions"); William Least Heat-Moon on "Nameless, Tennessee" or "Nowhere" (as a destination) (from *Blue Highways* [1982]); Redmond O'Hanlon, from *Into the Heart of Borneo* (1985); Paul Fussell's seminal history of travel, "From Exploration to Travel to Tourism," from *Abroad* (1980); old classics, such as Halliburton and Twain; and twentieth-century ones: Graham Greene, Beryl Markham, Mary McCarthy on Venice, Peter Matthiessen on Africa, Bruce Chatwin (on Patagonia), Paul Theroux (on England), Jan Morris on China, and more and more.

Thubron, Colin. *The Lost Heart of Asia.* New York: HarperCollins, 1994. A 1992 trip through post-Soviet Central Asia by the Britisher, also a novelist, *Lost Heart* stars the author as character: Thubron and his new best (drinking) buddies, and various Russians and other melancholics from Ubekistan, Samarkind, and other still-exotic locales (Samarkind conjures no earthly city. . . . [It] inhabits only the edge of geography" [145]). Again, as so often among travel writers, here is the seeming "destiny" of writer meeting region or peoples (or, as in the case of Chatwin, the nearly empty wild places).

——. *Where Nights Are Longest: Travels by Car Through Western Russia.* 1983. New York: Atlantic Monthly Traveler, 1984. From the Polish border ten thousand miles through Abkhazia and other ethnic groupings that prefigure post–Cold War Russia, as do the blindly patriotic Russians he meets. As usual in Thubron's travel writing, the people he meets speak and act so as to teach us their lands; Thubron "talks back" and interacts; and there is much detail (e.g., on mushroom hunting with Volodya [17–18]) and enriching, illuminating Russian history. Thubron's region also covers the Middle East: *Hills of Adonis: A Journey in Lebanon* (New York: Grove-Atlantic, 1990); *Jerusalem;* and *Journey into Cyprus.*

Tidwell, Mike. *The Ponds of Kalambayi: An African Sojourn.* New York: Lyons & Burford, 1996. Another of the Peace Corps volunteers who became writers, Tidwell, who tried to teach fish farming in south central Zaire, catches both the tragedies of disease, poverty, and isolation, and the nobility of his hosts and the humor of his intercourse with them: Tidwell, trying to spear-hunt; Tidwell trying—in vain—to stop the farmers from giving away half their fish to celebrate harvest. This is one of the new hope-giving "one world" odysseys.

Toth, Susan Allen. *My Love Affair with England.* New York: Random House, 1992; Ballantine, 1994. Toth's has been a thirty-year "love affair," and it will speak to and for U.S. Anglophiles. She has also written a guidebook, *England As You Like: An Independent Traveler's Companion* (1996); and other books on England are in the works: *England for all Seasons* and *England for Pleasure.* Toth broke through memorializing her Midwestern youth, and her *Blooming: A Small Town Girlhood* (1982) and *Ivy Days* (not in print in 1997) popularized the "half-memoir" (only "half" a life lived).

Tree, Isabella. *Islands in the Clouds: Travels in the Highlands of New Guinea.* Melbourne: Lonely Planet, 1996. Another poignant story not so much of lost nature as of fading tribal mores—and change.

Turner, Frederick. *A Border of Blue: Along the Gulf of Mexico from the Keys to the Yucatan.* New York: Henry Holt, 1993; Henry Holt Owl, 1994. An example of the strength of locally oriented travel writing, showing alliances only locals know, such as the U.S. gulf area's Caribbean leanings. Indirectly insightful contemporary American history, sociopolitical as well as cultural.

Twain, Mark. *Following the Equator.* 1897. Hopewell, NJ: Ecco Travels, 1992 (vol. 1), 1993 (vol. 2). Hawaii, the South Sea, Australia, New Zealand, India, South Africa, and so on, and the amazingly contemporary, yet incomparable Twain view. See Wetzel.

——. *The Innocents Abroad, or The New Pilgrim's Progress.* 1869. New York: Signet Classic, 1980. Classic satire of the "new barbarians": travelers from the United States. But, even more, a satire of pretensions of "antiquity." Covers Europe through "the Holy Land."

——. *Roughing It.* 1872. New York: Signet Classic, 1980. Twain in the Far West and even Hawaii, in the 1860s. (Como? Pshaw! See Lake Tahoe.")

Unsworth, Barry. "Among the Hellenes." Review of *Dinner with Persephone,* by Patricia Storace. *New York Times Book Review,* October 20, 1996, 9.

Urry, John. *The Tourist Gaze: Leisure and Travel in Contemporary Societies.* Thousand Oaks, CA: Sage, 1990. An important text on the democratization and growing intrusiveness of the traveler/tourist's gaze, pointing out how connected many economic, political, and sociological (class) issues are when looked at from the perspective of travel. Chapter 5 is central: "Cultural Changes and the Restructuring of Tourism," on how the "romantic ethic" in capitalist-consumer society has fed "post-touristic" individualism, the movements against boundaries and memory (i.e., history), and a new elitism—this one not of intellect or class, so much as of lifestyle.

Wakefield, Dan. *New York in the Fifties.* New York: Houghton Mifflin/Seymour Lawrence, 1992. A memoir of this novelist and journalist and therefore of literary figures such as James Baldwin and the "Beats," reporters such as Michael Harrington, and politicians from Joe McCarthy to Ike. But also of the place and time: jazz, torchy singers and piano bars, Spanish Harlem, and above all, the Village (Greenwich).

Walker, Dale. *Fool's Paradise.* New York: Random House, 1980; Vintage Departures, 1988. A look beyond the oil in Saudi Arabia, the fond view of an American English teacher looking at the wildness and ferocity of the tribes, but also at a "society . . . egalitarian, with a directness and simplicity unknown in the more hierarchical Western democracies" (69).

Walker, Ian. *Zoo Station: Adventures in East and West Berlin.* New York: Atlantic Monthly Press, 1987. Decadence! Shades of Dietrich, Weill, and spies that look like the dissipated Richard Burton or a haunted Alec Guinness. A historical work from the last days of the divided city.

Waller, Robert James. *The Bridges of Madison County.* New York: Warner, 1992. The footloose American who holds life at a (lens) distance, and the expatriate from Italy, who has grown deeply rooted in the fields of Iowa. See the introduction to this book.

Waugh, Alec. *Hot Countries.* 1930. New York: Paragon, 1989. Woodcuts by Lynd Ward. Tahiti, Ceylon, "Siam," Martinique, and the people and sociology of the time, particularly racism (in the genteel British style).

Waugh, Evelyn. Look for this travel writing master's essays in collections or in what works are in print—for example, *Tourist in Africa.* (1960; Westport, CT: Greenwood, 1977).

——. *When the Going Was Good.* 1934. Boston: Little, Brown, 1984. Excerpts from four Waugh travel books, 1929–1935, covering the Mediterranean, Abyssinia (for Haile Selassie's coronation), across Africa, on to South America, and back to Abyssinia (Ethiopia) after the Italian Fascists invaded it. Waugh represents the heyday of elite adventuring and the opening of the bloody end of the era in a place—Ethiopia—as opposite to "elite" as the globe shows.

Webster, Donovan. "The Looting and Smuggling and Fencing and Hoarding of Impossibly Precious, Feathered and Scaly Wild Things." *New York Times Magazine,* February 16, 1997, 26–33, 48–49, 53, 61.

West, Rebecca. *Black Lamb and Grey Falcon: A Journey Through Yugoslavia.* 1941. New York: Penguin, 1982. A classic journal of travel in the 1930s, published when Yugoslavia was "enslaved" by the Nazis (as West says in her dedication). Now Yugoslavia is wholly gone, for reasons rooted in the convoluted twisting together of its peoples and the perhaps incomparably bloody history West elucidates.

Wetzel, Betty. *After You, Mark Twain: A Modern Journey Around the Equator.* Golden, CO: Fulcrum, 1990. Hawaii, Fiji, New Zealand, Australia, India, Bangladesh, Sri Lanka.

Wharton, Edith. *Edith Wharton Abroad: Selected Travel Writings, 1888–1920.* 1995. Ed. Sarah Bird Wright. Preface by Shari Benstock. New York: St. Martin's Griffin, 1996. A welcome gathering of the sharp, sensitive sightings of one of the best of the American "elitists."

White, Randy Wayne. *The Heat Islands.* New York: St. Martin's, 1992; paper, 1993. The second Doc Ford mystery. See next two entries.

——. *The Man Who Invented Florida.* New York: St. Martin's, 1993. The third Doc Ford in Sanibel; wilder, funnier characters, but still the serious core, the environmental focus.

——. *Sanibel Flats.* New York: St. Martin's, 1990; paper, 1991. The first Doc Ford thriller, with a sensuous, "felt" locale of the Florida Gulf waters off Sanibel Island: the palm trees, pines, shells, birds, breeze. A serious, original story, an intelligent hero, and just plain unusually good writing.

Williams, Carol Traynor. " 'And Then I Saw the Monkey': Teaching Travel Culture." In *Preview 2001+: Popular Culture Studies in the Future,* edited by Ray B. Browne and Marshall Fishwick. Bowling Green, OH: Bowling Green State University Popular Press, 1995.

Williams, Raymond. *The Country and the City.* New York: Oxford University Press, 1973. The important structural analyst here explores scenic tourism, emphasizing its origins in eighteenth-century England.

Wilson, Edmund. *Upstate: Records and Recollections of Northern New York.* New York: Syracuse University Press Classics Series, 1990. The literary critic and stylist, who lived there, makes this region his own.

Winegardner, Mark. *Elvis Presley Boulevard: From Sea to Shining Sea, Almost.* New York: Atlantic Monthly Press Traveler, 1987. A popular culture jaunt across America: The Woody the Woodpecker Museum in Los Angeles, Route 66, the Bourbon Street Woolworth's, and, of course, at the center, Elvis memorabilia.

Winkler, Karen J. "Anthropologists Urged to Rethink Their Definitions of Culture." *Chronicle of Higher Education,* December 14, 1994, A18. See introduction to this book.

Winternitz, Helen. *East along the Equator: A Journey up the Congo and into Zaire.* New York: Atlantic Monthly Press Traveler, 1987. Winternitz traveled two thousand miles into Africa: to the home of the pygmies in the rain forest, the Mountains of the Moon, and, particularly, Zaire, under the dictator Mobutu. She was accompanied by another reporter, Timothy Phelps; in 1992, they would write *Capitol Games,* on the 1991 Clarence Thomas–Anita Hill story, which Phelps broke in *Newsday.*

Yeadon, David. *The Back of Beyond: Travels to the Wild Places of the Earth.* New York: HarperCollins, 1991. With Yeadon's drawings. The Outer Hebrides, Costa Rica, the Rann of Kutch, a magical house on a cliff *(El Roque),* Grand Canary Island, Iran, Goa, Thailand's "Golden Triangle," and much more, each place unique and unforgettable. Maybe this is the best travel writer today.

——. *Lost Worlds.* New York: HarperCollins, 1993. More "wild places," in the Venezualan Andes, Zaire, Tasmania, the South Sea, and so on. In 1993, he was even more worried about the wild places, whose magic he communicates so beautifully.

Zinsser, William, ed. *They Went: The Art and Craft of Travel Writing: A Collection.* Boston: Houghton Mifflin, 1991. A unique, invaluable text, including Ian Frazier on writing on the Great Plains of the United States; Mark Salzman (China); Vivian Gornick (Egypt and the role of the real in travel writing); and Calvin Trillin, on how novelists have caught some American cities, particularly New Orleans.

Index

About the Contributors

JUDITH ADLER is Associate Professor of Sociology at Memorial University of Newfoundland. Her field is the sociology of art, including in recent years, travel regarded as an art form. Her study of "Youth on the Road: Reflections on the History of Tramping" was published in *Annals of Tourism Research* (1985), and "Travel as Performed Art" appeared in *American Journal of Sociology* (1989).

BEATRIZ BADIKIAN was born in Buenos Aires, Argentina, and now lives in Chicago. She is the author of *Mapmaker*, a collection of poetry, as well as *Akewa is a Woman*, a chapbook of poetry. Badikian teaches literature and writing in Chicago.

MICHAEL BRYSON is an Assistant Professor of General Studies at Roosevelt University in Chicago. Besides travel and exploration, he is interested in American literature and history, interdisciplinary studies of the environment, and the relationship between literature and science.

RUTH CARRINGTON has taught in five countries, including eighteen months (1990–1992) in Sri Lanka as a Fulbright lecturer in English at the University of Peradeniya. For her Ph.D. at the University of Maryland she researched the later poems of Marianne Moore. She has published poems, articles, and reviews. Semiretired, she is an adjunct professor at Montana State University–Billings, near her home.

DAVID ESPEY is Director of Freshman English at the University of Pennsylvania, where he teaches courses in modern fiction and expository writing. He was a Peace Corps volunteer in Morocco and has held Fulbright lectureships in Morocco and Turkey.

TOM GUNNING is Professor in the Art Department and the Cinema and Media Program at the University of Chicago. Author of *D. W. Griffith and the Origins of American Narrative Film*, he has written numerous essays on early cinema and was a founding member of Domitor, the International Association for the Study of Early Cinema. His current research is on the relation between early cinema and modernity.

WILLIAM E. LENZ is Professor of English at Chatham College. In 1993 he first traveled to Belize and Guatemala, developing a research interest in John Lloyd Stephens and cultural identity. He is the author most recently of *The Poetics of the Antarctic: A Study in Nineteenth-Century American Cultural Perceptions* (1995).

JOHN W. PRESLEY is Dean of the College of Arts, Sciences, and Letters at the University of Michigan–Dearborn, where he has taught an introductory course on popular culture. He is a regular writer on travel culture, as well as on the intersection of popular and elite literary culture, particularly as this intersection occurs in the works of James Joyce and Robert Graves.

MARIELLE RISSE has recently completed her Ph.D. at the University of North Dakota. Her dissertation, "Explorations Within the Genre of Travel Writing," discusses the generic components of travel writing using examples from travel books across twenty centuries. Risse presented "White Knee Socks Versus Photojournalist Vests: Distinguishing Between Travelers and Tourists" at the 1997 Popular Culture Association Conference.

TERRI RYBURN-LAMONTE is the Coordinator of Parent Services at Illinois State University at Normal. A doctoral candidate in history, she is writing her dissertation on Route 66. She has guest curated an exhibit entitled "Route 66: Goin' Somewhere (The Road in McLean County, Illinois)" and received an award for the travel guide written in conjunction with the exhibit. She has recently been named to the Illinois Humanities Council "Road Scholar Speakers Bureau," based on her presentations about Route 66.

TAMARA TEALE is currently revising her dissertation for publication, "The Liberty-Genocide Paradox: American Indians in European and American Travel Literature," from which her essay on Lawrence and Beauvoir has been adapted. As a lifelong resident of Colorado Springs, she writes about tourism development in her hometown, as well as creative nonfiction about her parents' 1930s-style motel.

DAVID TOMLINSON is Professor of English at the U.S. Naval Academy in Annapolis, Maryland, where he has taught since 1970. He has served as chair of the English Department and president of the Maryland Association of Departments of English.

LYNN Y. WEINER is Associate Professor of History and Associate Dean of the College of Arts and Sciences at Roosevelt University in Chicago. Her publications include *From Working Girl to Working Mother: The Female Labor Force in the U.S., 1820–1980* (1985) and "Reconstructing Motherhood: The La Leche League in Postwar America (1994), which won the Binkley-Stephenson Prize of the Organization of American Historians. She is currently writing a book on the ideologies and practices of motherhood in twentieth-century America.

CAROL TRAYNOR WILLIAMS is Professor of Humanities at Roosevelt University and an administrator in the university's program for adults. The author of "*It's Time for My Story: Soap Opera Sources, Structure, and Response* (Praeger, 1992) and *The Dream Beside Me: The Movies and the Children of the Forties* (1980), she has also published on images of women, television, and other popular culture subjects. She is currently a vice president of the Popular Culture Association and chair of its travel culture section.

ISBN 0-275-95727-6
90000>
EAN
9 780275 957278
HARDCOVER BAR CODE